Montana and the West

MONTANA AND THE WEST

Essays in Honor of K. Ross Toole

Edited and with contributions by
Rex C. Myers and Harry W. Fritz

Pruett Publishing Company   Boulder, Colorado

First Edition
1   2   3   4   5   6   7   8   9

Printed in the United States of America

LIBRARY OF CONGRESS CATALOGING IN PUBLICATION DATA
Main entry under title:

Montana and the West.
   "An Uncommon hand: writings of K. Ross Toole": p.
   Includes index.
   1. Montana—History—Addresses, essays, lectures.
2. Toole, K. Ross (Kenneth Ross), 1920–1981—Addresses,
essays, lectures.   I. Toole, K. Ross (Kenneth Ross), 1920–1981.
II. Myers, Rex C.   III. Fritz, Harry W., 1937–
F731.5.M65   1984   978.6   84-15885
ISBN 0-87108-229-2
ISBN 0-87108-586-0 (pbk.)

Contents

Foreword

WALLACE STEGNER

Most of us spend our lives trying to find out who we are and what we are good for and what we believe in, and even after lifelong effort we may go out, as Theodore Dreiser complained, more bewildered than when we came in.

Not Ross Toole.

It is true that it took him the first twenty-seven years of his life to find out that history, specifically western history, most specifically Montana history, and most specifically of all Montana history in its relation to present-day Montana life, was what absorbed, excited, inflamed, and angered him. It is also true that after seven strenuous years as director of the Montana Historical Society he resigned in a rage and spent the next seven years wandering in the wilderness: first New York, then Santa Fe—each stint in the interest of history but far from his own turf—and finally back to his own turf in ahistorical terms as manager of a Montana cattle ranch.

But what drove Ross out of Helena and the Montana Historical Society was not a weakening of his interest in history. It was outrage that in spite of heroic efforts he had been unable to teach respect for it to Montana politicians and educators. He did not swerve, he was derailed. Once he got back on the track as professor of history at the University of Montana, he never took his hand off the throttle or his eye off the rail.

He was a historian of the West, and of a very western kind. Since there are several kinds of western historians, it is necessary to say which kind he was and which kind he was not.

He was not the kind of popular historian who tells adventurous true-life stories about the exploration and conquest of the lands beyond the hundredth meridian in nonfictional imitation of Louis L'Amour. He was not an objective and disinterested antiquarian, a digger and recorder and annotator of small facts. He was not a historian so in love with the western country that he turned history into a travelogue.

Neither was he an enthusiast reassembling pieces of the western myth, like the man in Rhyolite who made a house of bottles found among the ruins of that once-wicked town. People who believe in the western myth of self-reliance and rugged individualism and untrammeled freedom often turn out to be from the East. They perpetuate the myth in innocence. Others, less innocently, deliberately encourage the myth because it suits the purposes of chambers of commerce, legislatures, and large corporations to have ordinary Westerners forget that they have often been dupes and victims, and to have them think themselves somehow heroic, a breed apart. Some historians have been guilty of taking the myth seriously. Not Ross Toole.

Ross loved Montana—the country and the people—but not what had been done to it. He was a man whom study of his region's history had made mad. Instead of devoting himself to admiration for the lone man in buckskin or homespun or worn levis, he became an attentive student of the corporate (and often criminal) records of the great piratical corporations, eastern-financed but often western-generated, whose power in Montana's development was irresistible and ruthless. He understood that much of what was called development in the West was the economics of liquidation—that the West was, in Bernard DeVoto's phrase, a "plundered province." What is more, comparing present events with those of the past, he found the system little changed. The conclusions of his dissertation on the Anaconda Copper Company, 1880–1950, became the premises of his polemic on the rape of the Great Plains in the 1970s.

All of which is to say that Ross Toole belonged to the breed of historians most familiar to us in the person of Bernard DeVoto: historians who take sides, partisans, champions, defenders of western land and the forming western society against the forces busy looting and exploiting them. He was not diverted by the beards and ten gallon hats of Frontier Days. What interested him to the point of passion was the way in which Montana resources, both natural and human, had been exploited and manipulated by corporate power. He wrote out of a rage of love, his indignation constantly refueled by new outrages perpetrated on the body of his beloved. If Ross Toole showed himself during his hyperactive career a sort of Populist, he also showed himself that rarer thing, a patriot, a dedicated, single-minded, tenacious, impassioned, and passionately articulate patriot bent upon keeping the mistakes and rapacities of the past from being repeated in the present and future. And his commitment was full-time. There was no neutral in him, there was no way he could disengage his clutch and simply idle.

Once I called him the best talker in Montana. In my experience, he surely was. But I could just as well have said the best talker *about* Montana. Montana was his subject and his preoccupation, the place he knew and cared about. And his talking was not mere words. It was invariably a provocation to action—was actually a form of action in itself.

Whether he was talking to legislators and educators in an attempt to build up the Historical Society and nudge the state toward acknowledging the importance of its own history, or writing books, articles, or letters to the press, or lecturing those incredible classes of seventeen hundred undergraduates in History 367, talk and action were inextricable. Words were the instruments of conviction and conversion. Like the pronouncements of the Delphic Oracle, what Ross said affected men's actions, and he was passionately respected and thoroughly loathed in consequence. It is hard to bloody noses without making enemies.

Montana is a big state with big problems and a small population that is almost as mobile as that of Texas. People in Montana know one another, and most of them knew Ross Toole. His former students are scattered through the state, running everything from the governor's office to smalltown newspapers and grain elevators and ranches. His influence is pervasive and statewide, and has not even yet been felt in its full force. His dedication to history and his determination to learn from it and to make the state *act* on learning from it may well have deflected the course of Montana history. In the last months of his life, during a remission of the cancer that killed him in 1981, he devoted his final energy to lobbying the legislature in Helena in support of the bills, mainly environmental, that he felt to be crucial. As I write this, Joan Toole is still there, still working for the results that she and Ross hoped to achieve.

That is the consequence of developing a historian who is also a patriot and a champion: others find in him the cues to further words and further action. That is the best justification I can think of for such a *Festschrift* as this. By its means, the friends, colleagues, students, and disciples of K. Ross Toole will spread him a little further, illuminate a few more corners, inch the state Ross loved toward a fuller understanding of its history and a fuller realization of its responsibility to prevent history from continuing to repeat itself.

When Bernard DeVoto died, I managed, by luck and promptness, to procure his library and papers for Stanford University. It was a splendid acquisition for the university, as the collection of Ross Toole's papers is for the University of Montana. I think the best result of these respectful gestures we make toward the departed who have been leaders in their time is what was expressed in Avis DeVoto's letter when the deal for DeVoto's papers was finally closed. "I'm glad," she wrote me. "I'm glad he's going to be all together at Stanford. I wouldn't have liked to see his mind dispersed."

No more would most of us like to see Ross Toole's mind—and influence—dispersed. We will have no more champions unless we deserve them.

Introduction

K. Ross Toole taught History 367, "Montana and the West," for sixteen years at the University of Montana. It is fitting that a collection of essays in honor of Ross Toole bear the name of his famous course. Yet while "Montana and the West"—the class—reflected the vibrancy of a single person, this volume represents the combined efforts of students and associates. This is as it should be, for Ross Toole communicated an infectious enthusiasm for his native state and its history. That contagion is contained in the essays which follow.

No one who studies Montana history can escape either the personality or the themes that permeated "Montana and the West." In the opening essay, Harry Fritz discusses Toole, the man and the historian. The same threads that appear in Toole's rendering of Montana history form the fabric of this collection of essays.

For Ross Toole, corporate influence played the major role in the historic cause and effect of Montana. Thomas White, Rex Myers, and Donald Spritzer identify variations of that theme in railroad, newspaper, and public utility activities from 1864 into the 1950s. Questions of land use and abuse—Indian reservations, homestead promotions, and the wide open spaces of the tourist's West—have also profoundly affected Montana development. Respectively, Daniel Gallacher, Frank Grant, and Robert Athearn illuminate these issues. Ethnic and minority groups in Montana history are accentuated by Delores Morrow's discussion of Jewish businessmen along Last Chance Gulch. Montana's cultural heritage emerges from Richard Roeder's synthesis of novels dealing with Butte. Ross Toole also stressed the need to preserve not only traditional documents of pen and prose, but the legacy

K. Ross Toole. Courtesy K. Ross Toole Archives, Mansfield Library, University of Montana.

of physical evidence as well. George Lubick traces state efforts to save this part of the past through historic preservation.

Ross Toole's Montana contained the color and exuberance of the early frontier—Custer, Vigilantes, and the flamboyant entrepreneurs. Yet Toole did not permit his students—graduate or undergraduate—to linger in the past at the expense of the present. Nine of the ten essays in this volume deal with issues and events of statehood and the twentieth century. Finally, Toole left a record of his own views in the historiography of Montana. His prolific efforts literally evade quantification, but the selected bibliography concluding this volume samples the panorama of Toole's audience and interest.

A word on format may help the reader. After the initial article on Ross Toole's life, the remaining nine essays are arranged in a rough chronological order. Brief introductions clarify the place of each in the history of Montana and the West. Biographical information on contributors appears after the bibliography.

Publication of any edited work is obviously a cooperative effort. Fittingly, this preface offers a sincere thank you to the people who made it possible. Principal among these individuals are the contributors. It would be nice to say that they all met initial deadlines, but this is an honest preface. Yet if the actual manuscripts lagged in arriving, the enthusiasm of their authors did not. Phone calls, letters, and personal conversations produced needed revisions and editorial changes with remarkable alacrity. Each author had his or her own typist and although they remain anonymous to editor and reader, we appreciate their work. Our own typists, Clarice Koby and Julie McVay, suffered considerably. Dave Walter helped with the bibliography. Pruett editor Jerry Keenan also deserves a word of thanks for his patience. And if this book pleases a single person—Joan Toole—it will be worth it.

A final, personal word about K. Ross Toole. We both teach Montana history, not as Ross Toole taught it, but with an enthusiasm for the subject that "rubbed off." We think he would be proud of the essays in this volume; we know he would be pleased that examination and discussion of Montana and the West continues.

Rex C. Myers
Western Montana College

Harry W. Fritz
University of Montana

1 /

AN UNCOMMON MAN
K. Ross Toole, 1920–1981

HARRY W. FRITZ

In the spring of 1975 Mr. James Burk, supervisor of secondary education in Montana's Office of Public Instruction, recommended to his board that American history be dropped as a required course in the state's high schools. A University of Montana history professor took strong exception to the recommendation. He constituted a one-man "Committee to Retain U.S. History as a Required Course in Our Schools." He marveled to Burk that any "educator in his right mind would suggest such a palpably absurd proposition." He wired together a paper coalition of teachers, legislators, farmers, and veterans and mounted direct mail, petition, and speaking campaigns. Single-handedly he generated so much publicity adverse to Burk's proposition that he quickly dropped it. K. Ross Toole was in action.

It was not Ross Toole's first crusade, nor would it be his last. All his life he was a crusader. For thirty years, as director of the Montana Historical Society and Hammond Professor of Western History at the University of Montana, Toole was the state's foremost public proponent of the relevance of history. No ivory-tower scholar, he actively promoted his museum and library in Helena; he wrote forcefully and feelingly about the sordid lessons of the past, and he reached thousands of students and citizens with his classes, speeches, and papers. He engrained a version of Montana history so deep in the public psyche that it became part of the political culture. Not content with excoriating past evils, he strove to prevent new ones; in the 1970s he linked the environmental crusade to the best of the Montana heritage. By the time of his death in 1981 Toole was one of Montana's most outspoken public personalities, mourned statewide as the historian who told us who we were.

On both sides of his family, K. Ross Toole was a fourth-generation Montanan. One great-grandfather, the legendary Cornelius C. O'Keefe, had settled in the Missoula valley in 1859; another, Alan "Doc" Hardenbrook, first arrived in Montana in 1864. Toole's grandfathers, two powerful men, worked for the company that became his *bete noire.* John R. Toole was president and Kenneth Ross was general manager of the Anaconda Lumber Company at Bonner, Montana. In a sense, Toole's life's work constituted an extended parricidal foray. In his boyhood, Toole's parents exuded a "patina of aristocracy" befitting their pioneer heritage. Without realizing it, he considered himself an old-style patrician reformer, exposing the deeds and correcting the errors of the past. "This family has not been an ordinary one," he once wrote. "Which implies, of course, that it has been an extraordinary one."

Young Ross grew up in the quiet university town of Missoula. He was interested in creative writing, in poetry, and he loved Shakespeare; in high school he played Cassius in *Julius Caesar.* Upon graduation in 1939 he entered what is now the University of Montana in Missoula to begin an educational odyssey that lasted twelve years. Toole was not a scholar. In eight undergraduate years at four institutions he compiled a gentleman's C average. He began at Montana, transferred to the School of Foreign Service at Georgetown University (where he took his first history courses), then entered law school in Missoula. But Toole was not yet ready—if ever he was—for the daily grind necessary to master contracts, property, and torts. He lasted two weeks. Puzzled over the modern relevance of the Court of King's Bench, he stunned his family by quitting abruptly and leaving for Alaska, where he worked for the U.S. Army Corps of Engineers. Returning to Missoula after Pearl Harbor, he spent another five quarters at the University before enlisting in the Navy. The Navy sent him to school at Carroll College and at Columbia University, and he saw wartime service in the Mediterranean and in Hawaii. As an ordinary line officer these were desk jobs. When the war ended, he came back and finished his B.A. at Montana.

In his 1947–1948 graduate year, Ross Toole found himself in history. His grades ballooned to a straight A average, and he wrote his master's thesis on "Marcus Daly: A Study of Business in Politics." Paul Chrisler Phillips, since 1911 a member of the Montana faculty and the dean of the state's professional historians, directed Toole's work and promoted his interest in Montana history. Phillips was a "scientific" historian of the old school, a dates and documents man whose editions of primary sources have now sustained Montana scholars for more than sixty years. Toole never met Phillips's expectations of research and scholarship, but the old man set professional standards which the student admired. Toole respected Phillips. He called everyone else by their first names, but his first real mentor was always "Dr. Phillips."

Toole went on, in 1948, to begin doctoral work at the University of California in Los Angeles. "Let's face it," he said much later, "I was just buying time. I didn't know what I wanted to do, so I just kept going to school." But by all accounts he was an excellent student and a first-rate teaching assistant. Above all, the man he worked for provided yet another role model for his career. John W. Caughey was not only a competent scholar in Western and California history, but a public figure of some notoriety. By the time Toole left, in 1951, Caughey stood tall in liberal eyes for his battles over civil rights and academic freedom. Caughey's academic and public lives both influenced Toole. The mentor's text, *California*, while far more thorough, was, like Toole's later *Montana*, a professional history that dared to be interpretive. And Caughey's reputation as a leader of causes foreshadowed Toole's crusades.

In 1951, not yet thirty-one and still four years from his Ph.D., Ross Toole landed a job as director of the Montana Historical Society. The next seven years would be at once the most frenetic and the most productive of his life. During this period he brought the quiescent historical society to life. He installed the latest in museum displays, ceaselessly promoted and advertised his operation, and earned a national reputation for the society's historical quarterly. For a year Toole edited and published a liberal journal of opinion. He finished his doctoral dissertation. With Merrill Burlingame, he coauthored the last (and best) of Montana's subscription histories, and with John W. Smurr he issued *Historical Essays on Montana and the Northwest*. And he wrote *Montana: An Uncommon Land*.

The Historical Society of Montana, founded in 1864, was reorganized in 1949 with an expanded board of trustees and a closer relationship with the state universities. Prior to the reorganization and Toole's assumption of the directorship, it had been a sleepy, do-little organization dedicated to preserving the memory of Montana's Pioneers—and their Sons and Daughters. Toole changed all that. He had a modern, up-to-date conception of the function of a library, the role of a museum, and the relationship of both to institutions of higher learning. "Professors replaced pioneers as the most interested parties," writes current MHS Librarian Robert Clark. Toole sought to open the library's collection to a broader range of users. He particularly wanted to attract academic researchers. "The Library, and above all, the professional utilization of what is in it," he wrote, "is the part of the iceberg under the water; it is, in the long run, what matters most." He set up grants-in-aid for faculty members and graduate students. "It is very important that trained people use our materials," he told his board. "We are, after all, not collecting such materials or preserving them simply for the sake of preserving and collecting." Toole also created a teaching museum from a traditional collection of artifacts. "They had three skulls of Henry Plummer," he reminisced. But the new Veterans and Pioneer Memorial Building would house a series of modern historical displays, and Toole, who knew little of museums, turned to a man who knew a lot. John C. Ewers of the Smithsonian Institution, who had planned the Museum of the Plains Indian in Browning, came to Helena at Toole's behest in early 1952 and frantically organized the exhibits that documented the major chapters in the state's history. Toole boasted long and loud that the series of dioramas constituted "the finest museum in the West."

The new director's most ambitious project was the fledgling *Montana Magazine of History*. Launched under the editorship of Al Partoll before Toole's arrival, the *Magazine* replaced the old *Contributions* series—the last volume of which had appeared in 1940. Partoll's first two issues were six-by-nine-inch enlarged pamphlets, containing articles and reviews. Toole added photographs, and in 1953 issued the *Magazine* in an enlarged pictorial format. Two years later he proudly boasted that "The magazine you hold in your hands has the largest circulation of any magazine of history in the United States." In 1955 he broadened the coverage and changed the name to *Montana: The Magazine of Western History*. Before turning the editorship over to Michael Kennedy in 1957, Toole was instrumental in the quarterly's success. He actively solicited manuscripts, wrote a "Director's Roundup" column in each issue, and sometimes even reviewed books under pseudonymous names. The *Magazine* published a combination of professional and amateur scholarship that represented the best in popular history. It is going strong today.

The library, the museum, and the *Magazine* were the heart of the historical society, but they did not sell themselves. The director's biggest job consisted of promoting his business and marketing his products. Toole undertook these tasks with a flair for showmanship still remembered in Montana. He gave, by his exaggerated count, three speeches a week to service clubs, professional organizations, and anyone else who would listen. He installed a money-making curio shop, "sponsored square dances, calf sales, dog sales, radio and television programs, arranged for and sold bronze Russell castings, distributed colorful pamphlets, put out handbills, posters, signs, took booths at fairs, sponsored Indian dances and glee clubs." When the Malcolm S. Mackay family offered its priceless Charles M. Russell collection to the society, Toole orchestrated a statewide fund-raising campaign. He enlisted the press and a variety of speakers to proclaim the theme "shame on you [Montanans] for letting *Texans* steal our Russells." The Mackay Collection is now on display at the historical society. These activities, necessary but nonacademic, disturbed Toole. "I have become a huckster and whatever elements may once have been scholarly in my being are now thoroughly tainted with commercialism," he wrote. It was "a hard, often bitter, frequently humiliating job." Toole excelled at it.

For most men, running the historical society would be a full-time job. It was for Toole, but, almost incredibly, he had another career on the side—as scholar and editor. During his tenure in Helena he worked actively on five major projects, which together would establish his reputation as historian and gadfly.

The first was his doctoral dissertation. Ponderously entitled "A History of the Anaconda Copper Mining Company: A Study in the Relationships between a State and Its People and a Corporation, 1880–1950," it was a comprehensive account of "The Company." Though unpublished, its main arguments appeared in Toole's later books. Toole finished the job late in 1954, defended his work early in 1955, and finally, on June 16, became an official Ph.D.

Toole then turned his attention from past evils to present. He founded a short-lived journal, *Montana Opinion,* which subjected Anaconda and state institutions to muckraking attacks. "We are convinced," the *Opinion's* credo stated, "that the preceptive [*sic*] Montanan is sick and tired of living without a candid and intelligent press"; the lead article in the first issue, by a former Republican legislator from Billings, castigated "Montana's Captive Press." The journal folded after four issues.

Another project, one which lasted for five years, 1952–1957, resulted in the publication of a two-volume *History of Montana.* Co-edited with Merrill G. Burlingame of Montana State College, the volumes were in a long tradition of "mug books," or "subscription histories" of

Montana. Burlingame and Toole farmed chapters out to some twenty-one authorities. Few met their deadlines. Toole once boiled a three hundred page manuscript down to thirty pages, and Burlingame cut another nine. The editors ended up with ten chapters themselves. Toole did "The War of the Copper Kings," which contained the line "Much of the distrust and animosity that erupted periodically from 1906 to 1950 had its origin in the traumatic period of Amalgamated's activity." The Anaconda Company, which had sponsored the work, tried to censor the passage, but Toole did not budge.

In the middle of these projects, the University of Nebraska Press asked Toole to write a history of Montana "which would be scholarly, readable and interesting." "Can you imagine?," Toole asked Burlingame. "God forbid!" But he accepted the contract, completed the manuscript during the summer of 1957 at the family home on Seeley Lake, and sent it off in September. At the same time, in collaboration with J. W. Smurr, Toole had a *festschrift* for Paul Phillips ready to go to press at the historical society. There were problems with Toole's Montana history, among them the title. Nebraska thought of "The Forty-first Star," and Toole offered no ideas beyond his secretary's suggestion of "An Uncommon Land." Apparently the first draft failed to keep chronology and analysis in balance. But Toole quickly revised the work, and in the spring of 1958 it drew rave reviews from his editors. The University of Nebraska Press, however, was in the throes of an administrative shakeup, and Toole had feelers from another publisher, Savoie Lottinville of the University of Oklahoma Press. He asked Nebraska for a decision; despite its extensive editorial work, the press pleaded financial problems and a non-Nebraska topic. It released the work, and Toole immediately sent it off to Oklahoma. The following year it appeared as *Montana: An Uncommon Land.*

Montana: An Uncommon Land stamped Toole as the premier historian of the state. Frontier studies by Merrill Burlingame and James M. Hamilton stopped short of the twentieth century. Journalistic accounts by C. P. Connolly, Carl B. Glasscock, and Joseph Kinsey Howard were dramatic but episodic. Toole covered the sweep of the Montana past in critical, professional analysis. *Uncommon Land* combined the best of two historiographical traditions. One stemmed from the muckrakers and reached its height in Howard's *Montana: High, Wide, and Handsome* (1943). The other drew from the professional arguments of Walter Prescott Webb—the scholar who most influenced Toole's interpretation—and younger historians like Robert Athearn.

These disparate investigators shared a common thesis: that the West in general (and any western state in particular) suffered economic exploitation at the hands of eastern corporate interests. Toole borrowed this theme, applied it systematically and historically to Montana, and made it his own. It was a sophisticated economic interpretation in the finest tradition of Progressive historiography. Rich in resources, Montana relied on outside capital to exploit them. In a cyclical and repetitive pattern the interests came—for furs, gold, grass, copper, lumber, wheat, farms. They battled the elements, the workers, and the land itself, but because money is power, in the end they won. Montana remained a corporate-dominated state; *Montana: An Uncommon Land* remains its history. A recent survey of subscribers to *Montana: The Magazine of Western History* rated it the third best book ever written about the state.

Toole welcomed the reviews in New York City. In 1958 he quit the Montana Historical Society for a complex of reasons. He was tired of battling a parsimonious legislature—tired of beating the drums for the private money needed to run the society. His espousal of liberal causes in *Montana Opinion* had earned him the enmity of a cadre of legislators, trustees, and the public. He was probably looking for an excuse to quit. The excuse came on May 5, 1958, with the resignation of Carl McFarland as president of Montana State University. For five years Toole had been working with McFarland to establish a joint University/Society research center in Helena. The center would take the society beyond its public equation with the museum, gallery, and magazine into serious academic pursuits. McFarland had all but nailed down a $50,000 Ford Foundation grant when, under severe pressure in Missoula, he was forced to resign. Toole was outraged. In words that doubtless haunted him later, he blasted the State Board of Education: "I cannot personally and with good conscience be associated, even indirectly, with higher education in Montana." Seven years later he was a university professor.

In the interim, Toole headed the Museum of the City of New York, the Museums of New Mexico in Santa Fe, and a cattle ranch in Luther, Montana. His New York sojourn lasted only two years. He brought to the moribund museum there the same dynamic leadership he exhibited in Montana. He liked Santa Fe far more than the big city, but when his wife inherited a spread near Red Lodge he jumped at the chance to be president of the K-Bar-J Ranch. "While I had no great affection for cattle," he admitted later, "the ranch was a terrific place to raise children."

Meanwhile, the University of Montana had established the A. B. Hammond Fund for the promotion of western history. Melvin Wren, chairman of the history department, set out to hire an occupant for the University's only endowed chair. Toole was not his first choice; indeed, Wren shuffled through a long list of potential candidates, and even hired Edwin Bingham of Oregon for a year. Bingham did not want the permanent job, but he did recommend a fellow UCLA classmate, K. Ross Toole. Wren invited Toole to the campus and persuaded him to accept a one-year, trial appointment. Toole apprehensively took the job, but by February 1966 he was committed. "I won't go into the somewhat complicated circumstances that brought me back to the University," he told Carl McFarland, "except to say that the Hammond 'chair' was simply too tempting to turn down."

For the first time in his career, Toole found himself directing M.A. and occasional Ph.D. students in the history of his state. He put them to work on twentieth-century Montana history. "The historical literature," he argued, "is so heavily freighted with published works on the territorial period and the 'War of the Copper Kings' that a basic unbalance exists." But, for Toole, the twentieth century never extended much beyond 1925. Reviewers of *Twentieth-Century Montana: A State of Extremes* (1972) were puzzled by the opening line of the preface: "This book is not a history of twentieth-century Montana." It consisted of a series of "portraits" based on his students' work, and drawn mainly of the action-packed years between the "Great Shutdown" of 1903 and "The End of Progressivism." It bolstered the themes of extractive development and corporate domination he had outlined earlier. Partisans of the "Toole thesis" adopted it warmly.

A certain ambiguity characterized Toole's thinking about history. On the one hand, he was not an academic historian in the narrow, professional sense of the term. Beyond his M.A. and Ph.D. he did little basic research in manuscript sources. "I am unutterably bored with the restrictions of writing history," he once confessed. "But there are lots of things left to write—including polemics." He was capable of the most disparaging remarks about university faculties, historians in particular. They constituted a "priesthood, protected, profoundly ignorant...isolated, insulated, shortsighted." But he believed fervently in the uses of history. He used his special version of the past to explain the present. "I am interested," he once said, "in the utilization of history for practical purposes." His favorite quotation was the line of the philosopher George Santayana: "Those who cannot remember the past are condemned to repeat it." Toole never quite got it straight, but believed strongly that "It seems pretty silly to proceed into the future if you don't know where the hell you came from."

Toole never published a scholarly monograph. He struggled for years with "the book," a *magnum opus* that was to be an historical analysis of the Rocky Mountain region along the lines set down for the Great Plains by Walter Prescott Webb. This "major undertaking" was "an analysis of the adaptation, social, economic and political, of the frontiersmen when they left the Great Plains and moved into the mountains." For Toole the changes were "no less traumatic and no less ultimately significant" than those which afflicted Webb's plainsmen. But somehow other projects interfered, and *The Rocky Mountain West* never reached manuscript form.

Toole might have ended his career as a respected, slightly out-spoken, but essentially parochial historian had not two separate developments catapulted him into national recognition. When the student movement of the late sixties turned violent, Toole became angry, and when the Montana cycle turned up a new generation of corporate despoilers on the eastern plains, he became apoplectic. Anger and apoplexy found forceful expression in *The Time Has Come* (1971) and *The Rape of the Great Plains* (1976).

The Time Has Come began as a letter to his brother John, continuing and expanding a family discussion. Picked up and published by the Billings *Gazette* as "The Tyranny of Spoiled Brats," the essay marked the beginning of the conservative cultural counterrevolution of the 1970s. "I am fed up with nonsense," Toole exclaimed. "I am tired of being blamed, maimed and contrite. . . I am sick of the total irrationality of the campus rebel. . . It's time to call a halt." His exaggerated rhetoric boiled with rage, frustration, and a touch of fear. But beneath the angry polemics lay the wisdom of time, the call for perspective, and the sense of the possible. Only an historian could have written the piece.

Toole's observations struck a national chord of anguish and resentment. Five hundred newspapers and magazines reprinted the piece; twenty thousand letters poured into Missoula; talk-show invitations arrived from coast to coast. Toole capitalized on the publicity and the obvious market. The resulting book, *The Time Has Come,* was a

Book-of-the-Month Club alternate selection and paid "hefty royalties." In 1970 the man who called campus militants "arrogant slobs" seemed himself bitter and reactionary. Today his message reads like the soul of wisdom and common sense.

No sooner had the "tyranny" flap died down than another cause claimed Toole's undivided attention. The environmental movement, gathering speed in the late sixties, hit Montana with full force in 1971. In that year the Bureau of Reclamation in the Department of the Interior issued the *North Central Power Study,* which forecast the construction of twenty-one coal-fired power plants totaling 69,000 megawatts in eastern Montana. Soon afterwards, the Montana Power Company began building Colstrip 1 and 2, with 3 and 4 to come. Here was a salient contemporary issue that only Ross Toole's history could explain.

In Toole's Montana, the last great battle had been fought fifty years earlier by Governor Joe Dixon. Nothing much had happened in the intervening decades. The thirties were "gray," the forties were "dull," the whole period was "somnolent." The problem lay, however, not in the march of time but in the "Toole thesis." No dramatic wounds, no spectacular reversals had beset the state. But now, in the 1970s, the past came home. Corporate power poised to strike again. Coal, gas, and oil were the new resources whose exploitation threatened Montana's future. A new chapter in a timeless sequence was being written on the eastern plains. What better weapon than history to combat it?

The Rape of the Great Plains: Northwest America, Cattle and Coal is not an impartial work. It was not meant to be. "It is a polemical book," Toole admitted later. "I think in several places it misused history, blew history out of course." Toole intended it as a weapon in the fight for the land he loved. He meant to halt the corporate giants in their tracks. Montana was the last line of defense. "If we cannot stop the rape here," he asserted, "I do not think it can be stopped anywhere." In his book, in his articles and lectures, and in his support of such organizations as the Northern Plains Resource Council, he drummed up an army of environmentalists to do battle on the plains, in the courts, and at the statehouse. In the last decade of his life he enjoyed a public stature of advocacy usually denied to historians. Of all his writings, he was most proud of *The Rape of the Great Plains* and saw it as his enduring monument: "This book was secretly written," he explained, "not for you, nor me, nor reviewers, nor librarians, nor money. It was written for my progeny."

Was Ross Toole liberal or conservative? Depending on circumstances, he claimed to be either. He told two MHS board members, angry about *Montana Opinion,* that he was a conservative. "Toole, if you are a conservative, you are a conservative with a damned radical heart," one responded. Yet he opened his angry man letter of 1970 by declaring "I am a liberal." Elsewhere, he called himself a "middle of the road Democrat" and a believer in the free enterprise system "when it is free and enterprising." Actually he was something of a preacher, with a knack for expressing majority sentiment just when that sentiment was forming. "I have hit issues when they break over the point into what I suppose you could call consensus," he said. Toole caught the nascent conservative mood of the 1970s precisely at its moment of birth. He articulated mainstream environmentalism and rescued the movement from the "eagle freaks." Yet he was also an iconoclast. "I feel increasingly uncomfortable when concensus [*sic*] is around," he wrote. "There is perversity in that. Right, wrong or partly both, someone should make waves—or [at] least ripples. I dislike calm seas and smooth sailing....I have simply never enjoyed being in anybody's mainstream. Maybe because the water is too deep. It is much more fun to muck around in the shallows and throw mud balls at the mainstream boaters."

K. Ross Toole taught the most popular class at the University of Montana. History 367, "Montana and the West," began slowly in the 1960s, gathered steam in the 1970s, and peaked at more than seventeen hundred students (in two offerings) during Toole's last year. In any four-year period, he preached the gospel according to Toole to more than half of the UM student body. Ironically, he was not a spellbinding lecturer. But his straightforward presentations caught fire when he hit a villain, who invariably had "beady eyes," and he easily communicated his enthusiasm and his anger. Toole claimed not to believe in the "devil theory of history," but that's the way he taught Montana. He did not lecture with professional caution, and he abandoned scholarly detachment. Students loved it. His version of Montana history was theirs; it made sense in their time. The past was not dead; the cycle had not run its course; history was alive, it taught real lessons, and students learned them in class and out. To Ross Toole, the university was no ivory tower, but a platform from which to fire up the armies of the future.

For the last twenty years of his life, Toole toyed with death. He suffered a massive heart attack in 1963 (one of the reasons that impelled him to take an academic job); a minor coronary in 1972 followed by an artery catheterization; in 1976 he underwent open heart surgery to cure arrhythmia. In the *modus vivendi* he reached with his health, however, the accent was on the living. He never quit smoking or drinking. Life was too short to spend as a rutabaga. He willingly sacrificed a few extra years to enjoy the few he had left. He maintained an intellectual understanding of his frailties. When his diagnosis in February 1980 was oat-cell cancer of the lung, he underwent a debilitating chemotherapy treatment to buy one more year to work. "Goddammit, everybody is terminal," he asserted. "I am just a little more so. I am not dying of cancer, I am living in spite of it." Death was not a process to rue but a puzzle to master, and almost incomprehensibly he enjoyed mastering it.

He lived his last year to the fullest. When, in October 1980, the Anaconda Minerals Division of Atlantic Richfield announced that it was closing its copper-smelting operations in Anaconda and Great Falls, he lambasted the corporation in old-fashioned muckraking style. "We've been had—again," he thundered. "It's criminal and inexcusable. They really are a bunch of slobs" (his favorite epithet was "slobs"). Awards came his way—Outstanding Teacher at the University, Distinguished Service to State Government from the governor. "His contentious criticism," said former classmate Ted Schwinden, "draws attention to the cyclical 20th century patterns in Montana—patterns of boom and bust, resource exploitation, single-industry regions and power hungry corporations—patterns Montanans do not wish repeated." Toole spent his last winter in Helena, keeping watch over the legislature; his last article praised both parties for standing firm on the environment.

A man's life is not measured by the bits and pieces he leaves behind, but by the spirit in which he lived it. Ross Toole was a fighter. He fought "The Company" and its attendant evils, he fought meanness and bigotry where he found them, and he fought the destruction of the uncommon land. In his books and other writings, and in the life he led, he left a powerful understanding of Montana history. The way we think things happened in Montana is the way he told us they happened. No greater tribute can be paid to an historian. But he taught us to think not just about the past, but also about the future. "He gave us our history," one obituary read, but he warned us not to repeat it. Like the land he loved, he was an uncommon man.

BIBLIOGRAPHIC NOTE

My sources are both public and private. I'm indebted to Dave Walter and Bob Clark at the Montana Historical Society, where I consulted the Merrill Burlingame and Ross Toole files. Dale Johnson showed me the Toole papers in the UM Archives. I talked to Tom Haines, Al Partoll, Dana Toole, John Toole, and Mel Wren, and I corresponded with Edwin Bingham, Merrill Burlingame, Stan Davison, Lucie Clapp Hagens, Vivian Paladin, J. W. Smurr, and Norman Winestine. My greatest debt is to Joan Toole, who deposited Ross's papers in the Archives at the University of Montana—now named the Ross Toole Archives.

2 /

Jewish Merchants and the Commercial Emporium of Montana

DELORES J. MORROW

Mining in Montana Territory has captured much popular and historical attention. Yet as Delores Morrow, photo curator at the Montana Historical Society, observes in her study of Helena's Jewish merchants, many individuals "sought to dig not riches from the earth but profits from the diggers." Indeed, far and away the greatest number of successful entrepreneurs during the mining frontier era reaped profits in merchandising, transportation, and banking, rather than mining. This trend becomes obvious by focusing on Helena's Jewish pioneers, who facilitated the transition from placer boomtown to "commercial emporium of Montana."

Success for many of these merchants depended not upon capricious economic whims, but on close religious and family ties. Buying and marketing networks linked Jews in Helena with others in Denver, San Francisco, and New York City. Many of the wholesalers and retailers along Last Chance Gulch did not confine their distribution to that community, but traveled or extended services to camps throughout the territory. Among the services badly needed on the frontier was banking —converting gold dust to coin or currency and making loans. The combination of mercantile and financial growth facilitated by these Jewish pioneers helped Helena mature as an economic and social center.

At the close of the year 1877, the *Helena Daily Herald* gave front-page coverage to a directory of the town's businesses, schools, institutions, and societies. All six of the clothiers listed in the business section of this directory were Jews, and Jewish merchants monopolized the sale of other goods, including firearms and tobacco. Despite the numerous Jewish tradesmen recorded in its business columns, the newspaper accompanied its directory with an historical sketch that described Helena in 1877 as "the centre and distributing point for a happy and prosperous commonwealth, bound together by the amenities and civilization of Christian people."[1]

Although this publication chose to ignore the presence of non-Christians in the Territory, Jews played an important role in its settlement. Montana's Jewish pioneers were distinctive, not only for their religious practices, but also for their choice of occupations. Most Jews in Montana gold camps were merchants who "sought to dig not riches from the earth but profits from the diggers."[2]

Between 1862 and 1875, Montana placer mining produced nearly $134,000,000 worth of gold.[3] A substantial portion of this wealth passed through the hands of local bankers, merchants, and saloon keepers; many of these entrepreneurs, particularly in Helena, were Jews. They controlled a large part of the town's retail trade and served as distributors of manufactured goods to people in other mining camps. Through their widespread business and family connections, Jews often were able to overcome problems endemic to frontier merchants and to maintain prosperous businesses that survived the gold rush.

In addition to supplying goods to their customers, Jewish merchants performed needed financial services; they exchanged gold dust for coin, contracted loans, and extended credit to other business concerns. Through their role as economic middlemen, distributing both goods and capital, Helena's Jewish pioneers encouraged commercial development in the town and influenced Helena's safe transition from gold camp to "Commercial Emporium of Montana."[4]

The discovery of sizable gold deposits on Grasshopper Creek in 1862 touched off Montana's first placer rush. This strike and richer ones at Alder Gulch in 1863 and Last Chance Gulch in 1864 drew thousands of goldseekers to the Territory. Included in this migration were hundreds of Jews "attracted by the potentialities of the new region, by the rumors of wealth or motivated by the spirit of adventure."[5] Next to Alder Gulch, Helena (Last Chance Gulch) had the richest gold deposits in Montana. This camp soon topped the other camps in population and importance and counted among its inhabitants the largest number of Jewish immigrants.[6]

During Montana's placer boom (1862–1870), more than 160 Jewish men lived and worked in Helena.[7] Most of these Jews were single, in their twenties and early thirties, and recent immigrants from Germany and central Europe, primarily Bavaria, Prussia, and Poland.[8] The majority listed their occupations as merchants and clerks, but there were also butchers, tailors, saloon keepers, bankers, and assayers. (See appendix A.) Many came from families of tradesmen or had learned their mercantile skills as apprentices in businesses in Europe. Others began their merchandising careers in America, working for relatives already established in business or peddling goods in towns along the Atlantic coast and in mining camps in the West. For over sixty per cent of these men, Helena was not their first gold camp experience.[9] (See appendix B.)

During the early years of Helena's settlement, Jewish merchants dominated the retail sale of general merchandise and clothing in the camp. In its directory of city businesses, published February 28, 1867, the *Helena Herald* listed seventeen Jewish dry goods and clothing merchants to three Gentiles in the same business:

Dry Goods and Clothing

Ladies' Dry Goods Emporium. 36 Bridge street S Levy.
W Weinstein & Bro. 26 Bridge street, clothing store.
I Haas. 20 Bridge street, clothing establishment.
J Helfer & Co. 15 Bridge street, dry goods and clothing.
Poznainsky & Behm. 13 Broad [Bridge] street, dry goods and clothing.
Lavenburg & Co. 11 Bridge street, Temple of Fashion.
Ellis & Bros. 18 Bridge street. dry goods and clothing.
Honest Charley's auction and commission store. 16 Bridge street.
I Harris. Bridge street opposite Main. Dry goods and clothing, miners' outfitting store.
Emanuel & Co. Cor Main and Bridge streets, clothing, boots and shoes.
G Goldenburg [sic] & Co. Cor Main and Bridge street, California clothing store.
J P Nohm. West Main street, west side, dry goods and clothing.
Loeb & Bro. 8 Main street, clothing merchants.
Remish & Stenzel. 20 Main street, pioneer cheap John auction store.
Gens [sic] & Klien [sic] 28 Main street, clothing, boots and shoes, cigars and tobacco.
John How. 73 Main street, dry goods, groceries and hardware.
L Blumenthal. 43 Main street, clothing, tobacco.
J C Levy. Main street, clothing, tobacco.
A. Cohen. 5 Main street, clothing, boots and shoes.
John Morris & Bro. 3 Main street, clothing, boots, shoes etc.[10]

Two of the Jewish clothing stores, Gans and Klein, and J. C. Levy, also sold tobacco and cigars. After clothing and dry goods, tobacco products were the most popular merchandise carried by Jewish retail outlets. Three of the six tobacco store owners enumerated in the newspaper's directory were Jewish.[11] Almost exclusively, Helena's pioneer residents purchased dry goods, clothing, and tobacco from Jewish merchants.

Not all the business conducted by Helena Jews was confined to the retail trade. Some Jewish merchants expanded their operations to include wholesaling, while others, including Gumpert Goldberg and the Morris brothers, had two places of business, one wholesale and one retail.[12]

Jewish wholesalers urged merchants in neighboring gold camps to purchase their goods in Helena, offering their prospective customers numerous inducements: prompt service, low prices, and large selections of merchandise. One clothing and dry goods store, Loeb and Brother, promised "Orders from the Country promptly attended to,"[13] while another Jewish wholesale merchant, A. Weinshenk, announced his purchase of "the largest stock of ladies' dress goods ever brought to Montana" and offered to sell it to his retail buyers for very attractive terms. His advertisement read

> "...He [A. Weinshenk] will not be undersold. Country dealers will do well to give him a call at his wholesale house."[14]

Some "country dealers" were Jewish merchants from other mining towns who depended on Helena's wholesalers and journeyed there several times each year to purchase their merchandise. Their visits occasionally drew attention in the local newspapers.

> Charles Blum, that genial and popular Deer Lodge dry goods merchant, is over on both business & pleasure—purchasing such minor articles in his line as will insure him the most complete stock on the West Side, and shaking the hands of friends on every corner....[15]

Jewish merchants kept their ties with relatives and friends engaged in merchandising in other parts of the country. They utilized these ties to set up trading contacts that were beneficial, not only to build up their existent retail and wholesale businesses, but also to open new stores in other camps. For example, Charles Blum and several of his contemporaries, including William Weinstein and William Copinus, had operated clothing and dry goods stores in Helena in the 1860s.[16]

When they moved their mercantile establishments to other locations in Montana, they retained their connections with Helena wholesalers and friends.[17]

Many Helena Jewish merchants depended upon Jewish business associates both in Montana and in the trading centers of New York and San Francisco. They participated in merchandising networks, consisting of brothers, cousins, and friends in shifting partnerships. It was through such partnerships and trading contacts that many Jews found business success in Helena and in the West.[18]

A number of Helena's early general merchandise and tobacco stores were owned by Jewish men in partnerships with their brothers. In 1867 at least four of the seventeen Jewish-owned dry goods and clothing stores and one of the three Jewish-owned tobacco stores listed in the newspaper directory were family operations.[19] Also, at this time there were some Jewish firms identified only as Emanuel and Company or G. Goldberg and Company that were partnerships between either brothers, relatives, or Jewish friends.[20] One such store, for example, Lavenberg and Company, was owned by Alexander Lavenberg and his brother Isaac.[21] Four Helena dry goods and clothing stores, Auerbach Brothers, Loeb and Brother, Morris Brothers, and Sands Brothers, were owned in the late 1860s by Jewish brothers and continued to operate under these partnerships throughout the 1870s.[22]

Several stores run by Jewish merchants in Helena were branch operations or affiliates of firms in Denver, San Francisco, and New York. Often the merchants who managed these stores were related by blood or marriage to their partners in Helena and to their business associates in these larger cities. Morris Brothers, for example, was one Helena general merchandise store that was owned by three Jewish brothers and was operated initially as a branch house. In the 1860s John, Moses, and David Morris were operating a dry goods store in Denver, Colorado. They decided to expand their operation by opening two mercantile stores in Montana, one at Virginia City and one at Helena. John Morris ran the Virginia City store until 1863, when a fire destroyed the Morrises' business in Denver, and his brothers joined him in Montana. Eventually, the whole family moved to Helena and sold out its Virginia City interests.[23] By 1867 the Morris brothers operated one general store in Helena and had announced the opening of another store, a wholesale business, which they owned in partnership with their brother-in-law Gumpert Goldberg.[24] John Morris sold out his interest in the business in 1869 and moved to Cincinnati, Ohio, and soon after Mr. Goldberg was reported living in Corinne, Utah. In 1879 Morris Brothers, owned by David and Moses Morris, was still in operation on Main Street in Helena.[25]

Another firm with family trading connections was Koenigsberger and Brother, a branch of the Koenigsberger family firm in San Francisco. In 1867, this store was operated by Philip and Sebastian Koenigsberger, who sold cigars and tobacco at 13 Main Street.[26] Evidently it was a successful business, because on December 4, 1873, the *Helena Weekly Herald* noted the departure of one of its owners, Sebastian Koenigsberger, and his wife on a six-month vacation to Europe.[27]

On January 9, 1874, just one month after their departure, a fire destroyed numerous buildings in Helena, and Koenigsberger and Brother suffered losses totaling $35,000.[28] This fire, which occurred during the economic depression that followed the Panic of 1873, may have prompted the Koenigsbergers to close their business in Helena.[29] Sebastian never returned to Montana after his vacation, and in April 1874 Philip Koenigsberger also took his leave, returning to San Francisco.[30]

Poznainsky and Behm (right) were among Helena's pioneer Jewish merchants. Courtesy Montana Historical Society.

Success for Jewish businesses in Montana was not guaranteed by family or business connections, but the more prosperous firms in Helena in the early years were those whose owners kept in close contact with their relatives and friends engaged in merchandising in other cities. Both Auerbach Brothers and Sands Brothers were family operations that utilized their mercantile connections to their advantage and set up personal ties with their suppliers in New York and in San Francisco.

Auerbach Brothers was a general merchandise store established in Helena around 1869 by two Bohemian immigrants, William J. and Leopold Auerbach.[31] The Auerbach brothers had relatives and friends in San Francisco, so they planned any personal visits in that city to coincide with their trips to purchase goods for the Helena store. In 1872 the *Helena Daily Herald* announced the departure of Leopold Auerbach on a buying trip to San Francisco and commented at length on the firm's ability to purchase quality California goods for the Helena market because of its connections.

> The Auerbach Bros. are among the most considerable shippers to this Territory of California goods, and for several years past have done a large and lucrative trade in the metropolis, and in many of the mining camps east and west of the range. The firm purchase[s] the great bulk of their merchandise from first hands—their teas, coffees, sugars, and other staple gorceries [sic] from the importers direct, and the various products and manufactures of California, so popular in all of the mining and agricultural sections of the interior, from the leading firms in Frisco....[32]

Leopold Auerbach set up permanent residence in San Francisco in the late 1870s and Auerbach Brothers had a full-time buyer to attend to its purchasing needs.[33]

The Sands Brothers firm in Helena had its family and business connections in Denver and New York. Its owners, Abraham and Julius Sands, were Polish immigrants who had spent their early years in America engaged in merchandising in New York. When the brothers came west during the gold rush, they established a mercantile business in Denver and sent for their younger brother, Morris, to join them. In the 1860s Abraham and Julius started a general merchandise house in Bannack, Montana, and later transferred this business to Helena.[34]

In 1870 all three brothers were living in Helena and Julius Sands was making buying trips to the East.[35] In order to improve their connections with eastern wholesalers, Julius Sands became the resident buyer for

Sands Brothers in New York and attended to all the firm's purchases. He returned to Montana on yearly business trips, but left the management of the Helena store to Abraham and Morris. This arrangement proved advantageous to the firm, and by the late 1870s Sands Brothers was one of Helena's largest and most prosperous wholesale and retail stores.[36]

Unlike the successful Sands Brothers' firm, many Jewish-owned Helena businesses did not survive the placer boom; consequently, little is known about their owners or their family connections. Surviving records indicate, however, that Helena Jews engaged in a variety of business partnerships and operated commercial enterprises that were not owned exclusively by family members. Some Jews formed business associations with Gentiles, and others opened businesses with Jewish partners who were not relatives. The exact number of enterprises with this type of ownership is difficult to determine because few of these partnerships remained intact long enough to leave any record of their participants.[37]

Jewish merchant Louis Remish, for example, engaged in a short-lived, Jew-Gentile partnership. On February 21, 1867, just months after he was elected one of the trustees of the Hebrew Benevolent Society, Louis was identified by the *Helena Herald* as one of the owners of Remish and Stenzel, a clothing business. The newspaper also announced the expansion of the firm to include a branch store in the Salmon River country.

> Remish & Stenzel—These enterprising wholesale & retail clothing dealers on Main Street, have recently shipped from their house here, and from their branch in Virginia [City], some $20,000 worth of ready made first class clothing to the new Salmon River mines, where they have a large store already completed to receive them.[38]

Not long after this announcement, Louis Remish relinquished his share of the business and on April 18, 1867, the firm publicized his withdrawal from the partnership. Two months later, Louis was operating his own clothing store, Remish and Company, "one door below Wells, Fargo & Co.'s Office on Main St."[39]

During the early years of the gold rush, many Helena businessmen, both Jew and Gentile, engaged in a series of partnerships and business associations. The unpredictability of economic life in the gold camps made the operation of any enterprise a risk; newspapers of the period frequently reported business closures, partnership dissolutions, and costly losses suffered as a result of the frequent fires in Helena. Some merchants terminated their business partnerships and moved away from Helena to seek more lucrative business locations, while others remained in the camp and tried to stay in business, entering one partnership after another. In boom towns of doubtful longevity, most businesses faced a precarious future and Jewish-owned enterprises were no exception.

Isaac Marks and Moe Edinger were two Helena Jewish businessmen whose early business affiliations reflect the uncertainties of the placer period. On Febrary 28, 1867, the *Helena Herald* listed Isaac Marks and his partner, Moe Edinger, as the proprietors of Our Sample Rooms, a liquor store located on Main Street.[40] Three months later, the same newspaper announced the retirement of Mr. Edinger from the business and the addition of a new partner, W. J. Carnduff.[41] In the city directory of the following year, Marks and Edinger are listed once again as partners, but this time in another liquor business, the "Branch Saloon, Ike & Moe Proprietors, Main Street, Helena."[42] By 1870 Isaac Marks was the only member of this partnership still operating a saloon business in Helena. Moe Edinger was reported by the newspaper to be selling clothing at Cedar Junction, another placer camp.[43]

Like his contemporaries, Ben Falk had a series of business partners during his pioneer years in Montana. In 1865 he moved to Helena from British Columbia and opened a meat market on Wood Street.[44] During his first full year in business, Falk entered and ended at least two separate ownership arrangements involving the Empire Meat Market.[45] Despite these successive partnerships, the market remained in operation and by 1868 Ben Falk was its sole proprietor.[46] Falk ran the market successfully until April 28, 1869, when a fire swept Helena and destroyed numerous buildings, including his store. Following this disaster, Falk abandoned his business interests in Helena and moved to New York.[47]

Fires and fluctuating partnerships were not the only conditions that disrupted business activity in Montana's mining camps. A more significant risk to stable commercial operations in Helena was the practice of buying and selling goods on credit. Few merchants traded on a strictly cash-and-carry basis. Most sold merchandise to miners, prospectors and retail customers on credit. Often the merchants were badly undercapitalized and were themselves credit customers of wholesalers in New York and San Francisco. On the frontier, success in merchandising "required a skill, the luck of being in the right place at the right time, adequate capital and a line of credit."[48] The latter two ingredients were crucial elements for the prosperity of Helena's Jewish merchants, and lack of them precipitated bankruptcies and business failures.[49]

Many Jewish merchants preferred dealing with cash customers and used persuasive newspaper advertising to attract them to their stores. In 1870 Julius Sands, for example, ran numerous small ads in the *Helena Daily Herald*, including the following: "Buyers at wholesale and retail are invited to buy goods at their own prices, for cash." The Sands Brothers firm also offered their customers "a special discount of *five per cent* on all *cash* purchases."[50] Most Helena merchants started their businesses by selling goods "cheap for cash," but later extended their operations to accommodate credit customers.[51]

Julius Basinski was one Jewish merchant who established a successful credit business with several Helena Jewish firms. At the age of twenty-two, he emigrated to the United States from Poland and lived four years in New York before deciding "to leave for the Montana Mining fields."[52] Soon after his arrival in Helena in February 1870, Basinski realized that he did not have sufficient capital to open a business, one that could compete with the mercantile firms already operating in the camp. He presented a letter of introduction to the Sands brothers, but was unsuccessful in securing a clerkship in their store. Finally, with the assistance of Jacob and Dave Goldberg, Jewish clothing merchants, Basinski met a local cigar dealer with whom he transacted business.

Discouraged by his prospects in Helena, Julius investigated other business locations and decided to move to Radersburg, a mining town near Helena. He opened a candy and cigar store in that community and returned to Helena periodically to replenish his supply of goods. Basinski retained his contacts with the Goldberg brothers, and with their assistance established credit with some of Helena's leading business houses. According to his own account, he received liberal credit terms from Sol Holzman and Brother, Morris Brothers, L. Auerbach and Brother, Gans and Klein, and Koenigsberger and Brother, but "these credits were accepted only with one understanding—they are not to hurry me with the payments and [I] will remit to them as fast as business would justify." This credit arrangement proved satisfactory for all concerned and Basinski operated a successful business in Radersburg for several years. Finally, the community's lack of growth forced Julius to seek new opportunities elsewhere. He moved his goods first to Bozeman and later to Miles City, where he remained in the general merchandise business until the 1890s.[53]

Sands Brothers Dry Goods store occupied a prominent spot on Helena's Main Street. Courtesy Montana Historical Society.

Montana retail merchants were not always good credit risks. Some fell behind in payments to their Helena wholesalers and received threatening letters asking them to come forward and settle past due accounts.[54] Others were unable to pay for their purchases because of mismanagement or the loss of goods in a fire, and they became the subjects of court action.[55] Occasionally, too, a merchant had no intention of repaying his bills and deliberately defrauded his creditors.

On May 29, 1868, the *Montana Post* published a story about Abe Polak, a Jewish merchant "with an eye more to his own pecuniary interest and comfort than to that of his creditors." According to the newspaper, Abe had been employed at Louis Remish and Company for some time when he decided to embark on a peddling expedition. He purchased $3,000 worth of goods on credit from several local firms and left Helena to peddle his merchandise in several mining camps. Abe wrote his creditors once from German Gulch and reported his progress, but nothing more was heard from him until news reached

Helena that he had "shook the dust of Montana soil from his feet and into the faces of those who had befriended him."[56] He had sold his goods and was attempting to leave the territory without paying his creditors when he was robbed. The *Helena Daily Herald* reported the incident with a vindictive tone:

> Tit for Tat—Abe Pollock [Polak]...lost eight hundred dollars by the late robbery of the overland coach, near Pleasant Valley. We are informed that he had disposed of the goods and purchased a ticket for Salt Lake, with the intention of defrauding his creditors out of the money which he had realized from the sale thereof. This is what we would call 'tit for tat.'[57]

The editor of the *Montana Post* also published his own version of the story—describing the stagecoach robbers as "agents of retributive justice."[58] Understandably, local newspaper editors were sympathetic to the losses of the town's merchants and were quick to publicize any events that jeopardized business operations in the community.

Helena merchants suffered losses in their credit dealings, not only with retail customers, but also with their own wholesalers. Occasionally, a Jewish merchant failed to pay his debts and experienced a tightening of credit by his wholesalers in New York or San Francisco. Mitchel Block was one Helena merchant who encountered difficulties with his creditors. Less than a year after his costly experience with Abe Polak, the *Helena Weekly Herald* reported Block's latest misfortune:

> Persuant [*sic*] to instructions received in this city from New York and San Francisco house[s], the wholesale clothing establishment of M. Bloch [Block], Main Street, Helena, was closed last evening by writ of attachment to recover the sum of $27,000.[59]

Helena Jewish merchants took risks when selling or buying goods on credit, but they realized the importance of such financial arrangements. During these years of recession and recurring fires, many merchants had minimal capital resources, so they had either "to find credit or face bankruptcy."[60]

Jewish merchants had more difficulty obtaining credit than non-Jews because credit investigation agencies like Dun and Company usually considered Jews a poor credit risk. Jewish "religious affiliation more often than not carried with it the automatic assumption and assignment of 'poor' or 'not good' for credit." To obtain a favorable credit rating, a person must possess "character" as well as assets. Dun and Company investigators often ascribed the latter to Jews, but not the former.[61] Helena merchant, Alexander Lavenberg, for example, was described by a Dun and Company agent as "Very hard pay. 'L' lives here with a woman not his wife. He is a very hard case."[62] Such negative "character" reports meant that Jews received low credit ratings and often were denied access to credit and loans from customary lending institutions. To overcome ethnic and religious prejudice that often barred them from credit, Helena Jews had little choice but to borrow money from relatives and Jewish business associates. Without this credit network, Jewish merchants would have lacked the capital to open or expand business operations in the West.[63]

While Helena's Jewish merchants usually relied upon other Jews for credit and loans, they did not confine their financial transactions to their coreligionists. Gold was the medium of exchange in Montana in the 1860s and miners depended upon merchants and saloon keepers to convert their gold dust into coin and credit. Helena's Jewish merchants and their non-Jewish colleagues set the value for gold dust circulating in the camp, converted that dust into currency, and safeguarded valuables.[64] Jews who accumulated enough money from merchandising also made loans to individuals and invested their capital in other business enterprises.

Some Helena Jewish firms, including Auerbach Brothers, offered short-term, personal loans at comparatively low interest rates to both individuals and other firms.[65] Occasionally, the recipients of these loans were neighboring businesswomen, whose not so respectable occupations made access to credit from conventional sources difficult. Dry goods merchants Alexander and Selig Lavenberg extended mortgages to several of the camp's pioneer prostitutes and profited from these transactions. Jewish restaurateur Edward Zimmerman, on the other hand, suffered losses when his mortgages to Helena's fancy ladies went unpaid.[66] If they were fortunate, Jewish merchants who were loaning money received their payments when their notes were due, and used interest obtained from such loans to expand their merchandising activities or to pursue other investment opportunities.

Some Jewish merchants chose mining as an outlet for their investment capital. The earliest lode records for Lewis and Clark County verify the involvement of Helena's Jewish pioneers in mining ventures.[67] Louis Behm, a dry goods and clothing merchant on Bridge Street, recorded two placer mining claims, one on February 24, 1865, at the mouth of Grizzly Gulch and the other on May 2, 1865, in the Green Horn Lode.[68] Two other merchants, David and Moses Morris, recorded ten claims in Lewis and Clark County between April 12, 1867, and September 19, 1867.[69]

In addition to mining, ranching was another enterprise that appealed to Jewish investors. In 1867, the Morris brothers purchased ranch land in Lewis and Clark County and soon were engaged in raising stock. That same year, Louis Gans and Henry Klein, Helena clothing merchants, bought land for farming and raising livestock.[70] Other Jewish firms, including Sands Brothers and Greenhood and Bohm, invested in ranch properties and cattle, horses, and sheep. From these initial investments several Jewish merchants gradually increased their ranching interests, until by the 1880s they had extensive agricultural holdings throughout the Territory.[71]

The Jewish merchants who settled in Helena during the gold rush were influential participants in the business life of the Territory. They specialized in the retail sale of clothing, dry goods, and tobacco, and served as distributors of these items to local residents and people in other mining camps. As businessmen, Jews had an interest in the future of the community. They worked to solve civic problems and to promote cultural activities.[72] Jewish merchants also provided financial services badly needed in the region, offering credit to customers, loans to entrepreneurs, and investment capital to developing industries. An examination of Jewish involvement in Montana's early mercantile trade reveals both the difficulties of merchandising on the frontier and the unique aspects of the Jewish merchant experience in the West.

APPENDIX A
Occupations of Helena Jews, 1868, 1879*

Occupations	Number in 1868	Number in 1879
Assayers	4	2
Auctioneers	1	—
Bankers	5	2
Barbers	1	—
Bookkeepers/Accountants	1	2
Butchers/Meat Markets	2	1
Cashiers	1	—
Clerks/Salesmen	4	1
Express Agents	1	—
General Operators	1	—

APPENDIX A (cont.)
Occupations of Helena Jews, 1868, 1879*

Occupations	Number in 1868	Number in 1879
Grocers	1	—
Hide and Fur Dealers	1	—
Hotel Proprietors	1	3
Loan Officers	—	—
Manufacturers' Agents	—	—
Merchants	42	—
Clothes	1	13
Crockery/Glassware	—	2
Dry Goods	—	3
Fruits/Confectionery	—	—
Hardware	—	—
Miners	2	—
Pawnbrokers	—	—
Peddlers	1	—
Physicians	—	—
Ranchers	—	—
Restaurant Proprietors	—	—
Saloon Keepers/Liquor Dealers	4	1
Tailors/Dressmakers	3	1
Tobacconists/Guns and Liquors	—	4
Not Listed	1	1
Total Number	78	36 (Two with residences out-of-state)

*From *Business Directory of the Metropolis* (Helena, Mont.: 1868); *Montana Business Directory, 1879*

APPENDIX B
Previous Residences of Helena Jews, 1868*

Place	Number
United States	
Alabama	1
California	31
Colorado	8

APPENDIX B (cont.)
Previous Residences of Helena Jews, 1868*

Place	Number
Idaho	3
Illinois	1
Kansas	4
Louisiana	1
Nevada	1
New York	11
Oregon	3
Pennsylvania	3
Texas	1
Utah	1
Virginia	2
Washoe	1
Foreign Countries	
Germany	1
Poland	1
Prussia	2
Not Listed	2
Total Number	78

*From *Historical Sketch and Essay on the Resources of Montana: Including a Business Directory of the Metropolis* (Helena, Mont.: Herald and Job Printing Office, 1868).

NOTES

1. *Helena Daily Herald*, 31 December 1877, p. 1. This essay was adapted from the author's master's thesis, "A Voice from the Rocky Mountains: Helena's Pioneer Jewish Community, 1864–1889" (University of Montana, 1981). There are two other historical studies on Jews in Montana: Benjamin Kelson, "The Jews of Montana" (M.A., Montana State University, 1950); Patricia L. Dean, "The Jewish Community of Helena, Montana: 1866–1900" (B.A., Carroll College, 1977).

2. Peter R. Decker, "Jewish Merchants in San Francisco: Social Mobility on the Urban Frontier," *American Jewish History* 68 (June 1979):396.

3. *First Annual Report of the Bureau of Agriculture, Labor, and Industry of Montana for the Year Ended November 30, 1893* (Helena, Mont.: 1893), p. 287.

4. *Helena Daily Herald*, 31 December 1877, p. 1.

5. Benjamin Kelson, "The Jews of Montana," *Western States Jewish Historical Quarterly*, Vol. III, 1 (January 1971), p. 114.

6. *Ibid.*, Vol. III, 2 (April 1971), pp. 170–189.

7. This figure includes only those men who arrived in Helena between 1864 and 1871 and are known to be Jewish by their identification as such in local newspapers or through their membership in the Hebrew Benevolent Society and their contributions to the Alliance Israelite Universelle, a relief organization set up by French Jews in 1860.

8. U.S., Department of Commerce, Bureau of the Census, Ninth Census of the United States, 1870. Thirty-nine of the fifty-eight Jewish males listed had been born in Bavaria, Prussia, or Poland.

9. *Historical Sketch and Essay on the Resources of Montana: Including a Business Directory of the Metropolis* (Helena, Mont.: Herald and Job Printing Office, 1868); U.S. Manuscript Census, 1870.

10. *Helena Herald*, 28 February 1867, p. 1. Stenzel of Remish and Stenzel is not known to be Jewish. Two merchants, J. P. Nohm and John How are not Jewish. Honest Charley's auction and commission store might have been owned by a Jewish merchant, either Charles Friedman or Charles Blum. Both were merchants in Helena at this time, and not identified with a particular store.

11. *Helena Herald*, 28 February 1867, p. 1. W. Brown, M. Goldman, and Koenigsberger and Brother were all Jewish.

12. *Helena Herald Supplement*, 26 June 1867, p. 2.

13. *Business Directory of the Metropolis* (Helena, 1868), p. 169.

14. *Ibid.*, p. 135.

15. *Helena Weekly Herald*, 9 October 1873, p. 7.

16. *Business Directory of the Metropolis* (Helena, 1868), pp. 139, 141; *Helena Herald*, 28 February 1867, p. 1.

17. *Helena Daily Herald*, 14 June 1878, p. 3. William Weinstein moved to Philipsburg and William Copinus moved to Butte.

18. Robert E. Levinson, *The Jews in the California Gold Rush* (New York: KTAV Publishing House, Inc., 1978), pp. 32–35; William Toll, "Fraternalism and Community Structure on the Urban Frontier: The Jews of Portland, Oregon —A Case Study," *Pacific Historical Review*, 47 (August 1978):372–378.

19. *Helena Herald*, 28 February 1867, p. 1. The family-owned dry goods and clothing stores were W. Weinstein and Brother, Ellis and Brothers, Loeb and Brother, and John Morris and Brother. The only family-owned tobacco store was Koenigsberger and Brother.

20. *Helena Herald*, 28 February 1867, p. 1.

21. *Helena Daily Herald*, 27 March 1871, p. 3; *Deer Lodge New Northwest*, 1 June 1888, p. 3.

22. *Montana Territory History and Business Directory, 1879* (Helena, Mont.: Fisk Brothers, Printers and Binders), pp. 142, 152, 153, 157.

23. Michael A. Leeson, ed., *History of Montana: 1739–1885* (Chicago, Ill.: Warner, Beers and Company, 1885), p. 1238; Joaquin Miller, *An Illustrated History of the State of Montana* (Chicago, Ill.: Lewis Publishing Co., 1894), p. 202; *Progressive Men of the State of Montana* (Chicago, Ill.: A. W. Bowen and Co., 1902), pp. 764, 1742.

24. *Helena Herald*, 28 February 1867, p. 1; *Helena Herald Supplement*, 26 June 1867, p. 2.

25. *Helena Herald*, 12 February 1872, p. 3; *Ibid.*, 6 April 1877, p. 3; *Montana Business Directory, 1879*, p. 153.

26. *Helena Herald*, 28 February 1867, p. 1.

27. *Helena Weekly Herald*, 4 December 1873, p. 7.

28. Leeson, *History of Montana*, p. 717. In the earlier 1869 fire the *Helena Weekly Herald* reported that Koenigsberger and Brother suffered losses of $5,000, 6 May 1869, p. 7.

29. Michael P. Malone and Richard B. Roeder, *Montana: A History of Two Centuries* (Seattle, Wash.: University of Washington Press, 1977), pp. 130, 142.

30. *Helena Daily Independent*, 15 April 1874, p. 3.

31. Neither brother's name is listed in the 1868 Helena city directory. Both are listed in the Hebrew Benevolent Society minutes; William was elected to the society on 3 December 1869, and Leopold was elected a trustee of the society on 3 June 1869. Hebrew Benevolent Association of Helena Records, 1865–1943, Manuscript Collection 38, Montana Historical Society Archives, Helena, Montana. Only William Auerbach is listed in the 1870 census.

32. *Helena Daily Herald*, 14 February 1872, p. 3.

33. William Auerbach to Leopold Auerbach, 1877, L. Auerbach and Brother Papers, 1868–1880, Manuscript Collection 125, Montana Historical Society Archives, Helena, Montana. *Montana Business Directory, 1879*, pp. 142, 161.

34. Leeson, *History of Montana*, p. 1249, pp. 1351–1352; *Progressive Men of Montana*, p. 398; *Business Directory of the Metropolis* (Helena, Mont.: 1868), p. 155.

35. *Helena Daily Independent*, 15 December 1910, p. 5; U.S. Manuscript Census, 1870; *Helena Daily Herald*, 23 July 1870, p. 3.

36. *Helena Daily Herald*, 18 May 1877, p. 3; *Montana Business Directory, 1879*, p. 157; *Progressive Men of Montana*, p. 398.

37. A notable exception to this statement was the Stadler and Kaufman livestock firm. In the early 1870s, Louis Kaufman formed a partnership with Louis Stadler to provide meat for the gold camps. They went into the stock-raising business and opened a butcher shop in Helena. Their partnership was continuous until the death of Mr. Kaufman in 1933.

38. Hebrew Benevolent Association of Helena Records, 1865–1943, 3 December 1866; *Helena Herald Supplement*, 21 February 1867, p. 1.

39. *Helena Herald*, 18 April 1867, p. 2; Ibid., 19 June 1867, p. 5.

40. *Ibid.*, 28 February 1867, p. 1.

41. *Ibid.*, 9 May 1867, p. 1.

42. *Business Directory of the Metropolis* (Helena, Mont.: 1868), p. 94.

43. U.S. Manuscript Census, 1870; *Helena Daily Herald*, 11 February 1870, p. 3. Cedar Junction was located in the Cedar Creek (Montana) mining district.

44. Helen Fitzgerald Sanders, *A History of Montana*, 3 vols. (Chicago, Ill.: Lewis Publishing Co., 1913), 2:1160.

45. *Helena Montana Radiator*, 27 January 1866, p. 4; *Helena Herald*, 20 December 1866, p. 3.

46. *Business Directory of the Metropolis* (Helena, Mont.: 1868), p. 94.

47. *Helena Weekly Herald*, 6 May 1869, p. 7; Sander's *History of Montana*, p. 1160. A summary of Helena's early fires is presented in Leeson's *History of Montana*, pp. 712–718.

48. William M. Kramer and Norton B. Stern, "Early California Associations of Michel Goldwater and His Family," *Western States Jewish Historical Quarterly* 4 (July 1972):195.

49. Levinson, *California Gold Rush*, pp. 21, 52–53.

50. *Helena Daily Herald*, 10 February 1870, p. 3; *Ibid.*, 29 December 1875, p. 3.

51. *Helena Herald*, 6 December 1866, p. 1.

52. Julius Basinski Diary, 1883–1925, Biographies file, 14 pages, p. 3, American Jewish Archives, Cincinnati, Ohio.

53. *Ibid.*; Robert E. Levinson, "Julius Basinski: Jewish Merchant in Montana," *Montana the Magazine of Western History* 22 (January 1972):60–68.

54. Letterpress Book, 31 October 1876–12 March 1877, L. Auerbach and Brother Papers, 1868–1880.

55. Helena's Jewish merchants brought their complaints with customers, other merchants, and freighters before Montana's courts. Jews frequently utilized Montana's legal institutions and expected that their cases would be judged seriously and equitably. Note the number of Jewish plaintiffs in the proceeding accounts in the Helena newspapers of the period: *Helena Herald*, 14 March 1867, p. 5; *Ibid.*, 4 April 1867, p. 1; *Helena Herald Supplement*, 4 April 1867, p. 1; *Helena Daily Herald*, 9 March 1870, p. 3. For an examination of the treatment that other minorities received in Montana's courts, read John R. Wunder's article, "Law and Chinese in Frontier Montana," *Montana the Magazine of Western History* 30 (July 1980):18–31.

56. *Helena Montana Post*, 29 May 1868, p. 8. Polak is listed as one of the Helena Jewish contributors to the Alliance Israelite Universelle, *Cincinnati Israelite*, 17 April 1868, p. 6.

57. *Helena Daily Herald*, 28 May 1868, p. 8.

58. *Helena Montana Post*, 29 May 1868, p. 8.

59. *Helena Weekly Herald*, 25 February 1869, p. 7.

60. Decker, "Jewish Merchants in San Francisco," p. 398.

61. *Ibid.*, pp. 398–399.

62. R. G. Dun Reports, Vol. I, Montana and Nevada Territories, p. 240.

63. Decker, "Jewish Merchants in San Francisco," pp. 398–402.

64. Leeson, *History of Montana*, p. 704.

65. William Auerbach to Leopold Auerbach, 21 February 1877, p. 272, L. Auerbach and Brother Papers, 1868–1880.

66. Paula Petrik, "Capitalists with Rooms: Prostitution in Helena, Montana, 1865–1900," *Montana the Magazine of Western History* 31 (April 1981):30–34.

67. The first lode records are listed under Edgerton County and are housed in the Office of the Clerk and Recorder, Lewis and Clark County, Helena, Montana. The county name was changed in 1867.

68. Lode Record A, Lewis and Clark County, 24 February 1865, p. 6; Lode Record B, Lewis and Clark County, 2 May 1865, p. 7, Office of the Clerk and Recorder, Lewis and Clark County, Helena, Montana.

69. Lode Record C, Lewis and Clark County, pp. 242, 273, 274, 275, 291.

70. Ranches and Ditches, Record C, Lewis and Clark County, pp. 30, 264.

71. *Helena Daily Herald*, 16 May 1874, p. 3; Leeson, *History of Montana*, pp. 1214–1215; *Progressive Men of Montana*, pp. 255, 376, 398–399; Miller, *An Illustrated History*, pp. 203, 574.

72. Morrow, "Helena's Pioneer Jewish Community," pp. 62–108. This chapter discusses Jewish civic and cultural activities in Helena. It includes Jewish involvement in issues of concern to the mercantile community.

3 /

THE WAR OF
THE RAILROAD KINGS
Great Northern–Northern Pacific
Rivalry in Montana, 1881–1896

W. THOMAS WHITE

The role of outside capital in the development of Montana has attracted both journalistic and historic attention. K. Ross Toole and others focused principally on the mining phase of this phenomenon, culminating in the formation of the Amalgamated Copper Company. Similarly, Montana's major railroads acquired vast economic power by virtue of land holdings and transportation dominance across the state.

In this essay, W. Thomas White, curator of the James J. Hill Reference Library in St. Paul, brings the twin themes of corporate control and railroad development together. He places economic competition and concentration in Montana in regional and national context. White demonstrates that economic and political rivalry began between the Northern Pacific and the Great Northern even before the first transcontinental route across Montana was completed in 1883. This struggle involved most, if not all, of the key political leaders in Montana and affected not only railroad construction but also labor activity, the W. A. Clark-Marcus Daly feud, and the capital fight of 1894. Ultimately, the Great Northern emerged victorious when the Northern Pacific failed to survive the Panic of 1893 and Hill secured control of his competitor. Railroad consolidation paralleled the unification of Montana's mining industry and reflected corporate centralization throughout the nation during the late 1890s and early 1900s.

"The War of the Copper Kings" dominates the historical literature of Montana. Following in the interpretive tradition established by C. B.

Glasscock and Joseph Kinsey Howard, K. Ross Toole found that dispute of central importance to any understanding of Montana's past. Clark C. Spence continued the theme in his bicentennial history of the state, and recently Michael P. Malone has written incisively on *The Battle for Butte*.[1] That is as it should be, for the mineowners' battles are an integral part of Montana's political and economic heritage.

Yet there was another and not unrelated "war" which also had a substantial impact on the state's experience in the late nineteenth century. As they forged west from Minnesota, the Northern Pacific (led variously by Henry Villard, Thomas F. Oakes, Robert Harris, and Brayton Ives) and James J. Hill's Great Northern (before 1890, the St. Paul, Minneapolis & Manitoba) exported their rivalry to Montana as each maneuvered to become the dominant transcontinental in the Northwest.[2] Between 1881, two years before the NP was completed and five years before its rival entered Montana, and 1896, when Hill forced the bankrupt NP to end the long-standing feud, each road sought out its own allies in Montana, in the nation's capital, and in the great financial centers of the East. They fought on many fronts. The future of northern Montana, the shattering of the Northern Pacific-Union Pacific pooling arrangement, the construction of the Manitoba line through the Blackfeet Reservation, the early days of the Clark-Daly feud, the labor unrest of 1894, and the capital fight of 1892–1894 all involved the Railroad Kings and captured Montanans' attention—both their outrage and their approbation.

As early as 1881, less than three years after the St. Paul & Pacific completed its line to Winnipeg and opened the Red River Valley for settlement, Paris Gibson was urging James J. Hill to build west. They had met in Minneapolis where Gibson constructed the first merchant flouring mill (the Cataract, 1859) and the North Star Woolen Mill (1862). However the Panic of 1873 proved devastating for Gibson, and in 1879 (at the age of forty-nine) he struck out for Montana to recoup his losses. Within two years he was advising Hill: "All that triangular shaped country between the Missouri and Marias rivers and bounded on the West by the Marias range is very important to your company [and] no road can ever be built into Montana as cheaply as by the Northern or Milk River route." To the anxious Gibson, time already was growing uncomfortably short. Unless Hill moved quickly, much of northern Montana would "be gobbled up by the Northern Pacific Co. unless you [Hill] should reach it from Benton."[3]

When his long-time acquaintance showed no inclination to challenge the Northern Pacific in Montana, Gibson did an about-face, urging the NP to construct branch lines to the north. To that end, he wrote Hill "to put a flea in the right man's ear at once."[4] Gibson, known as the "Father of Great Falls," had some grounds for assuming that both Hill's and his own interests could follow such lines. Both men had a direct personal concern for the development of the area. By late 1882, they had concluded a partnership to purchase much of the remaining nonreservation land in northern Montana, including the "several Falls of the Missouri...and also the land adjacent to the Missouri River between the Falls and the mouth of the Sun River on the South bank of the Missouri River, and also certain lands adjacent to the River on the North bank, about twenty-five hundred acres in all."[5] However, Gibson, whose attention was focused wholly on the development of Great Falls, was able to alter his view of the NP's potential role in Montana. Hill, who had found himself at odds with the Northern Pacific in Minnesota and who, even then, was probably considering his own drive to the Pacific, viewed his stake in the future of Great Falls and the surrounding territory as peripheral to his broader concern for the well-being of his railroad.

Even Gibson's new hopes for the NP proved temporary. By the spring of 1883, he had begun to worry that the newly completed NP would, as his friend T.E. Collins reported of a conversation with Henry Villard, "build no branch lines unless compelled to do so to keep other RRds. out." On the local level, Gibson soon was "confident that the prominent Helena parties," jealous of any rival towns, "will do their 'level best' to influence N.P. Management to keep away from the mouth of the Sun River."[6]

Among the most prominent of the "Helena parties" was Samuel T. Hauser. One of the territory's major figures, Hauser, as Rex Myers has observed, "played the N.P. and the Hill lines against one another to his own advantage." While Hauser's loyalties remained unclear at first, Gibson was convinced—wrongly as things turned out—that Charles A. Broadwater (also a prominent figure in Helena and Montana) was an enemy, warning that he "will do Great Falls no good... and...will stand in with them [the 'Helena parties'] every time." Yet Gibson assured Hill that "Broadwater cannot play a two sided game to save his soul without my knowledge."[7]

Much of this ambiguity evaporated once Hill decided to build the Montana extension. Hauser became the NP's principal ally in the state, while Broadwater, Martin Maginnis, Joseph Toole, and later, Marcus

Daly and many of the other mineowners threw their support to the St. Paul, Minneapolis & Manitoba. The end of the NP-Manitoba truce, which clarified alignments in Montana, followed Hill's 1884 visit to the territory. The presence of coal deposits (confirmed by Columbia University School of Mines Professor J.S. Newberry), the potential for hydroelectric power at Great Falls to process the ores from the burgeoning mines of western Montana, the willingness of Hill's financial backers to support the extension, his own interest in the Great Falls Water Power and Townsite Company, and the agricultural potential of northern Montana all worked toward the decision to incorporate the Montana Central and contest the NP's and the UP's hegemony in the growing territory.[8]

By early 1885, Hauser clearly was alarmed by the prospect of Hill's entry. "Governor Hauser has been very busy in the East during the past three or four weeks in endeavoring to impress upon the directors and managers of the Northern Pacific the danger of allowing any rail company or interest. . .in[to] this territory which in the future might form a foothold for the entrance of any road and especially of the road with which you are connected," Maginnis informed Hill, following a conversation with Thomas C. Power. "Of course the Governor's notion is to kill or head off any scheme of local development of which he is not at the head." Although Maginnis felt, probably wrongly, that the NP and particularly Vice President and General Manager Thomas F. Oakes were inclined to be "apathetic" about the matter, since they could construct branch lines and easily protect their own interests, he did warn that "Hauser is a good talker and there is no knowing what he may *scare* them into."[9]

To the north, yet another rival emerged. Alexander Galt had secured encouragement and some financial support from the NP and a group of Fort Benton backers led by W.G. Conrad to construct a line from Dunmore on the Canadian Pacific Railroad south to Fort Benton. The proposed line threatened to cut Hill off from the northern Rockies, and he moved quickly to counter the maneuver. At his behest, CPR president George Stephen, who also had a substantial investment in the Manitoba line, easily quashed Galt's plans, which threatened both roads, and effectively delayed construction of the north-south line until after Hill had completed his road into Montana. On other fronts, the Northern Pacific moved to block the Montana Central's line to the Red Mountain mines in Lewis and Clark County and refused Hill's re-

James J. Hill in 1886. His decision to build a railroad to Montana produced economic and political changes in the region. Courtesy James J. Hill Reference Library.

quest to reduce the $35 per ton rate to $20 for the over 10,000 tons of rails he planned to ship over the NP line.[10]

However, because of the Northern Pacific-Union Pacific pooling arrangement which kept rates artificially high in Butte and Helena, both roads and their supporters were becoming increasingly unpopular.

Hill and his allies were able to play effectively upon this unpopularity and further discredit their rivals. They concentrated their efforts upon the Montana Improvement Company, a Hauser-led affiliate of the Northern Pacific, which, U.S. Land Commissioner William Andrew Jackson Sparks charged:

> was formed. . .for the purpose of monopolizing timber traffic in Montana and Idaho, and under a contract with the railroad co. running for 20 years, has exploited the timber from unsurveyed public lands for great distances along the line of said road, shipping the product of joint trespass and controlling the general market.[11]

By March, 1886, Hill had recruited a new ally to handle the anti-NP/Montana Improvement Company campaign from New York and Washington. R.B. Harrison, son of Senator (two years later, President) Benjamin Harrison, was president of the Montana Cattle Company and keenly interested in the early arrival of the Manitoba road. "On Seventeenth Van Wyck [Senator Charles H. Van Wyck, Republican, Nebraska] introduced resolution to investigate Montana Improvement Company. . .Unanimously agreed to by Senate. Hauser and [E.L.] Bonner here and much alarmed," Harrison wired Hill, counseling that "this resolution judiciously pressed. . .can be used to stop all opposition to you as an investigation will hurt N.P. land grant seriously if their connection with Improvement Company is clearly shown."[12]

Hill immediately ordered Broadwater "to have parties furnish the information" to publicly discredit his opponents. "If you could show that the Company has been loaded down with branches built by the Directors and officers of the Company, the bonds guaranteed by the Northern Pacific for double the cost of the road; also, such enterprises as Wickes' outfit [the Helena and Wickes Railway of which Hauser was also president] and the interest held by officers of the Company from the commencement," Hill suggested, "it would make interesting reading for the public. You, however, will know how to get these items forward and which ones to send."[13]

Meanwhile, Harrison fed the New York Associated Press the story of Governor Hauser's close ties to the NP and his role in the attempt to exclude the Montana Central from the territory. The local press played up the pooling arrangement the NP and UP had for controlling freight rates into Butte and Helena—the year before, Hill had complained privately to Stephen of that arrangement, by which the NP received "$500,000 per annum for keeping out of Butte."[14]

Consequently, when he returned from Washington, Hauser found "the people as a unit against him" in Helena. Even his friends, as Broadwater reported to Hill, "dare not have anything to do" with any organization formed to support either him or the NP. When Oakes "learned that [the] company has been rendered very unpopular in Montana," even he "expresse[d] himself...as desiring to throw Hauser overboard." The leaders of the Northern Pacific did not do so —as late as 1892, Oakes still considered him "our" man—but Hauser's apparent bungling of the road's anti-Manitoba campaign remained an irritant.[15]

It remains difficult to assess the Northern Pacific's precise role in the next round of the railroad war, which centered on the necessity for the Manitoba to secure a right-of-way through the Blackfeet Reservation in northern Montana. On July 7, 1886, President Grover Cleveland vetoed the first right-of-way bill, complaining:

> it ignores the right of the Indians to be consulted as to the disposition of their lands, opens wide the door to any railroad corporation to do what, under the treaty governing the greater portion of the reservation, is reserved to the United States alone; it gives the right to enter upon Indian lands to a class of corporations carrying with them many individuals not known for any scrupulous regard for the interest or welfare of the Indians; it invites a general invasion of the Indian country, and brings into contact and intercourse with the Indians a class of whites and others who are independent of the orders, regulations, and control of the resident agents.
>
> Corporations operating railroads through Indian lands are strongly tempted to infringe at will upon the reserved rights and property of Indians and thus are apt to become so arbitrary in their dealings and domineering in their conduct toward them that the Indians become disquieted, often threatening outbreaks, and periling the lives of frontier settlers and others.
>
> I am impressed with the belief that the bill under consideration does not sufficiently guard against an invasion of the rights and a disturbance of the peace and quiet of the Indians on the reservation mentioned; nor am I satisfied that the legislation proposed is demanded by any exigency of the public welfare.[16]

Cleveland's action dumbfounded Hill, who was one of the president's supporters and who had urged him to "delay [the] matter until fully understood [that an] adverse action would be unjust and disastrous without serving any public end." Paris Gibson intimated that although

The Montana Central was James J. Hill's railroad extension to Butte.
Courtesy Montana Historical Society.

the veto would probably "not delay matters much," it could "encourage the N.P. folks to undertake to do more mean work." "Cleveland may be qualified for sheriff or Mayor of Buffalo," Gibson added bitterly, "but beyond that, he is not safe." Harrison also suspected the hand of the NP, opining to Hill: "The President has been furnished information other than that [which] he received from the Secretary of the Interior to guide him in saying what he did on the subject of this vetoe [sic]. If such information has been furnished him, it will not be difficult to guess from what source it came."[17]

The Northern Pacific's actual role in the Cleveland veto remains a mystery, although it seems unlikely that the road did not actively try to obstruct the arrival of the Manitoba. Certainly the NP's principal ally, the Union Pacific, played a crucial role. Indeed, as Michael Malone and Richard Roeder have argued, Jay Gould personally intervened to urge the Cleveland veto. Furious, Hill reportedly warned Gould that he would "nail every one of your crooks to the doors of the Capitol by their ——— ears" if the UP again dared to intervene on the Northern Pacific's behalf.[18]

Despite this initial setback, the Hill forces, including former Territorial Delegate Martin Maginnis who received over $3,000 for his lobbying efforts,[19] did obtain a right-of-way several months later. Reconsidering matters, Cleveland signed the required legislation, and the Act of February 15, 1887 gave the Manitoba its right-of-way through the Blackfeet Reservation. By summer, Commissioner of Indian Affairs J.D.C. Atkins reported the road had "fully complied" with the legislation, and that "tribal compensation [had been] fixed, and damages to the individual Indians assessed, and paid to the Indians, and the road is now being rapidly constructed on the route defined."[20]

By the end of the year, the Manitoba had reached Helena via Great Falls, laying a staggering 643 miles of track over the Great Plains since the spring when the road's western terminal was in Minot, Dakota Territory. In October, 1886, Hill had pledged to Marcus Daly of the Anaconda Company "to have our engineers press a line from Butte to Anaconda." More importantly, he vowed to shatter the NP-UP pool, insisting that "what we want. . .is a heavy tonnage, and *the heavier it is the lower we can make the rates.*"[21] The completion of the Montana extension to Helena in 1887 and to Butte the following year enabled Hill to fulfill his promise. However, that victory proved to be the end of only one battle in the ongoing rivalry in Montana.

After 1887 the dispute was characterized by a growing competition for freight and a struggle over branch lines, which often spilled over into debates concerning the location of smelters in Helena, Butte, or Great Falls. Inevitably, such rivalries became intermixed with the Clark-Daly Feud, or the War of the Copper Kings, that erupted in 1888. Hill's alliance with Daly grew dramatically between 1887 and 1896, when he finally gained control of the Northern Pacific. By the early 1890s, he found himself firmly allied with the Daly-Broadwater-Anaconda forces and opposed to the Clark-Hauser-Northern Pacific-Helena interests.

None of this was entirely clear at the outset, however. Hill's alliance with Broadwater (until Broadwater's death in 1892), Joseph K. Toole, and Gibson did not necessarily imply any opposition to William Andrews Clark, whose business the Manitoba also sought. Hill and Broadwater, apparently unaware of Daly's secret maneuvering to ensure the election of Republican Thomas H. Carter, enthusiastically suppported the candidacy of Democratic mining magnate Clark in his 1888 bid for territorial delegate. Indeed, Broadwater thought Clark would be "almost invaluable to us in Washington officially—to say nothing of the value of his influence in his Butte business."[22]

The easy accommodation with Clark became more difficult as his feud with Daly intensified and, from 1892 until 1894, crystalized in the state capital fight. Hill joined with the Daly forces for the Anaconda site and against the Clark-Northern Pacific-Hauser forces pushing for Helena. Great Falls boomer Paris Gibson's long-time competition with Helena to attract smelters meshed easily with the hardening lines of the Clark-Daly Feud. "Helena people always have and still are wedded to the Northern Pacific road," Gibson reminded Hill during the 1892 capital fight.[23]

Gibson preferred that Great Falls be the capital, but since Daly was firm in his hopes for Anaconda, he and Hill deferred to him and threw their resources into the anti-Helena campaign. By November, Gibson felt "much encouraged as we are developing great strength among the laboring men [and] have a large force in the field and shall keep adding to it until the last day." The Helena forces, who "all work for the N.P. Co.," remained formidable, but Hill's rival could not "control *all* votes on their line."[24]

The 1892 election, which demonstrated the growing Populist power and the Democrats' disarray, proved inconclusive insofar as the capital fight was concerned. Neither Helena nor Anaconda commanded a majority among the roster of contenders that included Boulder, Bozeman, Butte, Deer Lodge, and despite Hill's and Gibson's withdrawal of support, Great Falls. In the run-off election, scheduled for 1894, Gibson perceived the main chance for his town, observing: "If Mr. Daly will locate these works ["the Refineries of the Anaconda Co."] here, Cascade Co. will give him a solid vote two years hence, and will do all that can be done to carry the vote of Northern Montana for Anaconda."[25]

Daly seemed eager to oblige. Yet as the 1894 contest neared, he complained of new obstacles to such an enterprise. "There is a power at work in New York to turn [James Ben Ali] Haggin[26] from the possibility of locating a refinery at Great Falls," Daly confided to Hill, adding: "This is what they dread more than anything else." From another quarter, Daly and Haggin had to ward off attempts to locate their "refinery" at Buffalo. "These things must be stopped. . . and I have no fears of the result," Daly assured Hill, asking him for advice and aid in that effort which was "not alone in the interest of the Great Northern, but to the mutual interests of both [the Great Northern and the Anaconda Company]."[27]

When the bottom fell out of the economy in 1893 (the same year the Great Northern reached the Pacific Coast), the Hill-Daly alliance faced new tests but emerged stronger than ever, despite each man's decidedly different view of the silver debate then sweeping the country. A Cleveland Democrat, Hill was a hard money, gold advocate, while Daly and most Montanans who were dependent on the state's mines were staunch silver advocates. Their dispute with the forces of the Northern Pacific again became apparent in the wave of labor unrest that swept the state, as it did the nation, in the spring and summer of 1894. The Great Northern Strike, the Coxeyite activity in Butte and elsewhere, and the Pullman Strike embarassed all the state's roads. However, the latter two events served to reinforce the widespread resentment of the NP, already in popular disfavor because of its pooling arrangement with the UP in the 1880s, its relationship with the Montana Improvement Company, and its attempt to claim much of the state's mineral lands as part of its land grant.[28]

The Great Northern did not emerge unscathed from its battle with the American Railway Union in the spring—indeed, most Montanans seem to have supported the ARU. However, Daly reported that much of the general hostility, including his own, was directed at local officials who had mismanaged the dispute and actually precipitated the strike. Although he tended to discount the rumor, Daly also felt it at least possible that "the other roads are working this thing up."[29]

The unpopular and bankrupt Northern Pacific was another matter, and in both the Coxeyite and Pullman affairs Hill's miner allies worked hard to inflame the anti-NP sentiment. Daly's *Anaconda Standard* dispatched a reporter to accompany William Hogan's "army" when it commandeered an NP train from the Butte roundhouse and raced eastward, and the paper gave even-handed coverage of the Coxeyites' popular reception in railroad towns along the route. Later, Daly-owned business concerns took out advertisements in the publication *Keep Off the Grass*, which Puget Sound Coxeyites printed in Anaconda to raise money for their own protest march on the nation's capital.[30]

During the Pullman Strike two months later, the *Standard* joined with most of the state's other newspapers—in marked contrast to their national counterparts—to defend the character of the American Railway Union strikers, insisting that the insurgent NP and UP workers "are showing constantly that they have the interests of the community at heart."[31] The Great Northern's hand in all this is not clear. However, it does seem reasonable to assume that Hill, however much he disliked ARU president Debs, drew considerable solace from the NP's troubles.

Certainly, the Anaconda Company's indirect support of labor insurgency on the Northern Pacific did not interfere with its alliance with Hill during the last act of the capital fight. In August, as a "first start in the campaign," Daly asked the GN president to write personal letters to the preeminent figures of northern Montana. "[It] will only be necessary for you to say you are in favor of Anaconda for the capital," Daly assured Hill, while he promised to "get [the] letters back."[32]

As the conflict intensified and came to overshadow all other political contests, the GN and NP became even more enmeshed in the Helena-Anaconda fight. "Since the Helena papers and the Helena speakers have denounced him as 'The Shylock of Wall Street,' and designated the Anaconda Company as a foreign corporation," Haggin has become "very much in earnest," Daly reported to Hill, adding: "The man who is not with us is against us." Further, the Anaconda president complained:

> the Northern Pacific is furnishing free transportation for the entire town of Helena, giving free excursions, and doing everything in their power to aid Helena. The Capital Committee of Butte—composed of businessmen and merchants of Butte—wished to pass resolutions boycotting the Northern Pacific Road, for their action in openly fighting Anaconda, which means the interests of Butte, as well. I appealed to them not to do so, and stopped it, at least for the present, as it would give them an excuse for the bitter fight they are making against Anaconda. The officials of the

road claim they are getting no business from the Anaconda Company and therefore are out to fight them. Now something must be done to stop any of the Great Northern people from fighting us also. I do not care to put this in as strong language as Mr. Haggin requested. You will understand the situation, and I trust you will take some action in the matter. There is no middle course to be taken in this case.[33]

To the dismay of the Daly-Hill-Gibson alliance, the Clark-Northern Pacific forces successfully recruited the Boston and Montana and the Butte and Boston companies, which had a smelter at Great Falls and were controlled by the Lewisohn Brothers of New York. Hill angrily called the New Yorkers to account, while his long-time acquaintance, Jacob Schiff of Kuehn, Loeb & Company, tried to mediate the dispute. Leonard Lewisohn, observing that "Mr. Hill must have sent this telegram when he was rather excited," denied any knowledge that Hill "was so much interested in having the Capital go to Anaconda." Schiff urged Hill to accept the explanation, adding that Lewisohn believed Daly had no intention "of opening works at Great Falls" and only promised to do so to enlist GN political support.[34]

The construction of the Northern Pacific gave Montana its first transcontinental railroad. F. Jay Haynes photograph. Courtesy, Montana Historical Society.

Despite such disclaimers, which probably were disingenuous, the Lewisohns' support remained an important factor in Helena's victory in November. Neither Hill's pressure in the East nor his personal visit to western Montana just before the election altered the outcome. As Paris Gibson put it in an election postmortem, Clark's "liberal use of money on the morning of election, together with the great effort of the Boston & Montana and Butte Boston Companies, did the business." Particularly galling was Gibson's report a few days later that, despite Daly's repeated promises, the Anaconda Company no longer was inclined to locate its "refinery" at Great Falls.[35]

However disappointing the results of the 1894 election, the Great Northern ultimately emerged the victor from its long controversy with the Northern Pacific. Neither the NP's alliance with the Union Pacific in the mid-1880s, its alliance with the Clark-Helena forces after 1888, nor its victories in the labor troubles and capital fight of 1892–1894 could save it from its own long history of missed opportunities, poor management, and repeated bankruptcies. While it failed to keep its own house in order, the Northern Pacific also failed to stop James J. Hill's entry into northern Montana and, later, his expansion to the Pacific Coast.

Consequently, when the NP fell into receivership in the summer of 1893, Hill and Lord Mount (George) Stephen were able immediately to join forces with J.P. Morgan and the Deutsche Bank of Berlin and secure *de facto* control of the road. The "London Memorandum" of April 2, 1896, spelled the end of the roads' long dispute, declaring the "GN and reorganized NP shall form a permanent alliance, defensive and in case of need offensive, with a view of avoiding competition and aggressive policy and of generally protecting the common interests of both companies."[36] By 1901, the Hill forces, through a series of stock purchases, effectively were in control of the Northern Pacific. Later that year, Hill, Morgan, the Rockefeller interests, and Edward H. Harriman created the mammoth holding company, the Northern Securities Company, to consolidate formally the NP with the Great Northern and the Chicago, Burlington & Quincy roads. Although the U.S. Supreme Court ordered the dissolution of the Northern Securities "trust" in a celebrated decision three years later, the 1896 alliance held, and the roads did not resume their tooth-and-claw rivalry.

Like the Anaconda Company, the roads had become a part of the general consolidation movement, formal and otherwise, that followed in the wake of the economic debacle of the 1890s. After 1896, James J.

Hill, no less than William Rockefeller, Henry H. Rogers, Cornelius Kelley, John D. Ryan, and the handful of other men who headed the newly consolidated and enormously powerful business concerns operating in the state, played a central role in Montana's development. With the consolidation of the state's principal mines and railroads, Montanans found themselves a part—some would say the victims—of the nationally centralized, new American order that emerged during the Progressive Era.

NOTES

1. C.B. Glasscock, *The War of the Copper Kings: Builders of Butte and Wolves of Wall Street* (Indianapolis: Bobbs-Merill, 1935). Joseph Kinsey Howard, *Montana: High, Wide, and Handsome* (New Haven: Yale University Press, 1943), 48–84. K. Ross Toole, *Montana: An Uncommon Land* (Norman: University of Oklahoma Press, 1959); and "The Genesis of the Clark-Daly Feud," *The Montana Magazine of History*, 1 (April 1951), 21–33. Clark C. Spence, *Montana: A Bicentennial History* (New York: W.W. Norton, 1978), 95–106. Michael P. Malone, *The Battle for Butte: Mining and Politics on the Northern Frontier, 1864–1906* (Seattle: University of Washington Press, 1981).

2. For the early years of the Northern Pacific and its rivalry with James J. Hill, see Albro Martin, *James J. Hill and the Opening of the Northwest* (New York: Oxford University Press, 1976), 181–300; John L. Harnsberger, "Jay Cooke and Minnesota: The Formative Years of the Northern Pacific Railroad, 1868–1873" (Ph.D. dissertation, University of Minnesota, 1956); Joseph Gilpin Pyle, *The Life of James J. Hill* (Garden City, New York: Doubleday, Page, 1916–17), I, 131–376; and Eugene V. Smalley, *History of the Northern Pacific Railroad* (New York: G.P. Putnam's Sons, 1883).

3. Paris Gibson to Jas. J. Hill, August 22, 1881, James J. Hill Papers, James Jerome Hill Reference Library, St. Paul. The Northern Pacific entered Montana from the east, reaching Miles City the same year that Gibson began sounding his warnings. For more on Paris Gibson, see James G. Handford, "Paris Gibson: A Montana Yankee" (M.A. thesis, Montana State University, 1952), 9–12 and *passim*; and Paris Gibson, "The Founding of Great Falls and Some of its Early Records" (Great Falls: n.p., 1914).

4. Paris Gibson to Friend Hill, December 25, 1882, Hill Papers.

5. Agreement between Jas. J. Hill and Paris Gibson, November 25, 1881, Hill Papers.

6. Paris Gibson to James J. Hill, April 21 and 12, 1883, Hill Papers.

7. Rex C. Myers, "Montana: A State and Its Relationship with Railroads, 1864–1970" (Ph.D. dissertation, University of Montana, 1972), 80. Paris Gibson to James J. Hill, March 26 and June 25, 1884, Hill Papers. For more on Hauser,

see John W. Hakola, "Samuel T. Hauser: A Case Study in Nineteenth-Century Frontier Capitalism" (Ph.D. dissertation, Indiana University, 1961), and Alan S. Newell, "A Victim of Monopoly: Samuel T. Hauser and Hydroelectric Development on the Missouri River, 1898–1912" (M.A. thesis, University of Montana, 1979).

8. Martin, *James J. Hill*, 332–49. Hakola, "Samuel T. Hauser," 162–66. For background on the Union Pacific, consult Robert G. Athearn, *Union Pacific Country* (New York: Rand McNally, 1971).

8. Martin, *James J. Hill*, 332–49. Hakola, "Samuel T. Hauser," 162–66. For background on the Union Pacific, consult Robert G. Athearn, *Union Pacific Country* (New York: Rand McNally, 1971).

9. Martin Maginnis to James J. Hill, January 15, 1885, Hill Papers.

10. A.A. den Otter, *Civilizing the West: The Galts and the Development of Western Canada* (Edmonton: University of Alberta Press, 1982), 125–52. Paris Gibson to James J. Hill, July 10, October 18, November 5, 10, and 15, 1885; T.E. Collins and C.E. Conrad to S.E. Atkinson, November 16, 1885; and C.A. Broadwater to James J. Hill, November 20, 1885, Hill Papers. Martin, *James J. Hill*, 340. Hakola, "Samuel T. Hauser," 152–88. See also Montana Central Railway and Montana Securities Papers, 1885–1886, *passim*, Hill Papers.

11. K. Ross Toole and Edward Butcher, "Timber Depredations on the Montana Public Domain, 1885–1918," *Journal of the West*, VII (July 1968), 354 and *passim*, which should be consulted with Dale L. Johnson, "Andrew B. Hammond: Education of a Capitalist on the Montana Frontier" (Ph.D. dissertation, University of Montana, 1976).

12. James J. Hill to Messrs. Wyckoff, Seamans & Benedict, March 22; and R.B. Harrison to James J. Hill, March 23, 1886, Hill Papers.

13. James J. Hill to C.A. Broadwater, March 23, 1886, Hill Papers.

14. James J. Hill to George Stephen, January 18, 1885; C.A. Broadwater to Hill, March 14, and R.B. Harrison to Hill, March 24, 1886, Hill Papers. *Butte Intermountain*, March 12, 1886. *Helena Independent*, March 25, 1886. Malone, *Battle for Butte*, 23–24. Myers, "Montana," 69–76.

15. C.A. Broadwater to James J. Hill, March 14; Hill to J.S. Kennedy, April 10; and Hill to Samuel Thorne, April 10, 1886, Hill Papers. T.F. Oakes to W.S. Mellen and to S.T. Hauser, November 23, 1892, Oakes Letterpress Books, v. 56, Northern Pacific Railway Company Records, Minnesota Historical Society.

16. U.S. Senate Executive Document No. 204, 49 Congress, 1st Session.

17. James J. Hill to Grover Cleveland, July 7, 1886, Grover Cleveland Papers, Presidential Papers Microfilm Series (Washington: Library of Congress, 1958), roll 36. R.B. Harrison to James J. Hill, July 12, 1886. See also, W.L. Scott to Hill, July 22; and Knute Nelson to Hill, July 15; and the Maginnis-Hill-Broadwater correspondence, April–July, 1886, Hill Papers.

18. Quoted in Michael P. Malone and Richard B. Roeder, *Montana: A History of Two Centuries* (Seattle: University of Washington Press, 1976), 134.

19. C.A. Broadwater to James J. Hill, August 16, 1886, Hill Papers.

20. *Report of the Commissioner of Indian Affairs*, U.S. House Executive Document No. 1, part 5, 50 Congress, 1st Session (Washington: Government Printing Office 1887), 36–37. See also, U.S. House Report 3487, 49 Congress, 2d Session; and U.S. Senate Report 1494, 49 Congress, 1st Session.

21. James J. Hill to Marcus Dailey [sic], October 12, 1886, Hill Papers. *Great Falls Tribune*, October 5, 8, and 15, 1887. *Helena Independent*, October 9 and 16, 1887. Martin, *James J. Hill*, 346–49.

22. C.A. Broadwater to James J. Hill, September 29, and Hill to Broadwater, October 11, 1888, Hill Papers. See also, Malone, *Battle for Butte*, 80–88; and Toole, *Uncommon Land*, 167–80. For territorial politics in general, see Clark C. Spence, *Territorial Politics and Government in Montana, 1864–1889* (Urbana: University of Illinois Press, 1975).

23. Paris Gibson to James J. Hill, May 11, 1892, Hill Papers. For the 1892–1894 capital fight, see Malone, *Battle for Butte*, 94–105; and Toole, *Uncommon Land*, 182–85.

24. Paris Gibson to James J. Hill, September 16 and August 3, and Hill to Gibson, September 19 and November 2, 1892, Hill Papers.

25. Paris Gibson to James J. Hill, November 10, 1892, Hill Papers. For the impact of Populism on Montana politics, see Thomas A. Clinch, *Urban Populism and Free Silver in Montana: A Narrative of Ideology in Political Action* (Missoula: University of Montana Press, 1970).

26. James Ben Ali Haggin was one of the principal figures, along with George Hearst and Lloyd Tevis, in the San Francisco syndicate that financed the Anaconda Company. Malone, *Battle for Butte*, 26–31. Toole, *Uncommon Land*, 158–59.

27. Marcus Daly to James J. Hill, January 16, 1894, Hill Papers.

28. Thomas A. Clinch, "The Northern Pacific Railroad and Montana's Mineral Lands," *Pacific Historical Review*, 34 (August 1965), 323–35.

29. Marcus Daly to James J. Hill, May 4 and 30, 1894, Hill Papers. W. Thomas White, "A History of Railroad Workers in the Pacific Northwest, 1883–1934" (Ph.D. dissertation, University of Washington, 1981), 47–81. Ray Ginger, *The Bending Cross: A Biography of Eugene Victor Debs* (New Brunswick: Rutgers University Press, 1949), 102–14.

30. Thomas A. Clinch, "Coxey's Army in Montana," *Montana: The Magazine of Western History*, 15 (October 1969), 2–11. White, "Railroad Workers," 13–46. See also Donald L. McMurry, *Coxey's Army: A Study of the Industrial Army Movement of 1894* (1929; reprint ed., Seattle: University of Washington Press, 1968), 197–226.

31. *Anaconda Standard*, July 1, 1894. W. Thomas White, "Boycott: The Pullman Strike in Montana," *Montana: The Magazine of Western History*, 29 (October 1979), 2–13; and "Railroad Workers," 82–123. For an earlier, general account of the strike in the West, see Almont Lindsey, *The Pullman Strike: The*

Story of a Unique Experiment and of a Great Labor Upheaval (Chicago: University of Chicago Press, 1942), 239–73.

32. Marcus Daly to James J. Hill, August 7, 1894, Hill Papers.

33. Marcus Daly to James J. Hill, September 29, 1894, Hill Papers.

34. L. Lewisohn to Jacob H. Schiff, November 5; E.T. Nichols to James J. Hill, November 5; and Schiff to Hill, November 7, 1894, Hill Papers.

35. Paris Gibson to James J. Hill, November 11 and 15, 1894, Hill Papers.

36. "London Memorandum," April 2, 1896, Northern Pacific Reorganization File, Hill Papers. Martin, *James J. Hill*, 439–64. Indeed, in 1970 the GN, NP, and Burlington roads again attempted a formal consolidation, forming the mammoth Burlington Northern Company.

4 /

THE CHEYENNE QUESTION
Conflict on the Tongue River Reservation

DANIEL F. GALLACHER

Throughout the long and desultory history of Indian-white relations in America, the native Americans are most often the losers. "They made us many promises," said Red Cloud of the Sioux, "but they never kept but one. They promised to take our land, and they took it." On the Tongue River Reservation in Montana, however, a different outcome ensued. There, Northern Cheyenne Indians not only survived the hostility of neighboring whites, but actually secured a favorable settlement to a number of long-standing grievances.

The keys to this development, as Daniel F. Gallacher explains them, were the murder trials of two Cheyenne boys, Spotted Hawk and Little Whirlwind. Their cases attracted national attention to the plight of the reservation Indians, and created a climate of opinion which favored reform. In 1902—eighteen long years after the creation of the reservation—the U.S. government was forced to make belated amends for its earlier failings.

Two years after the Sioux Wars of 1876, most Northern Plains Indians who participated in hostilities surrendered to the army. The Sioux were confined on Pine Ridge and other reservations in Dakota Territory, but the Indian office ordered Northern Cheyennes to join their southern kinsmen on the Cheyenne-Arapahoe Reservation in Indian Territory. The Northern Cheyenne, however, demanded a return north to their homeland. The government refused, and consequently in September of 1878, Dull Knife and Little Wolf, together with 200 followers, fled north. The United States military pursued them with orders to "kill or capture" escapees. Little Wolf's band reached the Powder River country, Montana, in January of 1879, and was soon moved to the Fort Keogh Military Reservation near Miles City.

Dull Knife and his people were less fortunate. After separating from Little Wolf's band in October of 1878, Dull Knife surrendered at Fort Robinson, Nebraska, where he and his followers were imprisoned. Threatened a second time with removal to Indian Territory, Dull Knife's band broke out of Fort Robinson on January 9, 1879, but, of the 150 who escaped, 64 died at the hands of the pursuing United States cavalry. Some survivors reached the Pine Ridge Agency; others found their way to Fort Keogh where they joined Little Wolf's people.

The escape attempt illustrated the Northern Cheyenne's desperate desire to remain in their homeland, and it succeeded in focusing government attention on their complaints. An 1879 Senate investigation recommended that Northern Cheyenne who preferred Montana be allowed to return. In 1883 a final transfer from Indian Territory occurred and on November 26 of the following year, President Chester A. Arthur issued an executive order establishing a small reservation for the Northern Cheyenne in southeastern Montana.

The order ended the Northern Cheyenne's fight for their own reservation, but it created new problems. Reservation boundaries failed to embrace lands along the Tongue River where many Northern Cheyenne had settled in the early 1880s. Also, the president's order contained no provisions for purchasing lands within the reservation settled by whites prior to 1884. These settlers, and other area ranchers, protested President Arthur's directive and demanded he revoke the order. Moreover, they accused the government of providing inadequate rations to the Indians which, they alleged, led to illegal cattle-killing. In turn, Northern Cheyennes accused white ranchers of grazing cattle illegally on reservation lands.

Tension between whites and Northern Cheyennes continued throughout the 1880s and 1890s. Feelings ran especially high in 1890, when ranchers accused Indians of killing two men, Robert Ferguson and Hugh Boyle. The Yellowstone County district attorney failed to obtain a conviction in either case, and the incident only served to exacerbate feelings between whites and Indians.

In the spring of 1897 trouble erupted that threatened, more seriously than ever before, to end Northern Cheyenne occupation of the Tongue River Reservation.[1] On May 7th, the Miles City *Yellowstone Journal* reported that area settlers suspected Cheyennes of killing a sheep herder named Hoover. A search party was unable to find the man's body, but located the carcass of a steer. Whites contended that Cheyennes killed Hoover after he discovered them butchering the animal. "The settlers have suffered long and if not patiently, at least doggedly," the *Journal* stated, "hoping with each new year, some solution of the Cheyenne question would be reached by the government." The paper warned that if evidence implicated the Indians, "the Cheyenne question will not long lack a solution."[2]

Two weeks later, the *Forsyth Times* printed a letter from Fred Barringer, Hoover's employer, repeating the *Journal's* charge. Barringer claimed Indians frequently killed cattle and shot at white men who caught them. An editorial in the *Times* supported Barringer and urged settlers to organize themselves, and in the absence of government assistance, to demand that the tribe produce the murderer.[3]

Searchers discovered Hoover's body on May 23, prompting Montana newspapers to speculate on how authorities would take the murderers into custody. The *Daily Missoulian* reported that ranchers on the Upper Tongue River and Otter Creek threatened to take matters into their own hands. The reservation agent, Captain George Stouch, failed to turn over the murderers. Responding to white threats, two troops of cavalry left Fort Custer on the 25th to prevent angry settlers from attacking the Tongue River Reservation. By the end of May, fears among white settlers caused many families to leave their ranches for the security of Miles City. On May 31, the *Daily Missoulian* announced that Cheyennes were ready to fight area settlers and soldiers and that there were "certainly grounds for fear" since Cheyennes were "determined, and...reinforced by renegade Crow." The same day the *Helena Independent* declared that "the Upper Rosebud country is deserted, ranches, homes and property, all left to the mercy of the redskins.... Settlers stand guard night and day holding the Cheyennes back from white women and children."

A June 1 *Great Falls Daily Tribune* editorial reported that Cheyennes had killed over a dozen men, adding sarcastically that the U.S. Army should "wake up to the gravity of the situation," and anticipating that eastern newspapers and "half-baked New England statesmen" would argue that "the poor Indians had his feelings hurt by the insolence of white men...and was therefore justified in committing a few murders just to relieve his noble indignation."[4]

The same day accounts appeared in the *New York Times* confirming these suspicions. The *Times* reported, however, that according to dispatches from the Departments of War and Interior, trouble on the reservation was not serious. "There is a disposition at the department," the *Times* asserted, "to attribute the affair to encroachments of the whites in the neighborhood upon the Indians." However, the following day the *Times* stated that Sioux Indians from South Dakota had joined Cheyennes in the hills near Ashland and that this would be the scene of battle if fighting broke out.[5]

Although Montana papers had published inflammatory stories for more than a month, Agent Stouch reported a less dramatic series of events. After Hoover's body had been found, Stouch met with White Bull, leader of the band whose members Stouch suspected of the murder. The agent stated that the entire band would be held responsible unless it turned over the guilty party. White Bull told Stouch that David Stanley, also known as Little Whirlwind Voice, confessed to the murder, but had no intention of surrendering. According to White Bull, Stanley wanted to fight the soldiers and die a warrior's death. Stouch refused the request and went to White Bull's camp to arrest Stanley, who had fled. Finally, on May 31, Agent Stouch arrested Stanley in a camp sixteen miles from the agency. The following day, Stouch met with Custer County Sheriff John Gibb, who demanded that Stouch release Stanley into his custody. Stouch refused, until such time as he had completed his investigation. When Gibb refused to leave, Stouch ordered him off the reservation.[6]

When word of Stouch's actions reached Helena, Governor Robert Smith telegrammed President William McKinley, complaining that Stouch and the military were resisting Sheriff Gibb's efforts to arrest the murderers. In response Cornelius N. Bliss, secretary of the Interior, advised Stouch to cooperate with civil authorities. Stouch assured Bliss that upon completion of his investigation, he would turn Stanley over to the sheriff at a location outside the reservation.[7]

Stouch questioned Stanley for four days, then turned him over to Captain Robert Read, who escorted the prisoner to Rosebud, Montana, and turned him over to the civil authorities. After Stanley's departure, Stouch reported to Bliss that the Indians were as calm as they had been throughout the past ten days, except on the day that Stanley proposed to fight. "They have shown no signs of being troublesome," Stouch added; "they have not been in their war clothes, nor have they had on war paint." The absence of hostilities between Indians and whites satisfied Stouch that there was no danger of an outbreak. He assured Bliss that newspaper reports of the incidents were "gross exaggerations."

Sheriff Gibb soon returned to the agency to arrest three more Cheyennes (White Bull, Yellow Hair, and Sam Crow) whom Stanley had implicated. When Stouch told the sheriff he would turn over any Cheyenne for whom Gibb had a warrant, the sheriff produced warrants for Sam Crow and Yellow Hair. Stouch immediately sent for them. Before Gibb left, the agent assured him that if there were other Indians to arrest he would assist in any way possible.[8]

In a second confession made during July, Stanley accused Spotted Hawk, his brother Little Whirlwind, and a fifteen-year-old boy named Shoulder Blade of complicity in Hoover's murder. He told the sheriff that they had killed a cow and were butchering it when Hoover appeared. According to Stanley they all agreed that they must kill Hoover to prevent him from reporting them; Spotted Hawk did the actual killing, then swore them all to secrecy.

Not everyone close to the situation believed Stanley's confession. Captain Read, who was on the reservation during the entire affair, suspected Stanley had killed Hoover. Read also said that Stanley had always been a "disturbing element" among the Cheyennes, and had been discharged from the military because of mental incompetence. Hamlin Garland, a noted western author, was in the room when Gibb and County Attorney Thomas Porter interrogated Stanley. Garland accused the two officials of coercing the Indian and of offering him a lighter sentence if he implicated others.[9]

Authorities arrested Spotted Hawk, Little Whirlwind, and Shoulder Blade on July 20 and returned to Miles City the next day. County Attorney Porter, however, had already filed charges against all six defendants on the 20th. Stanley was the only defendant present when Porter filed charges because Sam Crow and Yellow Hair had escaped from jail on July 19.[10] In this and subsequent hearings, Judge C.H. Loud appointed counsel for each defendant, accepted each plea of not guilty, and set trial dates.

Separate juries found Spotted Hawk guilty on November 9 of first degree murder and ordered the death sentence; Little Whirlwind guilty on November 27 of second degree murder, life imprisonment; and David Stanley, also guilty of second degree murder, ten years in prison. For giving testimony against Spotted Hawk and Little Whirlwind, the boy Shoulder Blade received immunity from the state and was released from custody.[11]

Shortly after the jury's verdict, Captain Stouch wrote George B. Grinnell informing him of the outcome and encouraging Grinnell to

Spotted Hawk, focus of controversy. Courtesy Montana Historical Society.

persuade the Indian Rights Association (I.R.A.), a Philadelphia-based organization, to intervene on Spotted Hawk's behalf. Stouch noted that if Spotted Hawk were sentenced to hang, "it would be judicial murder, for I believe him as innocent...as I am."

Grinnell wrote to Herbert Welsh, the Secretary of the I.R.A., enclosed Stouch's letter, and added that since he had known Spotted Hawk's family for many years, he believed him to be innocent. Grinnell urged Welsh to solicit $500 from the members of the association to cover costs for an appeal to the Montana Supreme Court. The urgency of the situation prompted Welsh to "appeal to some wealthy friends of the Indians whose sympathies...will be touched." Subsequently, Welsh wrote to prominent members of the I.R.A., apprising them of Grinnell's request. He also contacted Secretary of the Interior Cornelius Bliss, asking him if the government could assist.[12]

In response to Welsh's letter Francis Leupp, I.R.A. representative in Washington, D.C. asked the United States attorney general and Interior Department officials for help in the Spotted Hawk case, but they indicated that they were unable to intervene. Leupp informed Welsh that his inquiries were unsuccessful but that there was a possibility of Congressional reimbursement to I.R.A. members if Welsh could get someone to advance the money. In addition, he cautioned Welsh to have a citizen from Montana act as an intermediary, thereby reducing the I.R.A.'s involvement.

Immediately, Welsh wrote to George Stouch suggesting he ask Bishop L. R. Brewer from Helena to serve as intermediary. He then wrote another letter to Leupp questioning the necessity of secrecy concerning the I.R.A.'s involvement.

In a confidential reply to Welsh, Leupp explained that since "there are plenty of Congressmen, especially...such cattle as come to Congress from the frontier...who have it in for the I.R.A.," secrecy was best. He also noted that if Brewer handled the money, Stouch might request the Indian Office to attach a comparable sum to the Indian Appropriations Bill. Leupp believed that this arrangement would ensure reimbursement for eastern contributors because even the Montana delegates would help the thing along; whereas they would fight it tooth and nail if it were labeled Indian Rights Association."[13]

The Executive Committee of the I.R.A. appropriated half of the money needed for Spotted Hawk's appeal in early December. In an act of generosity, Secretary Bliss agreed personally to provide the rest. But despite the I.R.A.'s wish for anonymity, the Montana press discovered its involvement. The *Stockgrowers Journal* denounced the association and contended that "the interest in the case by...long haired men and short haired women of the east...is born of the union of a sickly mentality and ignorance." According to the *Journal*, the object of Indian rights was "to see that the courts omit punishment of Indian murderers simply because they are Indians."[14]

On January 8, 1898, Spotted Hawk's attorneys obtained a statement from Shoulder Blade refuting earlier testimony implicating Spotted Hawk and Little Whirlwind. Shoulder Blade admitted that Stanley had told him that he, Stanley, would never get out of jail unless he implicated the two Indians. C.L. Merrill and George Farr, Spotted Hawk's attorneys, wrote Grinnell that newfound evidence improved their chances for winning a new trial for Spotted Hawk. Accordingly, since Little Whirlwind was convicted on the same evidence as Spotted Hawk, they obtained two sets of affidavits, because if Spotted Hawk was innocent, Little Whirlwind would be equally guiltless.[15]

Herbert Welsh was not convinced that Merrill and Farr would be successful with Spotted Hawk's appeal. He suggested to Leupp and Bliss that the I.R.A. should retain George Milburn to handle Spotted Hawk's appeal because he was well-known and respected in Miles City. Bliss, however, preferred Merrill, and Farr and Welsh acquiesced.

After Judge Loud rejected Spotted Hawk's appeal for a new trial on March 23, his attorneys moved for an appeal to the state supreme court. They contacted Wilbur Fisk Sanders, a Helena lawyer and former United States Senator from Montana, asking for his assistance. Sanders expressed his surprise to Welsh that the appeal had been rejected, but he surmised that the anti-Cheyenne feelings in Miles City influenced the judge's decision.

Welsh contacted S. M. Brosius, Francis Leupp's replacement in Washington, D.C., and advised him that Sanders would assist with the appeal. He also suggested that Brosius contact Secretary Bliss and tell him to "be prepared to ask the President to pardon Spotted Hawk." "There is no question about his innocence," Welsh explained, "but the feeling in that part of the country is so intense against Indians that the Court might be willing to hang even an innocent man."[16]

In July, Farr obtained an affidavit from Lame Woman, Stanley's wife, stating that Stanley told her he was the only one involved in Hoover's murder and that Stanley's father, Badger, had convinced his son to implicate others. Farr relayed this information to Brosius and noted that Grinnell, who had been on the reservation that fall, secured an affidavit from a young man who "overheard the conversation between Badger and his family." Farr advised Brosius that although there was no rule of law permitting affidavits to be submitted after the initial trial, the Supreme Court accepted the documents "as a matter of justice."

In late November, Sanders wrote to Welsh that Spotted Hawk's appeal date had been postponed. In addition, Sanders offered to file on behalf of Little Whirlwind since that had not been done. He stated that there were several points of law that could be argued on Little Whirlwind's behalf. Welsh, however, believed Little Whirlwind's appeal would be severely limited because Milburn had already dropped the case. According to Welsh, Milburn failed to protect Little Whirlwind by ignoring opportunities for an appeal. Welsh claimed that Grinnell attributed Milburn's negligence to the refusal of Secretary Bliss and the I.R.A. to retain him and that he "neglected the case in order . . . to get even with the friends of the two boys here in the East."[17]

Sanders proceeded with Little Whirlwind's appeal in late November, 1898. The Montana Supreme Court agreed to hear the appeal and set the hearing date for April 3, 1899.

Spotted Hawk's attorneys presented their appeal for a new trial to the Montana Supreme Court on January 4, 1899, contesting ten points in the lower court's decision:

(1) Spotted Hawk was not committed to judge before the charges against him were filed.

(2) Charges failed to specify that the murder did not occur on the Fort Keogh military reservation, although they noted that the crime occurred outside Tongue River Reservation.

(3) The court had no jurisdiction over Spotted Hawk either inside or outside of the Reservation because he was a ward of the government.

(4) The defendant was absent from court when his defense presented the demurrer and motion to quash.

(5) The change of venue motion should have been granted.

(6) Stanley's testimony was not sufficiently corroborated.

(7) The court unduly limited the scope of the defense's cross-examination.

(8) Defense attempts to prove Stanley was mentally "incompetent" should have been allowed.

> (9) The court failed to heed the defense's request to instruct the jury as to the weight afforded an "accomplice's testimony."
> (10) The court erred when providing instructions to the jury regarding the term "premeditation."

On January 23, 1889, Chief Justice C.J. Brantley presented the court's opinion, upholding three of the ten points contested by Spotted Hawk's attorneys. Point five received the greatest attention by the court. Brantley indicated that a motion for a change of venue could not be granted if the only evidence in support of an allegation of prejudice was the opinion of those requesting the change. In Spotted Hawk's case, however, the defense had submitted evidence that covered "sixty pages of the record" including affidavits from L.A. Huffman, a prominent Miles City photographer, and from Sheriff Gibb, besides an abundance of local newspaper clippings. Brantley submitted the opinion that the court found sufficient evidence to conclude the lower court "should have granted the defendant's petition." Brantley asserted that the lower court's decision was "such an abuse of discretion" that a new trial should have been granted on this point alone.

The court also agreed with the defense attorneys on two other points. On point six, Brantley pointed out that since Stanley was an alleged accomplice, it was necessary that his account be corroborated by evidence other than the testimony of a principal in the case. Moreover, since Shoulder Blade's testimony did not indicate conclusively that the man who had caught them butchering the cow was Hoover and since Shoulder Blade had fled before the shooting, the court concluded that his testimony was insufficient corroboration.

Finally, the court supported point seven. Justices agreed that Judge Loud had denied the defense attorneys sufficient latitude in their cross-examination, and they argued that the lower court erred by disallowing the defense's attempt to impeach Stanley's testimony. Upholding three of ten points in the appeal, Chief Justice Brantley ordered that the decision be "reversed and remanded with directions to grant the defendant a new trial."[18]

Afterwards Sanders contacted Welsh detailing the court's decision. He explained that he doubted whether Judge Loud or the people of Miles City would seek a new trial, and consequently, he believed Spotted Hawk would be freed. Although Sanders worried about Little Whirlwind's appeal, he believed that "if the [Supreme] Court could find any excuse for granting him a new trial, consistent with its former ruling" it would do so.[19]

The high court heard Little Whirlwind's appeal in April 1899, but the defense could only contend procedural issues due to Milburn's bungling of the case. Little Whirlwind's new lawyer, W. F. Sanders, protested that the prosecution's decision to file charges rather than to seek a grand jury indictment had violated his client's constitutional rights. However, Associate Justice J. Hunt, who wrote the supreme court's decision, disagreed. He stated that since both methods of pursuing a case were constitutional as long as the prosecution followed the proper procedure prior to the trial, the defendant had no cause for complaint. The defense attorney contended also that it was mandatory for the defendant to be present when the district attorney requested permission from the court to file charges, but Hunt disagreed. "To say his presence is necessary would frequently abrogate the power of prosecution," Hunt explained, "because, if a defendant were a fugitive, or absent when petition for leave to file a charge is passed on, his presence could not be had, no warrant could issue."

Sanders went on to contest two points stemming from Spotted Hawk's case: (1) the district court's right of jurisdiction over Indians; and (2) that Little Whirlwind was absent during the hearing on the demurrers and the motion to dismiss charges. Hunt rejected both points, referring to the court's ruling in Spotted Hawk's hearing. Because the high court concluded that none of these points violated Little Whirlwind's rights, it upheld the judgement of the lower court.[20]

Two months later, Brosius traveled to Montana, where he visited District Court Judge C. H. Loud. While Loud admitted to Brosius that the evidence in the two cases was identical, he refused to make this statement on the record for fear of implying that he favored a pardon. According to Loud, "both should have been hung."[21]

In September of 1899, Sanders appealed to Governor Robert B. Smith seeking an executive pardon for Little Whirlwind. Smith, while agreeing that there were errors of law in the trial, did not believe they justified executive clemency.

Just before his death from tuberculosis in October 1899, David Stanley confessed that he was solely responsible for the murder of Hoover. Two months later, Darwin R. James and Merrill Bates, chairman and secretary of the Board of Indian Commissioners, again appealed to Governor Smith on Little Whirlwind's behalf. They argued that Stanley's confession and other evidence clearly indicated that Little Whirlwind was innocent. Still, Governor Smith replied that he had already considered the case carefully and that Stanley's confession failed to persuade him of Little Whirlwind's innocence.[22]

Finally, in June of 1901, Governor Joseph K. Toole, Smith's successor, reconsidered the case and recommended a full pardon. The Montana State Board of Pardons approved the governor's recommendation, and on July 1, 1901, Little Whirlwind gained his freedom.[23]

During the years and because of the trials of Spotted Hawk, Stanley, and Little Whirlwind, changes occurred on the Tongue River Reservation. On July 1, 1898, Congress directed an inspector to determine the feasibility of moving the Northern Cheyenne onto some portion of the Crow Reservation. In addition, the inspector was to determine the costs for fencing the reservation and buying out "bona fide" settlers who owned land within the reservation boundaries. Secretary Bliss appointed James McLaughlin as inspector. On November 14, 1898, McLaughlin submitted recommendations to extend the eastern boundary of the reservation to the mid-channel of the Tongue River, buy up the claims and improvements of "bona fide" white settlers, fence the northern and southern boundaries of the reservation, and purchase 1,000 heifers and 40 bulls for the tribe.[24]

However, the government waited until March 19, 1900, before acting on McLaughlin's recommendations. Then, President William McKinley ordered that the eastern boundary of the Northern Cheyenne Reservation be extended to the mid-channel of the Tongue River. Two months later, Congress approved the annual Indian Appropriations Act that included $171,615 to purchase the claims and improvements of settlers within the boundaries of the enlarged reservation. McLaughlin's other two recommendations—fencing the reservation and purchasing cattle —were subsequently implemented after Congress appropriated $35,350 in February, 1902.[25]

Between 1880 and 1902, several factors contributed to Indian-white conflict on the Tongue River Reservation. Inaction by the United States government played a major role in the development and continuance of problems on the reservation. As early as 1883, the government learned that white settlers claimed the Indians were killing white-owned cattle. In the same year, Milburn informed the secretary of the Interior that it was imperative for the government to provide adequate rations for the Cheyenne. With regularity, newspaper articles and letters reiterated to Washington authorities the whites' concerns that the Cheyennes were

Barringer's Ranch, Tongue River, Montana, 1899. L.A. Huffman photo. Courtesy Montana Historical Society.

slaughtering cattle—actions they believed to be related to farming failure and meager rations. Yet between 1882 and 1902, the government failed to provide the Cheyenne with sufficient rations or an alternate food source, such as cattle herds.

At the same time, Tongue River Indian agents continually drew attention to the friction caused by poorly defined reservation boundaries and the presence of white landowners on the reservation. Again, the government failed to take quick action; instead, it ignored the problem of whites living inside the reservation and the need to clarify the boundaries.

Local newspapers aggravated the situation in reporting events on the reservation. Editorials and news reports of incidents and issues were consistently inflammatory and inaccurate. Reports intimated that wide-scale Indian uprisings were imminent, and that the government ignored the needs of white settlers.

Individuals from outside Montana played a prominent role in promoting equal treatment of Indians. George Bird Grinnell and members of the I.R.A. used their influence to assist Spotted Hawk and Little Whirlwind and also recommended changes to alleviate many of the conditions that caused animosity on the reservation.

John Hoover's murder and the subsequent trials of Spotted Hawk and Little Whirlwind illustrated the extent to which Indian-white hostility had grown over a span of fifteen years. The record indicated that the press and Custer County officials were determined to convict "some" Cheyennes in retribution for what they considered previous Indian offenses. Clearly, Spotted Hawk and Little Whirlwind did not receive just treatment under the law until their cases reached the supreme court. Their cases culminated two decades of conflict, and together with I.R.A. involvement prompted the government to establish a more equitable policy for the Northern Cheyennes.

NOTES

1. For a detailed discussion of the Northern Cheyenne people after the Battle of the Little Bighorn, see George Bird Grinnell, *The Cheyenne Indians: Their History and Ways of Life*, 2 vols. (New Haven: Yale University Press, 1962); James Mooney, "The Cheyenne Indians," *American Anthropological Association*, I (1907); Donald J. Berthrong, *The Southern Cheyennes* (Norman: University of Oklahoma Press, 1963); Orlan J. Svingen, "The Administrative History of the Northern Cheyenne Indian Reservation, 1877–1900" (Ph.D. Dissertation, University of Toledo, 1982).

2. *Yellowstone Journal*, May 7, 1897.

3. *Forsyth Times*, May 20, 1897.

4. *Yellowstone Journal*, May 28, 1897; *Daily Missoulian*, May 28, 1897; *Billings Gazette*, May 28, 1897; *Helena Independent*, May 28, 1897; *Daily Missoulian*, May 31, 1897; *Helena Independent*, May 31, 1897; *Great Falls Daily Tribune*, June 1, 1897.

5. *New York Times*, June 1, 1897.

6. "Annual Report of the Commissioner of Indian Affairs, 1898." ["Report, CIA, 1898."] *House Executive Document* [HED] 1, 55 Cong., 3 sess. (Serial 3757), pp. 81–86.

7. Bliss to Smith [telegram], June 2, 1897, File 25–3, Box 25, Collection 35a, Official Correspondence of Governor Robert Smith, 1896–1901 [Correspondence Smith], Montana Historical Society Archives [MHSA].

8. "Report, CIA, 1898," HED 1, 55 Cong., 3 sess. (Serial 3757), pp. 86–87.

9. *Yellowstone Journal*, July 23, 1897; *Billings Gazette*, August 3, 1897; Garland to Welsh, "A Review of the Spotted Hawk Case," March 21, 1898; HOL microfilm [M], E91 I417, Indian Rights Association Papers [IRA], Microfilm Corporation of America, Sanford, North Carolina.

10. Sam Crow and Yellow Hair were recaptured on October 30, 1897. In the interim, the charges against them were reduced to escaping jail. They were tried, convicted, and sentenced to one year in the state prison at Deer Lodge. *Yellowstone Journal*, October 9, 1897; December 9, 1897; *State of Montana v. Spotted Hawk et al.*, Docket 1299 (January 1899), Records of the Montana Supreme Court, Helena.

11. Records conflict concerning Stanley's original sentence. Some sources state he was convicted of second degree murder and sentenced to life imprisonment, but that later his sentence was reduced to ten years. Other sources indicate that he was convicted of manslaughter and sentenced to five years in prison. The only official record found is cited, and is contrary to all others. "Convict Record," Record Series 167, Volume 55, Deer Lodge State Prison, MHSA; *State v. Spotted Hawk*; *State of Montana v. Little Whirlwind*, Docket 1339 (April 1899), Records of the Montana Supreme Court, Helena.

12. Stouch to Grinnell, November 20, 1897; Grinnell to Welsh, November 20, 1897; Welsh to Grinnell, November 22, 1897, Reel 13; Welsh to Eckley B. Cox, Leupp, W.W. Frazier, Miss Mary E. Dewey, November 22, 1897; Welsh to Bliss, November 22, 1897, Reel 74, IRA Papers.

13. Leupp to Welsh, November 23, 1897; Welsh to Leupp, November 24, 1897, Reel 74; Leupp to Welsh, November 25, 1897, Reel 13, IRA Papers.

14. "Fifteenth Annual Report of the Indian Rights Association," Reel 102, IRA Papers; *Stockgrowers Journal and Livestock Reporter* [Miles City], December 4, 1897.

15. Merrill and Farr to Grinnell, January 17, 1898, Folder 77, Microfilm 7, Grinnell Papers, Southwest Museum, Los Angeles, California.

16. Welsh to Bliss and Leupp, February 12, 1898; Welsh to Bliss, March 12, 1898, Reel 74; Sanders to Welsh, April 4, 1898; April 19, 1898, Reel 13; Welsh to Brosius, May 4, 1898, Reel 74, IRA Papers.

17. Farr to Brosius, October 24, 1898; Sanders to Welsh, November 23, 1898, Reel 14; Welsh to Reverend I. Newton Rittner, n.d., Reel 75, IRA Papers.

18. *State v. Spotted Hawk*, Opinion of the Court, pp. 2–35.

19. Sanders to Welsh, January 30, 1899, Reel 14, IRA Papers.

20. *State v. Little Whirlwind*, Opinion of the Court, pp. 2–7.

21. Brosius to Welsh, June 6, 1899, Reel 14, IRA Papers.

22. Smith to Sanders, September 1, 1899, "Correspondence Smith," File 32–3, Box 32, Collection 35a, MHSA; Darwin R. James and Merrill Bates to Smith, December 15, 1899; Smith to Darwin R. James, December 20, 1899, Ibid., File 32–5, Box 32, Collection 35a, MHSA.

23. "Nineteenth Annual Report, Indian Rights Association," Reel 102, IRA Papers.

24. "Proposed Removal of the Northern Cheyenne Indians," HD 153, 55 Cong., 3 sess. (Serial Set 3807).

25. Charles J. Kappler, ed., *Indian Affairs: Laws and Treaties*, Vol. I—Laws (Washington, D.C.: U.S. Government Printing Office, 1904), pp. 860–861; "Northern Cheyenne, Montana," HD 354, 57 Cong., 1 sess. (Serial Set 4337).

5 /

FROM CRAZYQUILT
TO GRAY BLANKET
Montana's Colorful Press

REX C. MYERS

Newspapers are a window to the history of Montana. Indeed, for much of the past, newspaper accounts provide the sole documentation of events and emotions. Few periods of Montana's journalistic history have attracted more attention than the long, twentieth-century era of corporate domination. As Anaconda's power became monolithic in Montana copper mining, so did corporate control of key state newspapers. This phenomenon lasted from the early 1900s to the late 1950s and attracted the attention of publicist and historian alike—K. Ross Toole among them. He argued that control of these papers by the Anaconda Copper Company spread a "Great Gray Blanket" over the meaning of "freedom of the press" in Montana.

Rex C. Myers, of Western Montana College, reviews that period in light of the colorful and flamboyant journalism that preceded it. He argues that Toole's "Blanket" became "Gray" when compared to the outspoken frontier journalistic style of early Montana. He concludes with two observations on contemporary Montana newspapers: The Anaconda Copper Company divested itself of newspaper holdings only when radio and television competition lessened newspaper impact. But ACM sold its holdings to non-Montana newspaper chains, thus continuing the pattern of outside corporate control begun during the mining era.

K. Ross Toole called it "The Great Gray Blanket." For Montanans from the early 1900s through 1959, the unsigned editor for seven of the state's daily newspapers was the Anaconda Copper Mining Company. Nonresident and resident alike decried the circumstances. Upton Sinclair guessed as early as 1919 that ACM controlled all but two of Montana's newspapers. He overestimated. John Gunther came closer in 1946 in *Inside the U.S.A.* when he estimated that seven of fourteen dailies fell under the copper company's aegis. *Time, The Nation, New Republic, The Denver Post,* and *The London Economist* varied on their estimates of control, but sang a unanimous chorus in opposition to what they saw in Montana's press. Outcries rose in the years following World War II, with descriptive phrases like "Chain of Copper," or "Captive Press," or "Monuments to Indifference."

Montanans knew "The Company" had been setting type well before World War II, but like outside reporters they could only speculate on extent. The economic fact of the matter was that when Standard Oil began to consolidate diverse copper producing facilities in the late 1890s, it acquired other holdings, including newspapers. Indeed, any entrepreneur worth his salt had a paper to help "clarify" his public views. W. A. Clark spoke through the *Butte Miner,* Marcus Daly on the pages of the *Anaconda Standard,* A. B. Hammond owned the *Missoulian,* and F. Augustus Heinze the *Reveille.* Montana's awareness of corporate control came into focus during the first decade of the present century, but the center of that portrait was copper, not newsprint. The process was the same. Montanans acquiesced or adjusted to "The Company" in mining, only gradually comprehending the same force in journalism.

Gadfly presses bemoaned the situation well before national media picked up the hue and cry. Labor papers like the *Butte Bulletin* and the *Montana Labor News* took adversary roles from Butte, as did weeklies like Helena's *Western Progressive* and *People's Voice,* or the *Western News* from Hamilton. There were other protests of shorter duration, and the 1935 legislature even flirted with the idea of an inquiry, but it fell short of action. Yet the theme lived on: Anaconda controlled newspapers and thus the news.

How much control was anybody's guess until 1951, when the Fairmont Corporation, mother hen to ACM's journalistic nest, tried to add a Great Falls radio station to its brood. The Federal Communications Commission required detailed information on Fairmont holdings, and suddenly more than three decades of speculation ended with alarming precision. ACM held the reins of seven of Montana's eighteen dailies: Butte's *Post* and *Montana Standard,* Billings' morning and evening *Gazette,* the *Livingston Enterprise,* Helena's *Independent Record,* Missoula's morning *Missoulian* and evening *Sentinel.* Add to that two of Montana's ninety-five weeklies; one each in Libby and Superior. On one side, pallid statistics—9 of the state's 113 newspapers. On the obverse, Fairmont circulation totaled 89,934; independent Montana journalists, 69,552. Internal and external clamor rose even higher; ACM withdrew from its attempted foray into radio broadcasting. Writers and historians like John M. Schiltz, Richard T. Reutten, and K. Ross Toole now had grist and ground out more precise, if not dispassionate, analyses of what had been going on under ACM editorial scrutiny.

Guilt, according to these writers, lay more with acts of omission than commission. None of these three, nor any of the other critics, could find a codified policy of news control. Neither could they agree on its extent. Clear, however, was the in-print manifestation: events, philosophies, and people antithetical to company interests received little or no attention in the columns of its papers. Miles Romney, editor of Hamilton's *Western News*, put it best: "not hydrophobic character assassination," but rather "innocuous desuetude." In short, ACM's papers lost their once vibrant editorial color to shades of corporate gray. An alpenglow of independent journalism lingered beyond actual dates of Anaconda acquisition, but the shades paled in contrast to the irridescence of the preceding decades.

Post-1951 critics of Anaconda's press accurately assessed the scope and nature of the control, focusing on adversary newspapers which sniped at the behemoth. However, they passed lightly over circumstances creating that control, and the variegated journalistic history which made the scene all the more wan in comparison.

Montana's individualistic frontier journalism exuded a flamboyance well beyond the chronological confines of territoriality. Identifiable are four separate, but not always distinct, periods of florid journalism. Dates are approximate at best.

1. Partisan political rhetoric of the Territorial period (1864–1889)
2. Private, self-interested journalism of business entrepreneurs (1888–1906)
3. Political wranglings of reform and county busting (1900–1925)
4. Economic and patriotic propaganda surrounding corporate consolidation and World War I (1910–1929)

Through these arbitrary eras run the parallel themes that gave Montana journalism life and color: personalism and style. Early editors identified with their towns, and the communities reciprocated. Thomas

Dimsdale edited Virginia City's *Montana Post*, the *Helena Herald* represented Robert Fisk, James Mills was Deer Lodge's *New North-West*, Joseph Wright handled Bozeman's *Avant Courier*, and so it went. Each called them as they saw them for friend and foe alike. If a rival editor was a "whiskey pickled girkin," a "jackanape," or a "cussed disgrace to Montana journalism," so be it. If the same applied to the current candidate for Congress or governor, so be that too. When Hiram Brundage brought out the first issue of Dillon's *Tribune* in early 1881, he did not hesitate to predict a greatness for his fledgling community rivaled only by Chicago and San Francisco. Dillon people liked that kind of support, just as people in other communities appreciated what the local ink-slinger said about the town he served.

Montana's Historical Society Library lists more than 900 separate newspapers published since the *East Bannack News Letter* and the *Montana Post* set type in 1864. They admit the number is an estimate and caution that matters of predecessors, successors, movable type, and equally movable editors make precision difficult. Postulating further, more than 240 separate Montana communities had newspapers of one sort or another with 225 or more published at a single time— during the height of the homestead boom, 1910–1920. Titles include traditional Newses, Times, Heralds, Gazettes, and Journals; for politics there were Republicans, Democrats, and Independents; business postures encompassed Reporters, Observers, Advocates, Leaders, Promoters, Pilots, and Messengers, to say nothing of special interest Farmers, Stockmen, Husbandmen, Gushers, Fruit Growers, and Producers. Yet even by title, some newsheets strayed toward uniqueness: Headlight, Beacon, Searchlight, Radiator, Mountaineer, Optimist, Acantha, Wave, Mail, or Border Call.

Journalistic size and scope mirrored the nature of Montana itself. Initially each paper appeared as individualistic as the community it represented and the scrivener who ran it. Probably the youngest editor was Helena's fourteen-year-old Lee Travis who started the *Montana Daily News* in 1875. There existed no upper limit on age, and certainly no restrictions due to sex, as many husband and wife teams pooled publishing and editing talents. At least two German-language newspapers and three Negro journals circulated as well, adding texture to a diverse enterprise. That texture and diversity marked the colorful journalistic beginnings that contrasted with the weave of Toole's "Gray Blanket."

Editors and printing presses followed on the heels of prospectors

The staff of the Alder Gulch Times, *Virginia City, MT. Courtesy K. Ross Toole Archives, Mansfield Library, University of Montana.*

rooting in the placer sands of Montana's western valleys. The 1860s mineral rush gave birth to camps like Bannack and aspiring cities named Virginia, Blackfoot, Diamond, and Helena. Creation of the new territory in May of 1864 gave political validity to the boom, but in no way lessened the isolation mountain residents felt from "the states." Even that phrase had dual meaning among gold camp denizens. Union and Confederate forces fought to support their beliefs, and out of sectional political differences came the initial period of editorial controversy among Montana's editorial fraternity.

At issue during the Civil War and the Reconstruction years which followed was partisan control of Montana. Republican-dominated Congresses, and generally Republican presidents, appointed members of their own party to govern the territory. Montana's general population tended to be Democratic. In consequence, elections and editorials became political brouhahas for party and sectional opinion. Some historians have seen the genesis of the dispute in political preference, others in more regional and ideological differences; but all agree that the columns of Montana's fledgling press provided one of the principal battle grounds. Republican, pro-union, pro-Negro suffrage papers included (in various degrees of conviction) Robert Fisk's *Helena Herald*, Thomas Dimsdale's and later James Mills' *Montana Post*, and Mills' subsequent paper, the Deer Lodge *New North-West*. In opposition, E. S. Wilkinson, Peter Ronan, and Martin Maginnis published the *Rocky Mountain Gazette* in Helena, while J. H. Rogers espoused his views in the Deer Lodge *Independent*, which moved to Helena in the early 1870s but retained its strong Democratic bent.

Gazette and *Herald* editors exchanged constant rebukes during the 1860s, criticizing each other's politics and personalities with little restraint. Fisk likened Wilkinson's writing style to a "gorged condor of South America which vomits the disgusting contents of its stomach in the faces of its several readers." The Democrat did not wince editorially, branding Fisk's political views as an "eye-sore to the body . . . , a stench to the nostrils of all honest men, a leprous contagion to be avoided more than the Ten Plagues of Egypt." Fisk unhesitatingly criticized even Republicans with whom he did not see eye-to-eye. When Mills' paper received several territorial printing contracts at the expense of the *Herald*, Fisk suggested that the *New North-West* had been the "recipient of a sweet suck at the public titty-bag and obtained a 'fat take.' " Fisk never did agree with long-time Territorial Governor B. F. Potts—"Hippo-Potts-imus" and the "most shallow and odorous of all the Potts of which we have any record."

Partisan politics and vibrant prose tinged most newspaper debate during the Territorial period. The focus varied: Negro suffrage, capital location, railroad subsidies, printing, contracts, public appointments. But the debate was constant; likewise the forthright editorial prose. Montana's newspaper readers savored the grandiloquence while respective editors enjoyed social and political prominence. Free passes and community-wide "best editor" contests were commonplace. Fisk and one of his correspondents, Cornelius Hedges, continued as Republican stalwarts; Wilkinson and Rogers served in the territorial legislature; Martin Maginnis enjoyed six successive terms as the elected delegate to Congress, and came close to an appointive U.S. Senate seat. Exposed as Montanans had been to editorial candor and vituperation, the second phase of journalistic rhetoric would be played for higher stakes, as editors spoke not only for themselves, but also for their bosses.

Names like W. A. Clark, Marcus Daly, and A. B. Hammond appeared during the first dozen years of Territorial existence, but in minor roles. By the mid-1880s, such names had become decidedly larger in the public eye, as had their respective economic resources. In mining, both Clark and Daly ascended to prominence in first silver, then copper. Tangential growth in lumbering, to build railroads and stoke smelters, brought Hammond to the fore both economically and politically. Each man controlled, in addition to capital and resources, political power which derived from employing large numbers of men. Access to public forums became a strong component of their rising influence.

Clark first exercised effective editorial leverage. In 1884, when both he and Daly campaigned for seats at the Constitutional Convention, Clark's *Butte Miner* extolled all Democrats, but in the final column inch count, Clark won. Both men secured seats, although Clark finished first in populous Silver Bow County and ultimately enjoyed chairmanship of the convention. Four years later, Clark again sought public office as the shoo-in Democratic candidate for delegate to Congress. Of course the *Miner* swung behind him with extensive coverage of his campaign. But the economic needs of Democrats Hammond and Daly superseded party loyalties. They turned on Clark and engineered a defeat that has intrigued historians as much as it apparently surprised Clark. The rebuffed candidate jumped quickly to the attack in his *Miner.* Two days after the election, the *Miner's* editor used the word "conspiracy" freely with succeeding intimations of Daly's complicity. Hammond responded in kind through his Missoula papers; first the *Gazette* and then the *Missoulian.*

Daly did not long remain at a loss for words in an editorial sense. Less than a year after the election, he had a paper of his own—the *Anaconda Standard.* Daly bought the best. For editor he secured John H. Durston who had a doctorate in language and literature. In short order, Durston and Anaconda had Montana's finest paper. Daly had a mouthpiece.

Clark's 1888 defeat served as a prelude for the political and editorial squabbling that occupied the 1890s. Clark and Daly, competing for economic supremacy in Montana, moved their battle to the political arena in two bouts—one over designation of a permanent state capital; the other involving Clark's desire to become a U.S. senator. No newspaper, no editor, and in truth few Montanans—regardless of economic stature—remained aloof or disinterested.

In the capital controversy, an 1892 primary narrowed contenders to

Helena and Anaconda. Clark and his *Miner* favored Butte in 1892, but swung unhesitantly behind Helena for the finale. Hammond's *Missoulian* likewise joined the Helena cause: "What has Anaconda ever done for Missoula anyway? If Christ came to Anaconda he would be compelled to eat, sleep, drink, and pray with Mr. Marcus Daly." Clark and pro-Helena advocates warned Montanans of the "Copper Collar" if Anaconda became capital. Butte, Helena, and Missoula papers kept up the drumfire.

Durston and Daly pointed an accusing finger at the "Helena Hog," set on gobbling up political and economic power in her own self-interest. Durston's talented assistant Charles Eggleston fired the most literate volley of the campaign in a stinging satire entitled "Helena's Social Supremacy," which emerged anonymously from *Anaconda Standard* presses to characterize Helena as the home of the effete social snob, and Anaconda as the bastion of working class interests. Helena editorial efforts included brief publication of *The Colored Citizen*, a newspaper aimed solely at securing the support of black voters in Montana. In his final front page editorial on election eve, *Citizen* editor J. P. Ball, Jr., reminded readers that the Anaconda Copper Company did not employ a single black worker.

Editorial impact defied quantification, but Helena won in the 1894 election. For his part, Clark reveled in a hero's welcome in Helena. He returned to Montana's state capital a few years later, this time with an equally self-interested goal—his own election to the U.S. Senate.

Legislators selected U.S. senators in Montana before 1912, hence Clark supported solons who had his candidacy foremost in their minds. Short of a clear majority, the mining magnate set out to buy a sufficient plurality. Amid bribery accusations from Daly's *Anaconda Standard*, counter claims of "frame-ups" from Clark's *Miner*, a grand jury investigation and ballotting continued apace through the session. The former proved inconclusive (compounded with Daly's accusation that jurors had been bribed $10,000 each), but the election finally turned in Clark's favor. Daly did not retreat. He approached the Montana Supreme Court and eventually the U.S. Senate Committee on Privileges and Elections. The latter investigated, then unanimously recommended Clark not be seated. To save his honor, if not his seat, Clark ultimately resigned.

William A. Clark's resignation was a hindrance, not a defeat. Before the last type had been set on this debacle, Clark readied his 1900 campaign. Other forces had been at work concurrently, setting the stage for yet another battle in the economic campaign to control

Montana's mineral wealth. A. B. Hammond retired from Montana politics and profits to move west and exploit the timber resources of the Pacific coast. Marcus Daly also relinquished his economic control. Standard Oil, under the direction of Henry H. Rogers, began to consolidate Montana's copper mining industry in 1898. Rogers acquired Anaconda Copper holdings and forged them, with other corporations, into the nearly monolithic Amalgamated Copper Company. Control of the *Anaconda Standard* went with its copper parent.

Politically, Clark formed an amalgam of his own. A crucial ingredient was another copper entrepreneur—F. Augustus (Fritz) Heinze. The German immigrant rose to prominence in Butte economic circles through his amoral acquisition of copper holdings. Unquestionably, Amalgamated and Clark dominated Butte mining, but Heinze's bold economic and legal parrying, coupled with his political charisma, gave him clout. He also had his own newspaper—*The Reveille*, under editor P. A. O'Farrell. With Daly's personal influence (and his life) waning, and Standard Oil's on the rise, Clark found Heinze a useful ally during the 1900 election. Heinze must have realized the short-term nature of the alliance, but he, too, found it useful as he challenged Amalgamated's growing power.

Central in the campaign of 1900 stood the press. Clark knew firsthand a newspaper's impact because of his earlier political forays. Amalgamated took Daly's experience, perhaps his advice, and began to secure its own journals. In addition to the *Anaconda Standard*, the copper company purchased control of the *Helena Record*, the *Butte Intermountain* (which, interestingly enough, printed the *Labor World* and the *Labor Union Journal*), the *Belt Valley Times*, and at least partial interest in the *Great Falls Leader*. The *Standard* also became the state's feeder to the Associated Press wire service. Clark added to his *Butte Miner* with ownership of the *Great Falls Tribune* and an extended (although not clearly defined) interest in the *Helena Independent*. He counted also as a journalistic comrade for this particular election Heinze's *Reveille*.

Clark's tactics worked. A sufficient majority of "Clark men" secured election to the Montana legislature in 1900, and when lawmakers convened early in 1901, Clark had his long-sought senate seat. Some critics and historians have suggested Clark struck a bargain with H. H. Rogers, whereby Rogers stayed off Clark's back and the copper magnate stayed out of Standard Oil's business—business as it applied to Amalgamated Copper. In any case, Clark had no more political use for Fritz Heinze,

F. Augustus Heinze's Reveille was among Montana's most outspoken newspapers in attacking the Amalgamated Copper Company. Courtesy Montana Historical Society.

and swung his newspapers parallel to Rogers's. The *Reveille* and Montana's other independents called this union the "Kerosene Press." The *Miner* soon labeled Heinze's paper the "Reviler" while O'Farrell vilified the Amalgamated/Clark marriage. Clark's original paper became "the Lying Miner" in *Reveille* columns; *Helena Record* editor Eugene Carroll was portrayed as a "sour-visaged, dull-witted, truculent tool of Standard Oil villainy." Other editors of "muzzled" newspapers fared no better.

From 1901 until Amalgamated successfully silenced Heinze in 1906, the newspaper war continued. Anti-Amalgamated forces equated "Company" and Clark. In some papers control was obvious; others like the *Reveille* and independents like the Lewistown *Democrat*, Cut Bank's *Pioneer Press*, or the Hamilton *Western News* could only intimate corporate influence based on editorial policy.

In 1902, the Amalgamated-owned *Helena Record* bought out its struggling competitor, the *Herald*. The *Herald*'s former firebrand editor Robert Fisk retired to California. In eastern Montana, the heavy corporate hand began to hold the *Billings Gazette*'s editorial pen, too. Amalgamated's control of coal mines near Belt explained ownership of that community's newspaper, as did lumber holdings in Libby or Superior and corresponding journals there. By 1903, the *Lewistown Democrat* lamented "What a misfortune it is to the people of Montana that there is not a single free and independent daily newspaper published in any of the large cities of the state." Other members of the "Unmuzzled Press" spoke of news strained through an "Amalgamated sieve," and editorial policy with the "odor of coal oil."

Matters changed little in subsequent decades. In 1904, William Bole and Oliver Warden purchased control of the *Great Falls Tribune* from W. A. Clark—his need of it now past. Joseph M. Dixon continued to direct the *Missoulian* and *Sentinel* in western Montana, as he had since 1900 when he purchased the publishing plant from A. B. Hammond. Yet when Dixon wearied of his editorial duties and responsibilities and retired in 1917, Anaconda Copper bought him out. When W. A. Clark sold his papers, the copper company bought those, too. The second era of Montana's colorful journalistic history ended when Heinze left in 1906. In consequence, newspapers that had once been the private domain and voice of ambitious entrepreneurs entirely ceased operation or fell under the growing power of the Amalgamated-Anaconda Copper Company, as it rose to journalistic as well as economic dominance in the state.

ACM put its press to use within a decade of Heinze's departure, but during the interlude there arose another colorful era of newspaper activity. Montana's eastern plains had been an obstacle to settlement and a barrier to transportation during the 1860s and 1870s. By the 1880s, they had become the domain of rancher and cowboy, weather challenged, but unbroken. By 1900, increasing numbers of homesteaders dotted the plains. The Enlarged Homestead Act of 1909, the Three Year Act of 1912, and relentless promotion from multiple railroads combined to produce a surge of settlers—Honyockers, Scissorbills, and Sodbusters.

Shacks of green lumber and tar paper sprouted in intervals of 320 acres as would-be farmers staked out their land and future. New towns took root as well, and every half dozen towns or so clamored for a new county. Geometric increases in people, towns, and counties almost defied precise enumeration. Observing all this, reporting its significance in and out of proportion, came a new batch of community newspapers and a new breed of outspoken editors.

The fifteen years from 1906 to 1920 produced more newspapers than any other single period in Montana's history—upwards of 225. Most appeared on a weekly or semiweekly basis, joining the eighteen dailies published in larger cities. Two issues dominated these sheets—progressive politics and local growth. This decade and a half in Montana witnessed the initiative and referendum in 1906; direct election of senators, open primaries, and corrupt practices and campaign expenditures acts in 1912; women's suffrage, first exercised in 1916; and prohibition, in 1918. It would be a mistake to credit all such reforms to rural population and newspaper surges, since progressivism also had strong support in urban areas, but eastern Montana support was important. Rural sectors did succeed in pushing into law a 1914 initiative to support state-funded farm loans. Free-spoken editors of long standing, like W. K. Harber of Fort Benton's *River Press*, Dan Whetstone from Cut Bank, Tom Stout in Lewistown, and Hamilton's Miles Romney, assumed significant advocatory roles. Their editorial attacks on the company press and their unfaltering support of reform influenced the state.

Of more local concern, but equal journalistic fervor and flavor, were "county-busting" fights which also enlivened the era. "Grass orphans," far removed from existing seats of government in large eastern counties, demanded more attention to their needs. The most obvious solution appeared to be the creation of a smaller, closer to home county. Naturally, existing county seats and their established newspapers opposed such divisive efforts by "disgusting, pin-headed, pencil-pushing" rival editors. Ink and prose flowed from the "slimy pen of Slippery Jim," and his "beastly, cussed, damnable, brutish" opponents. But the newcomers prevailed. From 1906 to 1920, the number of Montana counties more than doubled. Most of the political growth took place on the eastern plains. Battles over the "beautifully colored plum" of local government appeared anemic, however, compared to the literary warfare of Montana's fourth colorful journalistic period.

First Amalgamated, then Anaconda Copper Company strove to consolidate economic control in Montana following Heinze's 1906 departure. Its servile press assisted. In opposing matters such as workman's compensation, increased mine taxation, or pollution control in the Deer Lodge Valley, the ACM press maintained the tatoo of corporate interest and opinion. After the direct primary law of 1912, the company also found it necessary to take a more public role in political campaigns when occasional anticompany candidates surfaced. The rhetoric heated two years later when World War I began in Europe. The price of copper increased, and, correspondingly, the need to keep mining it without labor interruptions. In 1917, the United States entered the European conflict and journalism took on the garish hues of super-patriotism.

A 1917 strike by Butte's copper miners exacerbated an already tense situation. ACM journalists fired continuous editorial salvos into Butte and all Montana. In particular, they worked to heighten the patriotic fervor and to criticize militant members of Butte's various unions, including the International Workers of the World. From the *Helena Independent*, one inch high hysterical headlines: "Your Neighbor, Your Maid, Your Lawyer, Your Waiter May Be A German Spy." In labor activities, ACM's editors saw "red socialism" and worse. When "parties unknown" lynched I.W.W. organizer Frank Little in early August, procompany editors generally fell silent. To challenge ACM's journalistic domination in Butte, labor leaders formed the *Joint Strike Bulletin*, which later became the *Butte Bulletin*. Its writers and editors like Bill Dunne and R. B. Smith responded in kind to *Anaconda Standard* and *Butte Miner* attacks.

Dunne saw company supporters, like *Helena Independent* editor Bill Campbell, grow "lean and gray, or fat and bald in the service of big business," and deplored the company's "putrid tactics." Dunne ran for mayor of Butte and later for the state legislature. The *Standard* and *Miner* painted him as a "hissing young serpent of sedition," on a platform of "free love, free dynamite, lots of loot, no work, plenty of pay." Dunne was not the only target. Burton K. Wheeler won the Democratic primary for governor in 1920. Company papers derisively labeled him first as "Bolshevik Burt" for what they felt was a lack of patriotism; then "Boxcar Burt" when political opponents in Dillon threatened the candidate's life and he sought refuge in a railroad car. Wheeler lost. So did Bill Dunne. Causes were manyfold, among them press pyrotechnics, lively and colorful.

Former *Missoulian* editor Joseph M. Dixon, an anticompany politician in his own right, assumed the governor's chair as a result of the 1920 election. His four year term was turbulent, rocked by drought and economic decline in eastern Montana along with mine taxation controversy in the west. Newspapers under ACM control railed against the incumbent governor in 1924. He did not win reelection, but did succeed in passing an initiative to institute more equitable mine taxation. East of Helena, towns, banks, counties, and newspapers that had prospered in the preceding decade began to face lean times and economic starvation. By decade's end, only 150 weeklies and dailies still published.

Faded, too, was the colorful journalism that brightened newspapers during the first sixty years of Montana's history. Here and there the hysteric prose streaked the political sky as the *Anaconda Standard* painted gubernatorial candidate Wellington Rankin "At His Rankest," and Bill Campbell fabricated stories about Burton K. Wheeler and Tom Stout when each ran for the U.S. Senate. Campbell accused both of various sins against public morality and national prohibition. For the most part, however, company-controlled newspapers dealt with distasteful issues and politicians in silence. Campaigns of "undesirable" candidates received little or no coverage, in a style the *Denver Post* typified as "editorial Afganistanism." What color existed was to be found in the editorials of established weeklies like the *Western News* or in the goading, anti-ACM columns of such papers as the *Western Progressive*, which berated "copper-collared" editors, including the "pot-bellied, ill-natured gink" Bill Campbell.

Such tawdry harangues made the grayness of the editorial blanket which Toole described all the more noticeable. Montana had experienced six decades of open journalism in the most intense frontier style. Gradually, "name" editors and "town" newspapers ceased to exist. Smaller papers simply folded; larger journals became business, not personal, ventures. Critics deplored circumstances as they stood after 1930, in both philosophy and fact. Yet the historical progression of events that produced Anaconda Company's control of Montana's media bore the seeds of its own demise.

As the Fairmont Corporation exerted its influence through the printed word in the 1920s, a new communication medium appeared. Radio broadcasting began in Montana during 1922 and by the end of the decade most major cities had a station. The number of broadcasters and receivers grew steadily to exceed forty by 1953. That same year, Montana's first television station began transmitting out of Butte. Here, too, numbers and public support grew. These new communication media provided broad news coverage which exceeded the range of ACM's press. At the same time, the number of newspapers in Montana declined to just over 100 by 1950. Clearly, the dominant role of the published word, so essential in the political wars of the nineteenth and early twentieth centuries, diminished in direct proportion to the spread of electricity in Montana and the media that used it.

Equally clear was the fact that Anaconda Company control of newspapers had outlived its utility. In 1959, Fairmont sold its holdings to the Lee Newspaper chain of Iowa. Lee, in turn, divested itself of some papers (to other chains) and turned editorial direction over to local managers. The era Shiltz, Reutten, and Toole deplored had come to an end. The roweling press, which existed during the 1930s, 1940s, and 1950s to needle and enlighten, disappeared.

In truth, however, Montana did not return to the colorful crazyquilt of frontier journalism. Lee was but the first of several chains to buy into Montana's newspaper business. Today not one of Montana's eleven dailies and only a portion of its fifty-one weeklies are privately owned. Wire services and corporate policy have woven a fabric of their own. Gray? Copper? Perhaps not. But the threads of controversy, prose, and vibrant rhetoric are reduced to pastel hues.

NOTES

No historian can deal with Montana's history and ignore its press. This is markedly true in the years before 1930 when journalistic reporting often forms the basis of historical documentation. Consequently, any history of Montana becomes a source for its newspaper development. Among the best are Michael P. Malone and Richard B. Roeder's *Montana: A History of Two Centuries* (University of Washington, 1976), K. Ross Toole's *Montana: An Uncommon Land* (University of Oklahoma, 1959), *Montana: Our Land and People* by

William L. Lang and Rex C. Myers (Pruett, 1979), and Clark Spence's Bicentennial history, *Montana* (W. W. Norton, 1978). In special areas, Michael P. Malone's *The Battle for Butte* (University of Washington, 1981) covers the color and controversy of newspapering in Butte between 1864 and 1906. Clark Spence does an equally credible job in his *Territorial Politics and Government in Montana, 1864–1889* (University of Illinois, 1975) in accurately portraying the role of the press during the first twenty-five years of Montana's history.

The three scholarly writers who discussed Fairmont Corporation holdings were John M. Schiltz in "Montana's Captive Press," *Montana Opinion*, Vol. I, No. 1 (June, 1956); Richard T. Reutten in both "Togetherness: A Look into Montana Journalism," *The Call Number*, Vol. XXI (Fall, 1959) and "Anaconda Journalism: The End of an Era," *Journalism Quarterly*, XXXVII (Winter, 1960); and K. Ross Toole's chapter "The Great Gray Blanket: The Captive Press," in his book *Twentieth-Century Montana, A State of Extremes* (University of Oklahoma, 1972).

Many articles in *Montana: The Magazine of Western History* have dealt with newspapers directly or indirectly. James L. Thane, Jr., in "The Myth of Confederate Sentiment" (Vol. 17, No. 2, April, 1967) and Stanley R. Davison and Dale Tash in "Confederate Backwash in Montana Territory" (Vol. 17, No. 4, October, 1967) focus on the partisan and sectional rhetoric of the Territorial period. Also to be included in the magazines with significant information is the *Montana Journalism Review* and the articles reprinted from it in Warren J. Brier and Nathan B. Blumberg's edited *A Century of Montana Journalism* (Mountain Press, 1971). Daniel W. Whetstone's *Frontier Editor* (Hastings House, 1956), is also helpful for firsthand insights into early Montana journalism.

Last, and certainly not least, would be Montana's newspapers themselves. The Montana Historical Society Library in Helena has the most complete collection of these, covering all periods of Montana's history. As of this writing, they estimate that approximately ninety dailies and weeklies are being published in Montana, and they pride themselves in having over ninety percent of those that have ever appeared. They do, however, admit the difficulty in quantifying frequency and diversity. Annual statistics used for that purpose in this article have, therefore, come from the various issues of Ayers *Directory of Publications*, under its several titles since 1869. In any instance, students of Montana's colorful journalistic past should browse the pages of its newspapers from Absarokee's *Headlight* to Zortman's *Little Rockies Miner*, or from the *Montana Post* of 1864 Virginia City, to a modern daily in Billings or Kalispell. There is found the color and history.

6 /

TO HUSBAND THE LAND
Robert Sutherlin and the
Irrigation–Dry Farming Controversy

FRANK R. GRANT

Controversy over water on the arid Great Plains is as old as John Wesley Powell and as recent as the morning newspaper. One round in that ever-lasting battle occurred in the early twentieth century, when optimistic scientists joined other promoters in advancing the notion of "dry-land" farming. At issue was the livelihood of thousands of small farmers, who poured onto the plains searching for the Montana version of the American Dream—a self-sufficient, agricultural homestead.

One man in Montana stoutly warned against the vagaries of nature and weather. Robert Sutherlin, for fifty-five years the editor of a farmer's newspaper, the *Rocky Mountain Husbandman*, consistently decried the notion that skies over the plains yielded sufficient moisture to support intensive dry-land agriculture. He called instead for massive irrigation projects to bring river water directly to the land. The great drought which began in 1918 vindicated Sutherlin's stature as a prophet. Frank R. Grant, Sutherlin's biographer, explains this courageous stand.

On March 31, 1904 editor Robert N. Sutherlin announced that he had relocated the *Rocky Mountain Husbandman*, Montana's pioneer agricultural journal, from White Sulphur Springs to Great Falls "to better serve the interests of our patrons."[1] He was also broke. Sutherlin had invested heavily in a home, business block, theater, and land in White Sulphur Springs; however, the rail connection upon which he had gambled failed to materialize. He had become embroiled in a bitter newspaper war, had lost the county printing contract, and had de-

Robert N. Sutherlin long served as agriculture's spokesman through the pages of his Rocky Mountain Husbandman. *Courtesy Montana Historical Society.*

nounced the Amalgamated Copper Company for its high-handed politics in 1903. In return the company-controlled newspapers had attempted to discredit Sutherlin through vitriolic personal attacks. Although he retained an interest in White Sulphur Springs, conditions made a move imperative.[2]

Sutherlin changed locations; he did not change his editorial policy. With a defiant challenge to the Amalgamated Copper Company, he vowed the *Husbandman* would continue to promote the state's agricultural interests and oppose corporate despotism. "From this day forward Great Falls breaks the shackles of its copper thralldom and starts out on the broad and enduring basis of agriculture."[3] His agrarian conviction was still very much alive: the yeoman farmer on his own land was the one man on earth "who enjoys civil and religious liberty in its fullest sense," is "in no wise dependent upon the surging mass of mankind around him for the necessaries of life," and does "not have to bow to the caprice of some big syndicate of wealth."[4]

Sutherlin viewed the Homestead Act of 1862 as the essential element in the realization of his agrarian vision. It granted the poor man and his family a homestead, which promised to fulfill the ideology of personal liberty and freedom as well as provide an economic stake for the laboring classes of the nation.[5] Sutherlin's experience, however, indicated that successful homesteading in semiarid Montana depended upon irrigation, and he vigorously advocated putting water on the land. Through irrigation the opportunities for mixed husbandry, crop rotation, and intensive production increased. This, in turn, strengthened the homesteader's ability to husband the land as well as to establish and maintain an economically and politically independent agrarian way of life.

Even as Sutherlin proclaimed irrigation the key to a successful Montana homestead, promoters and agricultural scientists promulgated a "new technique" to guarantee adequate moisture for semiarid agriculture. Through proper soil cultivation, they claimed, the homesteader could conserve moisture from one season to the next, assuring sufficient water for farming in spite of limited precipitation. Sutherlin labeled these dry-land farming techniques a "false hope" for the homesteader; he warned Montanans that the promotion of dry-land homesteading courted disaster and delayed the development of a sound agricultural program based on irrigation. Sutherlin's efforts to disarm the dry-land farming propagandists and fortify irrigation sentiment constituted the *Husbandman's* major theme during Sutherlin's twenty-two years in

Great Falls. The controversy revealed Sutherlin to be a prophetic interpreter of Montana's destiny.

Throughout his newspaper career Sutherlin had been a leading exponent of irrigation farming. He considered irrigation to be one of Montana agriculture's "chief merits," for "the convenience of being able to throw water upon your crops whenever they require it should be esteemed as a great advantage."[6] He was optimistic regarding the potential for irrigation in Montana, and as the population increased Sutherlin's irrigation proposals evolved from encouraging individual farmers to advocating federal reclamation projects. By the late 1870s he was urging farmers to take cooperative action either through private corporations or irrigation districts to alleviate the problems of water storage, appropriation, and utilization. In the spring of 1886, predicting that Montana was entering a period of severe drought which threatened both stockmen and farmers, Sutherlin urged Montanans to follow California's lead and raise capital for irrigation through state appropriation.[7] Montanans did not heed his advice.

They began to listen more attentively when the "Hard Winter" of 1886–1887 dramatically revealed the limits to agriculture in Montana. Though the disaster to the Montana livestock industry was generally attributed to the severity of the winter, Sutherlin believed the two seasons of drought preceding it were the primary cause. "Stock did not fatten all the summer, and, it will be remembered, began to die before snow began to fly," he reminded his readers. "This loss would have been heavy had the winter been light, thus proving conclusively that the feed supply was at fault."[8] Sutherlin insisted on large irrigation projects like storage reservoirs, canals, and dams. Such projects were not within the reach of private interests; "government aid must come to the rescue."[9]

In the summer of 1888 Congress began debating a direct appropriation for irrigation works in the arid West. Sutherlin was skeptical that such a measure would be enacted, but he heartily approved the idea. Later, when Congress did appropriate funds for reservoir surveys, Sutherlin "rejoiced" to see the work begin. He was pleased that individual enterprise had created many "bright and beautiful oases" in the arid West, but with government aid this land of bunch grass "is destined to become the most productive and certain of agricultural belts in the United States."[10]

Sutherlin continued to promote more extensive irrigation projects and increased government support for reclamation throughout the

1890s, but it was not until the turn of the century that national sentiment was strong enough to pass supportive legislation. Sutherlin believed that federal irrigation projects would accomplish two purposes. First, they would transform a land of light growth into a garden spot. Second, they would furnish homes for "an industrious and deserving people who merely eke out an existence in the great trade centers and make a nation of independent freeholders rather than a population dependent on the push, progress and investments of the few."[11]

Sutherlin labeled the National Reclamation Act of 1902 "the greatest achievement of the age," but he believed the projections that federal irrigation projects would bring a million people to Montana were "optimistic." "It means a steady and gradual reclamation of the country such as will be calculated to insure steady and onward progress rather than a big boom and the consequent reaction that generally follows these unhappy periods of inflated values." He also hoped the Reclamation Act had put "a quietus upon land leasing and gives land monopoly a most effectual check." For Sutherlin federal reclamation was "the same line of policy intensified that was adopted when the Homestead Law was ushered in. It means a homestead still to the settler."[12]

When Sutherlin moved the *Husbandman* to Great Falls, his reputation as an irrigationist was well established. For over a quarter century he had vigorously promoted irrigation projects throughout the state, and he expressed the belief that Great Falls would become "the greatest agricultural city west of St. Paul" through the development of large irrigation projects in the area.[13]

The Great Falls *Tribune* matched Sutherlin's enthusiasm for irrigation. Claiming that there was more irrigable land in the Great Falls district than in any other district of the country, the *Tribune* editor envisioned extensive irrigated tracts in northern Montana. "Better than plans for another smelter for Great Falls is the plan for the irrigation of the Sun River bench so that it can be occupied by farmers," he enthusiastically proclaimed.[14] He recognized that large irrigation projects would develop slowly and urged Westerners to initiate additional measures, including direct congressional appropriations, to keep the reclamation program alive.[15] Thus Sutherlin entered Great Falls on a wave of irrigation enthusiasm, and it appeared that his vision of thousands of irrigated homesteads in northern Montana would be realized.

Sutherlin acknowledged that there were extensive sections of fertile land in Montana that could not be irrigated and that irrigation projects, no matter how large, were essentially oases in a semiarid region.

Montanans had cultivated thousands of these nonirrigable acres since the 1860s. During his years in White Sulphur Springs Sutherlin carefully recorded and evaluated the development of dry-land farming techniques, and from his experience he advocated the earliest possible seeding, fall plowing, and summer fallowing to improve the chances of raising a crop. However, since dry-land farming was primarily successful with cereals and grains, Sutherlin, who was dedicated to diversification, discouraged its general use. He acknowledged that crops could be grown through dry-land farming techniques, but he insisted that the dry-land farmer would always remain dependent on timely and adequate precipitation. This was not a system for the homesteader who needed a crop every year; the Montana homesteader must irrigate.

Northern Montana promoters, who rejected the arid image implied by the demand for irrigation, repudiated Sutherlin's insistence that irrigation alone provided a stable source of moisture for homesteading in Montana. Among Sutherlin's most vocal critics was Senator Paris Gibson, founder of Great Falls, close associate of James J. Hill, and long-time Montana agriculturist.[16] In 1904 Gibson claimed he had grown wheat and oats on unirrigated land near Great Falls for seventeen years and only twice had had a crop failure. There were thousands of acres south of the city that could be converted into homes for the people, he asserted, since there was adequate precipitation in spring and early summer to guarantee a crop. Though he was a strong advocate of government irrigation, Gibson believed "the citizens of Montana are not absolved from the duty of advertising to the world the free homes that can be established in many parts of Montana upon lands far more productive without irrigation, than the farm lands of the middle and New England states."[17] Gibson and many other northern Montana promoters were eager to do their duty.

When there was scant precipitation in northern Montana during the summer of 1904, Sutherlin reminded his readers that they were experiencing Montana's normal aridity. Though he did not have the "brazen effrontery to claim the dry season may prove to be a blessing in disguise," he hoped it would encourage more enthusiastic support for irrigation.[18] He did not intend to discourage dry-land farmers nor to antagonize Senator Gibson, but he did want prospective homesteaders to be informed of the true nature of Montana's seasons. "We simply say that the skies are fickle and uncertain and that the man who depends upon drifting winds and shifting clouds for a crop leans upon a slender reed."[19] When Sutherlin called the summer of 1904 Montana's "regular annual dry spell," he established the focal point of the growing controversy between the *Husbandman* and the dry-land farming promoters. He insisted that thirty years' experience in Montana had clearly revealed that aridity was the characteristic feature of Montana's climate; that although there were years in which precipitation was adequate and timely for farming without irrigation, homesteaders could not depend upon such precipitation. For the promoters to encourage thousands of farmers to enter homesteads on nonirrigated lands was therefore a great mistake which threatened participants with disaster.

The scientists at the Montana Agricultural Experiment Station in Bozeman had also recognized the problems of cultivating nonirrigable lands, and in 1898 they began experiments with the Campbell Soil Culture System, a set of techniques for cultivating semiarid lands developed by Hardy Webster Campbell on his South Dakota farm. Campbell had gained considerable notoriety for his work managing demonstration farms for midwest and western railroads. So widespread was his influence that "the Campbell System" and "dry-land farming" were frequently used interchangeably.[20]

The primary achievement Campbell claimed for his system was the conservation of moisture in the soil through a systematic procedure of summer fallowing, thorough cultivation, subsurface packing, and early spring planting. Through his system, according to Campbell, winter and spring moisture could be retained in the soil for the late summer dry season, and it was even possible to conserve the moisture of one season for the next. By identifying his procedure as "scientific soil culture" he implied that his techniques were based on scientifically validated principles. The railroads and local boosters used his persuasive words as propaganda; to the thousands of land-hungry homeseekers hoping to settle the semiarid lands of the West, Campbell's system appeared to be a godsend.[21]

After a season's experiments with the Campbell System, R. S. Shaw, assistant agriculturalist at the Experiment Station, believed that the system "should prove of great service on arid lands where water is unavailable."[22] A year later, after comparing crops grown by the Campbell System with those grown by general farm culture using irrigation, he concluded, "the Campbell System will not compete with methods of irrigation, though it may hold an important place in crop production in arid regions where water is not available."[23] In 1900 the station could give only qualified support to the Campbell System and dry-land farming.

The interest in Montana homesteading was growing, however, and in 1904 the Experiment Station began a more extensive investigation of dry-land farming potential. At Wayne Siding near Great Falls the station established a temporary substation with three objectives: 1) to test the methods of cultivation and kinds of crops that would yield the best without irrigation; 2) to determine how to construct a small reservoir to catch the flood water of the spring for stock water and limited irrigation; 3) to control the overflow from the reservoir and use it to irrigate spring and fall. The station personnel clearly envisioned a combination of irrigation and dry-land farming as a viable structure for Montana farming.[24]

A year later the station established four additional substations for which the Northern Pacific Railway, the United States Department of Agriculture, and the State of Montana provided funds.[25] The Northern Pacific was especially interested in determining the value of its remaining grant lands, so the substations were located to meet the railroad's needs.[26] F. B. Linfield, Experiment Station director, expressed the hope that the work could be extended for several years and was encouraged by additional contributions from the Great Northern, Northern Pacific, and the state in 1905.[27]

By 1907 the scientists at the station had completed initial dry-land farming studies and began publishing their results. The conclusions drawn by Linfield were unexceptional; they affirmed what the experience of Montana farmers since 1870 had shown.

> The crops on the dry land are going to be affected to a considerable extent by this variation in rainfall. In the wetter seasons crops will generally be extra good; the average rainfall should also bring good crops. However, when the rainfall is below average, as it was in 1904 and 1905 at Havre, . . . we may expect under such conditions partial or complete crop failure.[28]

Though Linfield was cautious in his statements regarding dry-land farming success, the Experiment Station was assuming a role of leadership in the dry-land farming movement. In addition to the growing commitment of station resources to the dry-land farming substations, station personnel were emphasizing dry-land farming in the Farmers' Institutes the station conducted throughout the state.[29]

The *Sixth Annual Report of the Montana Farmers' Institutes*, published by the station in 1908, was devoted entirely to dry-land farming.[30] In addition to a discussion of Experiment Station work the *Report* contained some of the more speculative propaganda of H. W. Campbell and his disciples. Campbell argued that through his systematic tillage procedures crops could be consistently and successfully raised without irrigation in regions where the rainfall averaged less than fifteen inches per year, for "the crop growth and grain yield was governed largely by the physical condition of the soil." By using his techniques, he continued, a farmer could "grow larger crops of grains and vegetables under a fifteen-inch rainfall on the average high level prairie than is now grown by the man who farms by irrigation."[31]

W. X. Sudduth, one of Campbell's most enthusiastic Montana disciples, made even greater claims for Campbell's system. He testified that Campbell had so perfected his system that "where his methods are intelligently followed, he affirms that there need never be a crop failure, even where the annual precipitation is as low as seven inches." What a promise! If true, nearly every tillable acre in Montana could be farmed successfully year in and year out.[32]

The Experiment Station scientists were giving Montana farmers a confusing message. Their own experiments indicated that dry-land farming success was largely dependent on timely precipitation, yet they had published statements by Campbell and Sudduth, who acknowledged no such dependency. Furthermore, the station used these same promoters as speakers at the Farmers' Institutes.[33] The station was endorsing claims for dry-land farming that had not been verified by its own experiments.

Linfield's own words and actions exemplified the confusion. He refused to acknowledge any special value in the equipment designed by Campbell, and for this refusal Campbell personally assailed him.[34] At the Billings Dry Farming Congress in 1909 Linfield opposed attempts to change the name of the organization from "Dry Farming Congress" to "Scientific Farming Congress," arguing that it would mislead settlers regarding the arid nature of the land.[35] Yet at the Cheyenne Dry Farming Congress, in an address entitled "Progress in Dry Farming in the West," Linfield painted a very flattering portrait of dry-land farming success.

> . . . for the past two or three years thousands of people from the east have been spreading themselves over this western country. [The new settler] is conquering the desert by inches. . . . He has called to his aid the scientist near and far and now gradually with firm and safer step the settler is again traveling westward, conquering the desert as he comes.[36]

The implication of Linfield's remarks was that the successful techniques through which dry-land farmers were "conquering the desert" were based on scientific experiments.

For Sutherlin there was only one way to conquer the desert: put water on it. He believed the station's dry-land farming emphasis to be a misguided effort that encouraged an agricultural program already proven by experience to be unsound, short-sighted, and destructive. Although he acknowledged that dry-land farming techniques were practiced successfully on larger holdings in some years, he insisted that dry-land farming created too many problems to be a viable option for the homesteader.

Sutherlin argued his case on four grounds. First, dry-land farming specialized in "soil robbers," wheat and cereals, and threatened the homesteader with increasingly poor crop return. Second, dry-land farming required extensive acreage to produce a profitable crop. Sutherlin had no doubt that crops could be raised on nonirrigated land, but if he were going to farm in the dry-land areas, he would want "a thousand acres and a steam plow."[37] Third, extensive plowing created soil erosion. Sutherlin suggested that there were sections of Montana where the wind blew so hard and steadily that it was impractical to fallow the land. Such sections, he said, should be seeded to grass for permanent pasture or hay if they could not be irrigated.[38] Fourth, and most important, successful dry-land homesteading depended on consistent and appropriately timed annual precipitation. In Montana such consistency was not the pattern; the spectre of drought was ever present.

Sutherlin rejected the optimistic attitude that dry-land farming problems would be solved through scientific experimentation. He deeply resented the "self-styled experts" and "palace car farmers" who based their conclusions on limited information and ignored Montana experience, and he added: "We believe a third of a century's experience is worth more than all the new-fangled propagandas the age can invent."[39] For Sutherlin there was only one conclusion: no matter how diligently the dry-land homesteader practiced all the "scientific" techniques of dry-land farming, his success depended upon the quantity and timely occurrence of rainfall. By promoting dry-land farming the station was encouraging agricultural practices that robbed the soil of its fertility, required extensive operations, caused soil erosion, and imparted a false sense of security to the homesteaders. And most critical of all, he believed the dry-land farming emphasis delayed irrigation development.

Therefore he viewed the Experiment Station's commitment to dry-land farming as a betrayal of the established Montana farmer and the immigrant homesteader.

Linfield protested Sutherlin's accusations. "Now I believe I am as enthusiastic a believer in irrigation as the *Husbandman*. But that being so, I can see no inconsistency in calling attention to the possibilities of the dry farm." Linfield acknowledged that "many men are going to fail on these dry farms, . . . but tens of thousands have failed in the humid East; whole sections in the New England States have been deserted; thousands have failed under irrigation. . . ." He did not measure success through numerical verification. "One success as a demonstration of what can be done is worth a thousand failures and there are many [dry-land farming successes]." He believed the station had a duty to locate favorable dry-land farming sections of the state and to determine methods of cultivation and crop management that give the best results on nonirrigable land.[40] There were thousands of immigrants coming to Montana in search of homes. "Shall we tell them they are not wanted, or shall we direct them to those favorable sections of the state where successful dry farming is a possibility?" Linfield asked.[41]

Though he acknowledged serious problems, Linfield's enthusiasm for dry-land farming was readily apparent by 1910. "In light of the facts presented, I believe we are justified in claiming that dry farming may be made a success," he told the Montana Woolgrowers' Association.[42] And in a statement ready-made to fuel the railroad's promotional fires, he reported to Thomas Cooper, land commissioner for the Northern Pacific, that the dry areas of the state were quite limited, the rainfall of the year came mainly in the growing season, well water for domestic use was readily available and inexpensive, deep retentive soil was located throughout the state, and three transcontinental railroads crossed the state giving Montana farmers access to world markets.[43] All that was needed was proper cultivation to make Montana blossom.

Sutherlin had no quarrel with the station's surveys of potential dry-land farming areas or its experiments with new crops and cultivation methods. What angered him was the promotional emphasis that the station placed on dry-land farming experiments while the irrigation studies languished. Linfield might deny the antagonism between irrigation and dry-land farming, but Sutherlin insisted that the antagonism was at the heart of the conflict. The dry-land and irrigation departments vied for the station's meager resources, and the station's annual reports clearly indicate that the dry-land department received the lion's share of the funds.[44] More significantly, when the scientists claimed that dry-land homesteading was successful and that irrigation was unnecessary, they undermined further national support for federal reclamation by implying that the investment in reservoirs, dams, and canals could be curtailed. Sutherlin put it bluntly: "Our greatest fight with Montana's Experiment Station people is their determination to abandon irrigation for the fickle and uncertain method of depending on the skies. . . ."[45]

In spite of good crop production on the state's unirrigated lands between 1906 and 1909, Sutherlin refused to temper his position. His experience indicated that Montana's climate was erratic; on this he would not waver. A series of dry years often followed the wet seasons, though he had discovered no regular cycle. His solution to the controversy was simple.

> The great influx of dry farmers this year [1910] and the universal effort will in a few years tell some kind of a story. But nothing short of time and experience will do this. A million acres of dry land will be plowed this year and the effort will be such that the verdict will be easily determined.[46]

The effort of the following decade did indeed "tell some kind of a story." Between 1911 and 1918 there was generally enough moisture throughout the state to grow good crops without irrigation, and in 1915 and 1916 dry-land farms produced bumper crops. Furthermore, the war in Europe created a bull market for wheat, and Montanans sold all they produced. By 1916 the trial appeared to be over; the verdict was in. Dry-land farmers more than survived; they reaped surplus grain and cash balances; and real estate people, implement dealers, bankers, and businessmen invested enthusiastically in the dry-land farming future.

In 1917 enthusiasm began to wane as precipitation fell to below average levels in many Montana localities. A few farmers began to abandon their land. As the drought continued through 1918, the emigration from Montana's dry-lands increased. In 1919 the true verdict on Montana's dry-land homesteading experiment became excruciatingly clear. M. L. Wilson of the Experiment Station described the bitter results.

> The year 1919 came as a great climax of drought to set the seal of broken hope upon a majority of homes in [northern Montana]. There was no reserve of moisture from the two previous dry years; grass made practically no growth—there was no pasture for feed. Most of the grain that was seeded did not germinate, and as a result the farmers began shipping out their livestock.[47]

In northern Montana the drought that began in 1917 lasted through 1922. Though there were farmers who survived, the enduring legacy of the dry-land homestead boom was abandoned farms, failed banks, shattered expectations, and disillusioned homestead families. Wrote Wilson, "There was little more in the way of defeat that could be experienced."[48]

Sutherlin had forseen these results of unrestrained homesteading on Montana's nonirrigated lands. He had warned Montanans of the inevitable drought and had cautioned them to avoid careless land exploitation and speculation. And always, he insisted that dry-land farming was precarious and that it should be the homesteader's goal to put water on the land.

Sutherlin's pleas for restraint, words of warning, appeals for caution, and insistence on irrigation went unheeded. The dry-land farming frenzy, fueled by abnormally high precipitation, an excellent grain market, and intense propaganda, overwhelmed the voices of reason and moderation. Sutherlin was not heard; Montana's early experience was not considered.

The reckless promotion of land settlement and the careless cultivation of the land were American traditions that Sutherlin had long recognized and combatted.[49] He expected to challenge boosters and ignorant farmers. But he was thoroughly dismayed at the Experiment Station's alliance with such exploitation, and the institution which he thought would be a staunch ally became an ardent opponent. He urged restraint in portraying dry-land farming success; the station reduced funds for its irrigation department. Sutherlin denounced the railroads for their propaganda regarding Montana's agricultural potential; the station cooperated with the railroads to provide leadership for the dry-land farming movement. Instead of being a strong voice of reason, scientific skepticism, and improved farming, the station personnel acquiesced to the dry-land farming promotion enthusiasm and added their voices to the siren song luring thousands of homesteaders to disaster on Montana's nonirrigated lands. Only after drought had driven thousands of homesteaders from the land in 1919 did station personnel acknowledge their blindness to the warning signs of disaster.

The dry-land farming boom and disaster was a bittersweet affirmation of Sutherlin's prophetic insight. He had urgently warned against dry-land homesteading, and in 1919 he gazed across the northern Montana landscape where native vegetation had been uprooted, weeds were spreading across fallowed fields, and empty houses stood as tomb-

stones marking the homesteaders' shattered dreams. He had urged
Montanans to put water on the land, but in their enthusiasm for dry-
land farming, the state's commercial, agricultural, and political leadership had delayed irrigation development. Envisioning Montana as a
haven for the homesteader whose land was a hedge against economic
insecurity and corporate despotism, he saw his vision corrupted, for the
dry-land homesteader was the antithesis of the free and independent
yeoman.

Though the drought had driven thousands of homesteaders from
the land, it had also revitalized interest in irrigation. Sutherlin opti-
mistically believed the long-range outcome would be a more stable
and enduring agricultural system that acknowledged the arid nature of
the region and recognized the importance of irrigation. F. H. Newell,
consulting engineer for the Reclamation Service, warmly supported
Sutherlin's determined persistence. "You are one of the few men who
have unswervingly held to the line in spite of the allurements of dry
farming," he wrote in 1921. He hoped the businessmen of the state
would recognize the importance of reclamation, for "irrigation and diversification means stable though small profits and the development
of a stable population and stable business conditions."[50]

Irrigation was more than a technique for improving agricultural
production; it was the symbol of Sutherlin's enduring agrarian conviction that the welfare of society is best served through a commitment to
the interests of the yeoman and the determination to husband the
land. It was this overriding conviction that molded his editorial policy
for half a century, encouraged him to challenge corporate despotism,
turned him into a harsh critic of the Agricultural Experiment Station,
and made him one of the most prescient interpreters of early Montana
history.

NOTES

1. *Rocky Mountain Husbandman*, March 31, 1904. Robert and Will Sutherlin
began publishing the *Husbandman* in Diamond City, Montana Territory, on
November 25, 1875. In 1879 the brothers moved the press to White Sulphur
Springs. See Frank R. Grant, "Embattled Voice of the Montana Farmer," *Montana: the Magazine of Western History*, Vol. XXIV, No. 2 (Spring 1974), 34–43.

2. William G. Brietenstein, "A History of Early Journalism in Montana, 1863–
1890" (Masters Thesis: University of Montana, 1915), 22; *Husbandman*, September 1, 1904; November 26, 1925; Butte *Intermountain*, February 13, 1904;
March 23, 1904.

3. *Husbandman*, March 31, 1904; October 20, 1904.

4. *Husbandman*, November 22, 1878.

5. For a discussion of the relationship of the yeoman farmer, ideology, and land policy see Henry Nash Smith, *Virgin Land* (Cambridge: Harvard University Press, 1950) chapters 12, 15; Mary E. Young, "Congress Looks West: Liberal Ideology and Public Land Policy in the Nineteenth Century," in David M. Ellis, editor, *The Frontier in American Experience* (Ithaca: Cornell University Press, 1969) 74–112.

6. *Husbandman*, June 29, 1876.

7. *Husbandman*, November 14, 1878; May 27, 1886; July 22, 1886. For an introduction to early Montana irrigation policy see John W. Hakola, "The Development of a Policy Toward Irrigation in Montana to 1908" (Masters Thesis: University of Montana, 1951).

8. *Husbandman*, June 6, 1889.

9. *Husbandman*, January 6, 1887. See Ernest Staples Osgood, *The Day of the Cattlemen* (Chicago: University of Chicago Press, 1929) chapter 7, for a discussion of the alliance between irrigation development and range management changes following the "Hard Winter" of 1886–1887.

10. *Husbandman*, July 12, 1888; September 20, 1888. Everett W. Sterling, "The Powell Irrigation Survey, 1888–1893," *Mississippi Valley Historical Review*, XXVII, No. 3 (December 1940), 421–434.

11. *Husbandman*, July 11, 1901. For a critical view of the growth of irrigation sentiment see Stanley R. Davison, "Hopes and Fancies of the Early Reclamationists," in Michael Malone and Richard Roeder, editors, *Montana's Past: Selected Essays* (Missoula: University of Montana Publications in History, 1973), 317–334. The notion that homesteads in the West would provide a "safety valve" to ease population pressures in the urban East is examined in David Emmons, *Garden in the Grasslands* (Lincoln: University of Nebraska, 1971), chapters 4 and 5.

12. *Husbandman*, June 19, 1902. The National Reclamation Act, or Newlands Act, approved by Congress on June 17, 1902, established the Federal Reclamation Program. The act set aside money received from the sale of public lands to fund the proposed projects. It directed the secretary of the Interior to withdraw lands susceptible to irrigation from entry until reclamation works could be completed. The land would then be opened for entry under the terms of the Homestead Act.

13. *Husbandman*, April 5, 1904.

14. Great Falls *Tribune*, January 7, 1904; January 26, 1904; January 19, 1904; April 5, 1904; June 16, 1904.

15. *Tribune*, June 19, 1904. Many reclamationists believed the monies from the sale of public lands would be far too inadequate to fund extensive federal irrigation works. They turned to Congress for supplemental funding through direct appropriations.

16. *Husbandman*, February 28, 1889; March 14, 1889; June 27, 1889. Suther-

lin's differences with Gibson over dry-land farming were long standing. In 1889 he challenged Gibson's claim that there were large areas of northern Montana that could be farmed without irrigation. "There is no section west of the 100th meridian where farming can be carried on successfully one year after another without irrigation," wrote Sutherlin in response to Gibson's assertion. For Gibson's promotional activities see James G. Handford, "Paris Gibson: A Montana Yankee" (Masters Thesis: University of Montana, 1952).

17. Paris Gibson, "Letter to the Editor," *Husbandman*, July 21, 1904. The *Tribune* recognized Gibson as the driving force behind the irrigation development of northern Montana. "He was one of the main factors in getting the National Irrigation Law passed; and he has been the main factor in getting it applied to Northern Montana projects." *Tribune*, April 27, 1904.

18. *Husbandman*, August 4, 1904.

19. *Husbandman*, October 6, 1904. Sutherlin made a radical change in his position on the arid nature of Montana between 1875 and 1889. In 1877-1878 he criticized W. B. Hazen's remarks on the limited area of arable land in the Territory. But experience had convinced him that Montana was generally deficient of moisture for farming without irrigation. See W. B. Hazen, "The Great Middle Region of the United States, and its Limited Space of Arable Land, *North American Review*, CXX (January 1875), 17-18; *Husbandman*, January 31, 1878; Wallace Stegner, *Beyond the Hundredth Meridian* (Boston: Houghton Mifflin, 1954), 1-8, 212-231.

20. Montana Agricultural Experiment Station, *Sixth Annual Report*, for the year ending June 30, 1899. Montana Agricultural Experiment Station Bulletin No. 24 (White Sulphur Springs, Rocky Mountain Husbandman, 1899), 146. See also Mary Wilma Hargreaves, *Dry Farming in the Northern Great Plains* (Cambridge; Harvard University Press, 1957). Hargreaves claims promotionalism was the key innovation of the movement.

21. Mary Wilma Hargreaves, "Dry Farming Alias Scientific Farming," *Agricultural History*, XXII (1948), 39ff.

22. Montana Agricultural Experiment Station, *Sixth Annual Report*, 146.

23. Montana Agricultural Experiment Station, *Seventh Annual Report*, for the year ending June 30, 1900. Montana Agricultural Experiment Station Bulletin No. 28 (White Sulphur Springs: *Rocky Mountain Husbandman*, 1900), 10-11.

24. Montana Agricultural Experiment Station, *Eleventh Annual Report*, for the year ending June 30, 1904 (Bozeman: Experiment Station, 1904), 191.

25. Montana Agricultural Experiment Station, *Twelfth Annual Report*, for the year ending June 30, 1905 (Bozeman: Experiment Station, 1905), 241.

26. F. B. Linfield, "The Dry Farming Experiments for the Season of 1910." Montana Agricultural Experiment Station files, AG-1, AA-F17. Copies of Linfield's numerous articles, reports, and speeches are located in the Experiment Station files at Montana State University, Bozeman. Unfortunately, many of the papers are not dated and the location of publication is not noted. In most in-

stances the reports and articles on file appear to be final copies rather than rough drafts.

27. Montana Agricultural Experiment Station, *Twelfth Annual Report*, 237. Although Linfield was the spokesman for the station, Alfred Atkinson, station agronomist, appears to have been the most enthusiastic dry-land farming supporter on the staff. Sutherlin called Atkinson "The Chief law giver and oracle writer in Montana dry farming." *Husbandman*, April 21, 1910.

28. F. B. Linfield, *Dry Farming in Montana*. Montana Agricultural Experiment Station Bulletin No. 63 (Bozeman: Experiment Station, 1907), 11.

29. Hargreaves, *Dry Farming in the Northern Great Plains*, 148–155.

30. Montana Farmers' Institutes, *Sixth Annual Report*, for the year ending June 30, 1908. Montana Farmers' Bulletin No. 1 (Bozeman: Republican-Courier, 1908).

31. *Ibid.*, 75–77.

32. *Ibid.*, 81. Edmund Burke, *A Report on Montana Climate*, Montana Agricultural Experiment Station Bulletin No. 99 (Bozeman: Experiment Station, 1914), 45–65. Burke indicates that rarely was there less than seven inches annual rainfall in Montana at any location.

33. Linfield, *Dry Farming in Montana*; Hargreaves, "Dry Farming Alias Scientific Farming," 42–43.

34. H. W. Campbell to F. B. Linfield, February 2, 1907; F. B. Linfield to H. W. Campbell, February 6, 1907; H. W. Campbell to F. B. Linfield, February 12, 1907. Montana Agricultural Experiment Station files, AG-1, AA-F11.

35. Hargreaves, "Dry Farming Alias Scientific Farming," 48–49; F. B. Linfield to John W. Haw, March 2, 1937, Montana Agricultural Experiment Station files, AG-1, F17.

36. F. B. Linfield, "Progress of Dry Farming in the West," Montana Agricultural Experiment Station files, AG1-F17.

37. *Husbandman*, June 23, 1904; June 18, 1908.

38. *Husbandman*, September 22, 1904.

39. *Husbandman*, November 3, 1910.

40. F. B. Linfield, "Response to *Husbandman*," Montana Agricultural Experiment Station files, AG-7, AA-F18.

41. *Ibid.*

42. F. B. Linfield, "Success of Dry Farming." Presentation to Montana Woolgrowers' Association, 1910. Montana Agricultural Experiment Station files, AG-1, AA-F18.

43. F. B. Linfield, "Report on Dry Farming," Montana Agricultural Experiment Station files, AG-1, AA-F18. Montana Agricultural Experiment Station, *Fourteenth Annual Report*, for the year ending June 30, 1907 (Bozeman: Experiment Station, 1907), 170.

44. At the turn of the century the Annual Reports indicate a strong irrigation emphasis at the station. By 1909 the irrigation department had been divided and placed under the engineering department and the agronomy department. Little

information is provided on the actual irrigation work being done while there is extensive comment on dry land farming experiments and financial support. Montana Agricultural Experiment Station, *Fifteenth Annual Report*, for the year ending June 30, 1908 (Bozeman: Experiment Station, 1908); *Sixteenth Annual Report*, for the year ending June 30, 1909 (Bozeman: Experiment Station, 1909).

45. *Husbandman*, December 29, 1910.

46. *Husbandman*, April 21, 1910.

47. M. L. Wilson, *Dry Farming in the North Central Montana "Triangle,"* Montana Extension Service Bulletin No. 66 (Bozeman: Extension Service, 1923), 19.

48. *Ibid.*, 22.

49. *Husbandman*, December 2, 1875. Throughout his career Sutherlin criticized the farmers for their destructive land use habits. He quoted from an English writer, "In the American System of agriculture, the settler subdues a piece of land, flogs it to death, and abandons the carcass; and then he repeats the operation on a new subject." Sutherlin believed this image of the American farmer to be "nearly correct."

50. F. H. Newell to R. N. Sutherlin, October 6, 1921. *Husbandman*, November 1, 1921.

7 /

The Tin Can Tourist's West

ROBERT G. ATHEARN

Most historical literature records significant political leadership and dynamic economic development. For Montana and the West, much of the record rests in the nineteenth century. Thus the appearance of historical work on twentieth-century popular culture is a welcome departure. No historian was more qualified to tackle the subject of early tourism than Robert G. Athearn. His ten professional histories, all with western themes, centered on the topics of transportation, migration, and settlement. He wrote for extended audiences, and he worked on the broadest of all regional subjects, the mystique of the West.

Athearn's "tin can tourist's West" does not differ altogether from the larger and more familiar political and economic history of the region. Large eastern corporations quickly learned to siphon off tourist dollars in a mass version of economic colonialism. Just as quickly, the West "wilded up" and did what the East wanted it to do—cultural colonialism continued. These deftly-woven themes provide a substantive base to the entertaining essay that follows.

What was one day to be the day of the "tin can" tourist developed relatively slowly. The early automobiles were unreliable, expensive toys that found very few good roads to traverse. This was especially true in the West and it would remain so for some time to come. By 1903 three automobile "trails" had been blazed across the continent and that designation was accurate; they were little, if any, better than those used by covered wagons. It was almost another decade before any of the "name" highways would emerge.

Around 1901 some Colorado women proposed to a state motorists' convention at Pueblo that a coast-to-coast Lincoln Memorial Highway should be designated and lined with trees representative of the states through which it passed. In 1911 legislation was introduced into Congress that envisaged seven national highways, including one transcontinental. In the following year the Yellowstone Trail (later U.S. 10 and then Interstate 90–94) was created and a year later the Lincoln Highway (later U.S. 30 and then Interstate 80) came into being. These beginnings set in motion a development that saw a rapid spread of roadside facilities for the new auto traveler. Within a decade these and similar highways were reasonably well supplied with auto camps and cottages; by then the automobile was said to have revolutionized the average American's vacation.

It also moved that vacation westward.

But before it became common to load the family car with camp kits and kids and set forth on a nomadic summer jaunt, a new breed of motorists did the pathfinding. And pathfinding it was, for as a survey of 1904 showed, there were very few roads in the West that could be classified as "improved." That constantly violated term could mean anything; at best it conveyed the existence of shallow ditches on each side of the pathway, intended as barrow pits, and enough scraping on the intervening space to call the road "graded." In the region under consideration—the plains and mountain West—Utah led with 608 miles, the other contenders having around 200, but Montana and Nevada each had only about 65, Nebraska 23, and New Mexico a mere 2. Nationwide some seven percent of the roads were said to be improved; in the West the figure was slightly over two and a half. The westward passage still provided its challenges.

That exploring the wilds in one of the new gas buggies was a venturesome undertaking came home to Milford R. McClellan in 1911 when he took his new Moline Dreadnaught—retail price, $1,850— across the plains from Iowa to Montana. He found the steppes of North Dakota to be so devoid of road signs that he had to fall back upon a crude sort of navigation, relying on railroad timetables and maps to estimate distance and a "Blue Book" motorists' guide that offered only vague suggestions as to compass headings. This handy volume advised the motorist to start at some known point and then proceed so many miles by the odometer, then take a fix on a red barn, or a white church, after which a right or left turn was in order.

Taking into account stops for red barns and other identifiers, Mc-

Clellan managed to make a hundred miles a day, occasionally pushing the Dreadnaught up to thirty or forty miles an hour when the terrain was not too choppy. He logged a little over fifteen miles to a gallon of gasoline that cost twelve cents, and paid thirty-five cents for dinner at North Dakota's better cafes. There were some hidden expenses that later tourists avoided; crossing the Missouri River at Bismarck necessitated paying the ferryboat operator twenty-five cents. Later, he spanned the Little Missouri for nothing by using the Northern Pacific Railroad bridge and watching carefully for any oncoming unscheduled trains.

Despite navigational problems on the plains, Milford McClelland made a relatively easy passage. And a cheap one. This could have been misleading for others who aspired to adventuring in the modern manner. While McClellan was burning up the Dakota sod, others were not enjoying the West that much. A driver who made it deep into the Nevada desert wrote that some of those he met along the way swore they must have found the last land on earth in this sea of sagebrush and that no power under heaven ever would induce them to endure such heat or dust again. Some of the explorers, dressed in khaki and wearing goggles, simply gave up and shipped their cars to Reno.

Despite such talk from the pessimists, those who boosted the new freedom of movement for travelers stressed, among other things, that automobile trips across yesterday's frontier were safe for women and children. When social arbiter Emily Post ventured out into the wilds, in the spring of 1915, her readers learned that a whole new world awaited the so-called "weaker sex." Of course, these presumably delicate creatures had to be prepared for some rather primitive going if they took up modern trail travel. For example, the "highway" between Sterling, in northeastern Colorado, and Denver presented a picture of impassable mud, a landscape of innumerable autos glued to earth by gumbo, around which scene Mrs. Post circled and approached the mountain country by way of Cheyenne. It was advisable, she said, to select an American-made car for use in such country because its ten-inch clearance minimized high-centering. She also mentioned the desirability of taking along ropes, shovels, spare parts, tire chains, and extra links for chain-driven cars. Extra gas, oil, and water, stored in the running-board rack, were a must.

There were rewards for the persistent motorist. After a hard trip, Mrs. Post luxuriated at Denver's Brown Palace Hotel and later at the Antlers of Colorado Springs. These were well-known places, but any-

Tourist camp, Hamilton, MT, 1915. Courtesy K. Ross Toole Archives, Mansfield Library, University of Montana.

one who had taken pleasure in thirty-five cent Dakota meals was in for a shock. Lunch at the Brown could run to $3.50 or more. Double rooms cost $6.00, with coffee and toast room service available at seventy cents. Breakfast cost ninety-five cents. As one descended the map and stopped off at such ordinary places as Trinidad, Colorado, room with bath at the Hotel Cardenas came to $4.50, with meals proportionately cheaper. But then Trinidad was just a place to stop and restore. Colorado Springs, or "Li'l Lunnon" as it was called earlier, was more than that; it was a destination, a spa, a watering place, a resort that catered to folks disinclined to haggle over price. Emily Post found it charming, if a bit gay, and even a little racy.

Aside from the desire to play with the new gadget called the automobile, and go exploring where covered wagons once rutted the sod, two events that had nothing to do with the lure of the mountain West's scenic attractions occurred about this time. One was the outbreak of war in Europe, in August of 1914, and the other, a year later, was the opening of the Panama-Pacific Exposition at San Francisco and the Panama-California Exposition at San Diego. Both of these drew tourists westward, most of them by train, but a number of adventurous souls decided to make an outing of it and go by car.

As early as 1911 an advance party of automobilists was sent out to advertise the ease with which families might go to the West Coast in their family cars and attend the upcoming fairs. John G. Monihan, secretary of the Ocean to Ocean Motor Tourists, reported that because the expositions were bound to attract a flood of tourists, many of them by automobile, a convoy of twelve autos driven by their owners had that year completed the trip. The entire party, including wives, children, and friends, numbered forty, and Monihan stated proudly that the continent thus had been spanned, and without a single accident. Automotively speaking, the way west lay open.

The European war probably diverted only a limited number westward, its influence being more useful as a device to advertise the West as an attractive alternative. Vacationers were advised that European spas were not then beneficial places for nervous health-seekers or the curious. Instead, they were told, now was the appropriate (and patriotic) time to "See America First." By venturing across the old American Desert and cresting mountains so beautiful as to be mistaken for the Alps, modern adventurers were promised pleasure in the Pacific's Mediterranean climate as well as excitement and education at the fairs.

The war and the "See America First" movement's acceleration also coincided with the creation of the National Park Service. The parks were not new to the West; Yellowstone had existed since 1872 and by now over 400 miles of government road there were being used by tourists. This and other parks were under the control of the War Department while the Interior Department ran such parks as Glacier and Rainier. The National Park Service Act of 1916 drew the parks together under the Interior Department. Stephen T. Mather, who was appointed to direct the system, at once initiated a campaign to attract tourists. Coincidental to such advertising was the steadily increasing number of national parks opened to motorists. During the first three decades of the twentieth century, seventeen of them were added to the existing one, national forests were expanded to around 160 million acres, and strong emphasis was placed upon outdoor family recreation.

The American public responded. During those years national per capita travel increased sixfold, most of the gain being due to the wider use of the automobile. In this respect the West again was a frontier, a place that promised excitement, new experiences, and informative sight-seeing. Best of all, the new frontiering was a family matter.

Much of the change took place in a decade. In 1924 the author of an article on auto camping talked of the transition since the opening of the Yellowstone Trail and the Lincoln Highway a little over ten years earlier. The automobile, he said, had revolutionized the average American's vacation, sending out between five and ten million "motor gypsies" in the preceding year, and wherever they went—especially in the West—auto camps now beckoned them.

Denver is a good example of the oases that awaited the emerging "tin can" tourist. Calling Colorado one of the pioneers in tempting this fraternity to come its way, a *Saturday Evening Post* writer said that Denver's up and coming business leaders equated the importance of an auto camp with that of a railway station, hence, the city's $250,000 Overland Motor Park. Support for such a statement came in a statistic: in the summer of 1923 over 600,000 campers were said to have used the park's facilities. This was twice the number of people who lived in Denver at that time.

By the early twenties Overland Park offered a three-story clubhouse that also contained a modern grocery and meat market, grill and lunch counter with steam table, a billiard room, a barbershop, comfort stations, and a laundry room. The second floor featured a large lounge with dancing floor, phonograph included, as well as a restaurant and a soda fountain. Above that were women's toilets, showers, and lockers. An auto repair shop and a movie were nearby. The complex had about a thousand small camp lots, or room enough for around five thousand tourists a night. Here the "motor nomads" found one of the West's new watering holes, here they rested, replenished supplies, and repaired their vehicles. Then off again, off to the wild, wild yonder, for somewhere out there lay another auto camp.

The West, in general, was quick to see the potential of this new source of income. The business of nursing along a few rich tourists had been rewarding in a limited way; now, with a mass market before them, westerners got downright hospitable and held out the latchstring to any who wanted to soak up some of that fabled western atmosphere. By the early twenties there was hardly a town that had not joined in the most recent gold rush. Sometimes the offering was no more than some open space, with running water, but it could be tent frames and even small cabins. Towns got into wars with each other in their all-out effort to sidetrack some of the eastern money that passed by. They strove for one-upmanship in offering fringe benefits to those who would stop and spend a dollar or so. For example, Boise furnished free hot and cold water as well as free electricity for cooking, washing, and ironing.

The theory was that the outstretched hand of western hospitality would come back filled with money placed there by appreciative visitors. As one writer put it, to reap them you had to get them and to get them, you had to advertise. He said that enormous sums were spent to publicize the relative merits of these facilities, much of it appearing on highway signboards.

But hopes of gold prospectors have been dashed before and it happened again. To the great disappointment of the towns, some of their guests took the blandishments seriously and settled in, putting their children in the public schools and basking in the low-budget hospitality dispensed by these traditionally friendly frontiersmen. The hosts responded by demanding money of their visitors, whom they now designated as "vagabonds." The newcomers then engaged in just enough work to pay for their new western abodes, amidst outcries from the citizenry about cheapskates, tightwads and nonspenders. Ignoring the possibility that the western image might become a little tarnished by such mercenary attitudes, city fathers put their faith in private enterprise and turned these failing municipal hospitality houses over to private parties who better understood the best methods of corraling two-legged mavericks. And thus was born a string of establishments later known as motels, the owners of which shortly treated the advocates of public hosting to some illuminating lessons in monetary extraction. No wonder the campers began to grumble about the disappearance of the Old West.

One can't accuse western business types of not knowing a good thing when they saw it. It was estimated, in 1924, that two million "summer Bedouins" were roaming the Rocky Mountain West carrying around money that other highwaymen might get from them. The idea that tourists were entering Yellowstone Park at the rate of one car a minute was enough to excite anyone who had ever seen a cash register. By calculating the cost of supplying food, housing, repairs, and fuel for that number of motor-driven nomads even a westerner who could bulldog only a simple problem in arithmetic came up with mind-boggling totals. Montanans estimated that their share of the tourist take that year was $6,000,000, while Arizona guessed its figure at $10,000,000. With numbers like that floating around it was not necessary to yell "Tally Ho" to signify that the prey was in sight.

Unhappily for westerners, the results were about as rewarding as that of the hunting dog who deposits the game at his master's feet: a pat on the head. Finders were not keepers. When it finally dawned on outsiders that the West possessed yet another treasure that could be extracted, they moved in, and thus not a little of the gold that was rattled out of the tourists' pokes increasingly went to motel and restaurant chains, to corporate-owned gas stations and to outside suppliers in general. As always, the masters of the purse let the colonials hold the money for a brief moment, long enough to give them a feel for it, but then they moved it out for safekeeping. This is not surprising; what is surprising is that it took them a while to realize that the rustics had stumbled across another paying mine.

The emergence of the rubber-tired rovers did more than to motivate only those who wanted to set up deadfalls to trap unwary pilgrims who might wander their way. Westerners, in general, were so anxious to get things rolling that they were willing to pay dearly for more and better roads, and to lobby more fiercely for additional federal aid from those tight-fisted folks in Washington who were always trying to enslave them. The natives were, so to speak, anxious to pave the way for this emergent group of contributors and at the same time to free their own bailiwicks from the seasonal gumbo fetters that isolated them during inclement weather. Nationally this phase of internal improvements was known as the Good Roads Movement, and it was one to which those becalmed on the western seas of grass enthusiastically subscribed.

The coming of the blacktop, or "oiled" roads as westerners called them, was anticipated with nearly as much longing as had been the appearance of the railroads, both of which promised all-weather transportation. The West is big, very big, and its sparse population provides a small tax base with which to finance these expensive highways. They were slow in coming and painfully achieved.

The well-known author, E. B. White, noted in 1922 that "Your popular conception of a national highway would be blasted were you to ride . . . into the capital of North Dakota on a road which had a grass center. . . . All the roads here are 'natural.' " Ten years later a fellow motorist noted that Montana, then the third largest state in the Union, had but forty-seven miles of macadam, or hardtop. Wyoming had but thirty-five. At that time New York had 300 times as many miles of surfaced road as did Wyoming.

The little towns of the plains and Rockies regarded it as a matter of civic pride to provide cement sidewalks and paved streets, these refine-

Camping via auto in Western Montana (Hamilton), 1920. Courtesy K. Ross Toole Archives, Mansfield Library, University of Montana.

ments being equated with the number of schools, churches, libraries, free tourist camps, and other amenities they mentioned in their advertising. A passerby remarked that Bozeman, Montana, of 1924, was much improved in this respect since he had seen it nearly two decades earlier. Now it boasted fifteen miles of paved streets that served the town's 20,000 residents. Similarly, Phoenix now had paved streets, but rather than being praised for it, the eastern visitors, apparently wanting the Old West to stay muddy, said the place had lost its charm because the burghers no longer were interesting. They explained that these westerners were doing what other people wanted them to do "rather than what they damn-please." It was very hard to satisfy the critics.

Despite depression and great financial difficulties in the dismal thirties, there was a gradual improvement in roads as the hardtop network began to spread across the West. The results often left something to be desired, but blacktop of any kind was a great improvement over gumbo, or even gravel. In Montana, for example, with money short and the need very great, the highway department "stretched" its available funds for blacktopping by making the highways as narrow as possible. Since traffic wasn't heavy and Montanans were given to driving on either side of the road anyway, the "slim-Jim" highways were no handicap to them.

Understandably, tourists used to paved roads in the East stuck to these smoother trails despite the dangers imposed by the natives who, even when sober, could be a little wild behind the wheel. The unwillingness to forsake the "straight and narrow" annoyed westerners who had things to sell but were off the main highways. One of the "beaters" of the tourist hunters complained that during 1935 there were almost three million visitors in his state of New Mexico and half of them passed through the "Land of Enchantment" complaining that there just wasn't anything worth looking at. "They wouldn't get a yard off the highway," he complained. "We fooled 'em one place by building a highway right past White Sands, one of the natural marvels of the state, and they just had to look at it." Westerners were determined to make their scenery turn a profit if they had to rub the tourists' noses in it to get their attention.

Those whose tourist-oriented businesses were paying off belied the chronic complaint of low-paid westerners that "you can't live on scenery." Thousands of them did, and do today. By the late twenties a newspaper photographer remarked, "Now every desert road is crawling with the flivvers of immigrants, and the flivvers are crawling with babies, tin cans and folding phonographs." From Montana to Arizona, all along the mountain ranges, the modern trappers set up their snares and awaited the annual opening of the hunting season. In Arizona, said one reporter, "I find in all the trading posts great preparations to take care of the...tourist." It paid off. By 1939 Arizona, for example, claimed tourism as one of its thriving industries, one that added about fifty million dollars a year to its income.

By "taking care" of the tourists—a term that could have some nuances—it was generally understood that this implied the furnishing of food, shelter, and perhaps some form of entertainment. Scenic beauty, of course, was one of the attractions, but in addition to this, the time-tested health and morale appeal used earlier on railroad tourists consigned to western spas also was applied to this newer and larger group, the motorists. During the thirties there was an increasing emphasis in tourist advertising upon the West's free and open life-style, the purity of the air, the wholesomeness of the food, the freshness of the water, and opportunities for restful quiet. Additionally, said one publicist, there was a hidden dividend, an important one, in "the way the people take you, if you're the right sort." Even among the tin can tourists there were easterners for whom acceptance by the bronzed westerners was important.

Lamentably there were those among the new migrant masses who had no taste for or sense of history, for whom even honorary membership in this elite meant nothing at all, but westerners shrugged this off as one of the gambles of the game. Playing upon the sentiments of those who were properly tuned in, the residents of the Stetson Shangri-La dug deep into their nostalgia bags and came up with memorabilia that could be converted into cash from more appreciative guests. Admittedly, said a magazine writer, the West had no monopoly on romance, but somehow visitors to that legendary place were emotionally receptive to it; as a matter of fact, to them it was part of the promised package. "Westerns," in print and on celluloid, had done their work.

As always, the natives were ready to capitalize upon any resource, intangible as it might be, and they saw no reason to disappoint the dudes. That the western atmosphere was charged with some special kind of magic for easterners long had been recognized in the country beyond the wide Missouri. Teddy Roosevelt had shown them that a generation or more earlier. And for some time they had acknowledged what they regarded as a unique past with commemorative celebrations that recalled its color and excitement. They staged rodeos, usually for the sport of it, but in time this activity was merged with pioneer day activities to include the heroes of the open range. Besides, chaps and cowboy hats, not to mention prancing cow ponies, spruced up

Clinton Garage, 1920s. Courtesy K. Ross Toole Archives, Mansfield Library, University of Montana.

any parade. Now, in the 1930s, the pioneer day custom was put to a wider use, was publicized, dramatized and above all, commercialized. A mass market required mass production.

There now occurred a period in the region's history that will be known as the "wilding up of the West." Every place beyond the Big Muddy took part, the purpose being to give the visitors their money's worth. Even dull and desolate places closer to the river, those with almost no "wild West" heritage, lent a hand, knowing full well they had no mountains to sell but well aware that those en route to the hills carried money and any stops along the way would cause them to part with some of it. Dutifully the natives dressed up, wore hot and uncomfortable costumes on scorching August days, suffered beards and bonnets, and tried to look like carefree pioneers. Occasional profanity unintentionally lent an air of realism to the pageants.

Business districts were roped off, and the original Deadwood stagecoach—of which 156 were identified—was put on display. Communities that missed out on this opportunity made up for it by parading an old Conestoga wagon drawn by a couple of beasts that passed for oxen. Historical accuracy would have called for a representation of the ordinary farm wagon, accompanied by bib-overalled men carrying pitchforks, but this would have been as unthinkable as the sight of two plow horses dragging a manure spreader down mainstreet. Rather, these wheat-growing communities preferred to think of their West in terms of horsemen, and so mean looking "cowboys" now lurked about town, occasionally staging fake gunfights, after which a frock-coated gent wearing a black plug hat measured the victims and had them boxed for shipment to a local "Boot Hill" the place never had possessed.

There were, of course, some unexpected setbacks in the restoration of the old West. Just when the program was hitting its full stride, and the dudes were glassy-eyed with delight, it was revealed by some subversive soul that treacherous Shoshoni Indians on a Wyoming reservation were running a canning factory. "Some relief director, with a warped outlook on life, had got them putting beets and carrots and spinach into cans...," moaned one reporter. "Committees were at once named to get the miserable Shoshonis out of the kitchen and back to the ranges where a scalp or two might still be had, in a refined way." It was explained to the warriors that almost no money-bearing tourists carried can openers.

Despite such minor flaws the program went forward, the hawking of nostalgia and yore often being carried to extremes, while spokes-men for the region repeatedly swore that the Old West hadn't been tamed as rumored. This in face of the fact that there was a disturbing decline in gunfights on saloon-lined dusty streets and hitching racks were getting hard to find. Even the dusty streets were gone and apolo-gies had to be made for the pavement, a necessary nuisance progress-minded city fathers were said to have foisted upon unsuspecting resi-dents. Then there was the matter of the dude ranchers, who had spent a good deal of effort and no little advertising money to show how safe the place was. They took a dim view of perpetuating the image of wildness.

But the tourist-trappers had become used to the sound of the cash register, had tasted blood, and nothing would stop them from continu-ing the charade. To keep the kettle boiling they accelerated their adver-tising. Pinedale, Wyoming let it be known that the town was 105 miles from a railroad, a fact that would have been buried six feet deep in an earlier day. Tombstone, Arizona's newspaper, the famed *Epitaph*, labelled its obituary column "Hell's Bells" to suggest that the bad old days still were around, while Cheyenne rather pathetically reported a gun battle that any other place would have recorded as an ordinary shooting. Not to be left behind, a Colorado mining town repealed an ordinance that prohibited the gunning down of strangers on Sunday.

There is yet another twist to the tale of the tourist. By getting color-fully mean, and mimicking the orneriest old down-eastern who ever snarled at those brave enough to venture near the coast of Maine, some of the westerners took up the pastime, lambasting the dudes. Charley Russell, the cowboy artist who never quite made it into the twentieth century in an emotional sense, heaped his scorn on the tourists who fre-quented his summer neighborhood at Lake McDonald, Glacier Na-tional Park. Irvin Cobb, the humorist, visited there and gleefully wrote of the artist's bad disposition in this respect, saying that "Charley reserved the most sulphurous corner of his private Gehenna for tour-ists..." because they cluttered up beauty spots with banana peels and empty pop bottles. Those who remember Cobb's visit recall with amusement the efforts to hoist the bulky writer aboard a docile trail pony so that he, too, could ride the West.

Coloradans who did not make a living milking the tourist trade had their objections to these strangers, or said they had. When World War II intervened, and shut off some of the seasonal influx of visitors, Denver poet Thomas Hornsby Ferril wrote that the prospect of slim pickings really ought to "delight all civilized people." It was, he said, a compensation for the tire shortage, and he allowed that tourists "always should have been rationed anyhow." Why? Because, he judged, "There aren't more than a hundred choice spirits east of the Mississippi who deserve to come to Colorado in any year."

Exactly, said the tourists. This was the kind of talk they liked to hear from the aristocratic West. It showed discrimination. No peasants allowed. In this wonderful, democratic land one had to rise to royalty by his own efforts, to become one of the chosen through loyal and good works. Far from being upset by such gruff talk from the denizens of never-never land, they loved it. Steve Frazee, the Salida novelist, understood this when he wrote his prickly, humorous *More Damn Tourists.*

Despite the cuffs and curses, real or pretended, the tourists kept on coming west. By 1970 *U.S. News and World Report* found it necessary to advise travelers "Don't let those reports of bumper-to-bumper traffic in the national parks scare you away from a trip to the American West. This is still a big country."

The legend of the Big Sky country still lived.

NOTES

Earl Chapin May wrote about the 1909 Colorado women in "The Argonauts of the Automobile," *Saturday Evening Post,* Vol. 197, No. 6 (August 9, 1924), p. 89. Reference to the 1911 legislation to establish seven national highways is from *Harper's Weekly,* January 6, 1912, p. 12. Statistics concerning roads, as of 1904, are in Oscar O. Winther, *The Transportation Frontier* (New York: Holt, Rinehart and Winston, 1964), p. 159.

The motor convoy to the West Coast, in 1911, was described by John G. Monihan in "Across America by Auto," *Harper's Weekly,* January 6, 1912, pp. 11–12. For an account of some of the "trails" opened to autos see Frank E. Brimmer, "Autocamping—the Fastest Growing Sport," *The Outlook,* Vol. 137, No. 11 (July 11, 1924), p. 437. Milford R. McClelland talked of crossing the Dakota prairies in "Only Fifty-one Years Ago," *Montana: The Magazine of Western History,* Vol. 12, No. 3 (Summer, 1962), pp. 34–42. The "last land on earth" comment is from Hamilton Laing, "Bucking the Desert Trail," *Sunset,* Vol. 36, (March 1916), pp. 81–82. Emily Post's exploration of the high plains is recounted in her book *By Motor to the Golden Gate* (New York: D. Appleton and Company, 1916). See pp. 113, 243, 270–71 and 345.

References to the European situation of 1914 and 1915 came from "Go West," *Review of Reviews,* Vol. 51, No. 2 (February, 1915), pp. 131–37 and "Westward the Course of Tourism," *The Independent*, Vol. 80, No. 3436 (October 19, 1914), p. 82. The comments about Yellowstone Park are by Maurice O. Eldridge, "Touring Yellowstone Park on Government Highways," *The World To-Day*, Vol. 19, No. 5 (November, 1910), pp. 1263-4. A good description of the National Park Service's origins is in Donald C. Swain, "The Founding of the National Park Service," *The American West*, Vol. 6, No. 5 (September, 1969), pp. 6-9. The entire issue is devoted to National Parks. The growth of the park system is mentioned in Marion Clawson, et al., *Land for the Future* (Baltimore: Johns Hopkins Press, 1960), pp. 144-45.

There are several good accounts of Denver's early efforts to attract campers. Quite detailed is Edgar C. McMechen, "A Home for the Migratory Motorist," in *Outing*, Vol. 72 (June, 1918), pp. 161-63. See also Garet Garrett, "How in the West?" *The Saturday Evening Post*, Vol. 197, No. 21 (November 22, 1924), pp. 77-78; May, "The Argonauts," cited above, p. 89; Brimmer, "Autocamping," cited above, pp. 437, 439.

The figures for Yellowstone Park's entry rate in 1924 were quoted by Garrett, "How in the West?", cited above, pp. 77-78. The "vagabonds" remark is from the same source, as is the statement about Boise. Figures for travel in Montana and Arizona for 1924 were taken from Albert W. Atwood, "Wealth in the Outdoor West," *Saturday Evening Post*, Vol. 199 (January 8, 1927), p. 149. E. B. White's comments about North Dakota roads are found in Dorothy Lobrano Guth, ed. *Letters of E. B. White* (New York: Harper and Row, Publishers, 1976), p. 51. B. H. Kizer, "In Defense of the Sagebrush States," *Atlantic Monthly*, Vol. 149 (June 1932), p. 748, provided figures on blacktop mileages. The pavement in Bozeman information was from May, "The Argonauts," cited above, p. 25. Winifred Hawkridge Dixon, *Westward Hoboes: Ups and Downs of Frontier Motoring* (New York: Charles Scribner's Sons, 1926), p. 103 gave the Phoenix pavement reaction and the "what they damn please" comment. The conservationist worried about the Good Roads movement was Aldo Leopold. His "Conserving the Covered Wagon," *Sunset*, Vol. 54 (March 1925) article was subtitled "Shall We Save Parts of the Far Western Wilderness from Soft 'Improvements'?". See p. 21.

Western cuisine was evaluated by Bernard DeVoto in "The Easy Chair," *Harper's Magazine*, Vol. 193 (November, 1946), p. 432. The complaint that dudes would not leave New Mexico's pavement was set forth in Jim Marshall, "Untaming the West," *Collier's*, Vol. 97, No. 15 (April 11, 1936), p. 64. It was Atwood in "Wealth, etc.," cited above, who wrote that the roads were crawling with flivvers. See p. 150. The author who made the observation about being "the right sort" was Arthur W. Little, Jr., in "The Tall Walls of the Rockies," *Scribner's Magazine*, Vol. 101, No. 6 (June, 1937), p. 88.

The "wilding up of the West" material is from Marshall, "Untaming the West," cited above. See pages 52, 64, and 66. Atwood, in "Wealth," cited above, mentioned that tourists were in a receptive frame of mind for "wilding up." See

p. 150. Bernard DeVoto's "The Anxious West," *Harper's Magazine*, Vol. 193, No. 1159 (December, 1946), pp. 384–85 described "frontier day" celebrations. The "anti-tourist" material is by Irvin S. Cobb, in *Exit Laughing* (Indianapolis: The Dobbs-Merrill Company, 1941), p. 415, and Thomas Hornsby Ferril, *I Hate Thursday* (New York: Harper & Brothers, Publishers, 1946), pp. 36–37. The *U.S. News & World Report* article was entitled "Vacations Out West: 1970 Style" and may be found in Vol. 68, No. 25 (June 22, 1970), pp. 62–65.

ONE RIVER, ONE PROBLEM
James Murray and the Missouri Valley Authority

DONALD E. SPRITZER

Ever since Lewis and Clark poled their way along its entire length, the Missouri River—and its tributaries—have been central to Montana's economic development. In the 1940s the river became a political issue as well. In the wake of the highly successful Tennessee Valley Authority, the Missouri Basin became a candidate for long-range federal direction. No stronger advocate of the proposed Missouri Valley Authority emerged than Montana's longtime Democratic senator, James E. Murray.

Donald E. Spritzer, whose full-length biography of Murray is being prepared for publication, recounts here the long and futile travail of the senator in trying to win congressional approval for the MVA. A formidable array of enemies, including investor-owned utilities, backers of unrelated projects encompassed in the alternate Pick-Sloan Plan, the U.S. Army Corps of Engineers, and even the president of the United States, thwarted his efforts. In a day when competing interests still clash over use of the basin's water, Spritzer's essay provides an important historical perspective.

From its source at the headwaters of the Jefferson River, some 13,000 feet above sea level, the Missouri River when combined with the lower Mississippi flows for more than four thousand miles, making it the world's longest river. Together with its tributaries it drains over five hundred thousand square miles in ten states. Over the years each of those states has jealously guarded its share of the river's water from outsiders, whether they were other states or the federal government.

Twice each year the Missouri rises dangerously—in the spring from mountain snowmelt and again in early summer from heavy rains. In 1943 the river's annual rampage was the worst in more than sixty years. In April it ripped out millions of dollars worth of Army Corps of Engineers' flood control installations and inundated thousands of acres. Most of Omaha went under water; its airport was ruined, and six people lost their lives. Then in mid-May the devastating rains hit and seven million dollars in land and houses were washed away. Three more people died. In June, still another flood struck the middle reaches of the basin in Iowa and northern Kansas, flooding another million acres of farmland.[1]

The 1943 floods and a similar calamity a year later brought the total losses in the basin to over 110 million dollars in less than two years. The disasters led Congress to realize that quick action had to be taken to prevent still more of the basin's wealth from washing to the sea. With two-thirds of his home state lying inside the upper Missouri drainage, it was only natural that Montana's junior senator, James E. Murray, took a deep interest in decisions affecting the region. An avowed New Dealer, Senator Murray began his political career as an influential member of the powerful Irish Democratic organization in his home town of Butte. He did not focus his attention on the plight of the Missouri Basin's farmers in eastern Montana until his appointment in 1933 as a state director of President Roosevelt's Public Works Administration. As a PWA administrator, Murray labored tirelessly to secure federal irrigation and reclamation projects for the drought and depression stricken counties of Montana's plains. His work in this area continued unabated following his election to the U. S. Senate in 1934.[2]

Another problem that the senator determined to solve through federal action was the shortage of hydroelectric power in the upper basin. In 1944 only one-fourth of Montana's farms had electricity; in the Dakotas fewer than one farm in ten enjoyed this luxury. During the early 1940s Murray pushed the Senate to approve huge hydroelectric dams such as the one at Canyon Ferry on the upper Missouri near Helena.[3]

In emphasizing the use of basin water for irrigation and hydropower, Murray reflected the majority interests in the upper basin states. Beginning with the passage of the Reclamation Act of 1902, when the federal government first entered the water development field on a large scale, upper Missouri irrigationists had been squaring off with lower basin interests whose main concerns were flood control and navigation. The sectional rivalry soon took the form of a heated contest between the U. S. Army Corps of Engineers, whose main area of jurisdiction was navigation and flood control, and the U. S. Bureau of Reclamation of the Interior Department, which engaged mostly in irrigation and conservation projects.[4]

Occasionally the two agencies cooperated on multi-purpose ventures such as Montana's massive Ft. Peck Dam, but more often they were at loggerheads. So it was to no one's surprise that each agency in the 1940s came up with its own plan on how best to tame the raging Missouri. Following the 1943 floods, Colonel Lewis A. Pick, the army engineer in charge of the corps' Missouri River Division, drew up a thirteen-page document calling for a series of levees along the river's lower portion, together with several dams designed for flood control and navigation.

As expected, the Pick plan aroused a storm of protest in the states of the upper Missouri. It was not long before their own interests were put forth by W. G. Sloan of the Bureau of Reclamation's regional office in Billings, Montana. Sloan's report called for ninety reservoirs, most of them on the tributaries. The dams would provide irrigation for five million acres and power production for the region. The Pick and Sloan plans differed from each other in nearly every particular. Pick wanted massive dams on the Missouri's main stem in the Dakotas at Garrison and Gavins Point; Sloan felt that these projects were unnecessary. The Pick plan virtually ignored power production while Sloan called for seventeen power plants to generate three billion kilowatt hours of electricity each year. Neither plan mentioned soil conservation or wildlife preservation.[5]

In December Colonel Pick submitted his plan to the House of Representatives. The Corps of Engineers' ideas found favorable ground among congressmen from the lower basin whose districts stood to benefit from the pork-barrel projects embedded in the scheme. They attached the Pick Plan to the 1944 Flood Control bill. When the measure reached the hearings stage the governors of Montana, Wyoming and North Dakota rushed to Washington in a vain attempt to persuade the House to scrap the corps' program and substitute the Sloan plan. Senator Murray shared the upper basin governors' concern that irrigation would be sacrificed in order to enhance navigation on the lower Missouri. He argued that a plan should be developed to coordinate all of the basin's rival interests and designate the respective areas of jurisdiction of the Corps of Engineers and the Bureau of Reclamation. On May 9, 1944, the House passed the Flood Control bill with the Pick plan still intact.

In May, at the height of the controversy, the St. Louis *Post-Dispatch* suddenly injected a new element into the fray. In an editorial entitled "One River-One Problem" the newspaper called for creation of a Missouri Valley Authority as the only way to end the "futile struggle between one interest and another" and to develop the valley "to the full measure of its resources." The *Post-Dispatch*, which earlier had endorsed the Pick plan, now concluded, "with unity we can conquer the one problem which the one big river challenges us to solve."[6]

The idea of a Missouri Valley Authority was not new. During the 1930s Nebraska's Senator George Norris had sponsored legislation similar to his Tennessee Valley Authority bill to create an agency for the Missouri Basin. In June 1937 President Roosevelt in a message to Congress proposed dividing the nation into seven watershed regions in order to coordinate multi-purpose resource development.

The *Post-Dispatch* editorial converted James E. Murray to the Missouri Valley Authority idea. After reading *Democracy on the March* by TVA chairman David E. Lilienthal, the senator asked the TVA chief for advice "as to the essentials of such legislation." Lilienthal gladly assisted Murray and his staff in drafting the first Missouri Valley Authority bill, which the senator introduced on August 18. The measure followed the established TVA pattern. It called for an independent government agency headed by a board of three presidentially appointed directors. This group was to have jurisdiction over the dams and other federal projects within the region. The MVA headquarters would be located somewhere within the basin. The bill designated a citizen's advisory committee of local residents to act as a curb on the board. Still, the directors would hold sweeping powers to make contracts and to acquire the property necessary for MVA projects.[7]

Calling the task of basin development "the most important national project since the Louisiana Purchase," Murray presented his bill to the Senate. He denounced the conflicting programs of the Bureau of Reclamation and Corps of Engineers, and concluded: "So long as we hack the river to pieces and parcel it out to this agency and that agency, to this interest and that interest, stalemate, inaction, and a declining economy will be our reward." He anticipated one of the strongest arguments against the MVA when he promised that the proposed authority would use "to the fullest extent possible" the help and advice of the people, organizations, and governing bodies of the region.[8]

Murray's bill received an immediate boost in September, when President Roosevelt sent a message to Congress endorsing the establishment of a Missouri Valley Authority. Murray's aides together with Benton

James E. Murray (left) and Hubert H. Humphrey (right), 1955. Courtesy K. Ross Toole Archives, Mansfield Library, University of Montana.

Stong of the National Farmers Union had drafted the statement at the request of the White House. Yet even with the president's endorsement, the Murray bill did not create a wave of popular support. Shortly after Representative John Cochran of Missouri introduced the companion measure in the House, South Dakota's Francis Case called for its defeat. He pointed out that the bill demanded two more years just to draft plans for the first projects, while both the Army Engineers and the Bureau of Reclamation were prepared to implement their plans at once.[9]

Navigation interests of the lower valley and upper basin irrigationists forgot their differences long enough to denounce the MVA. The Omaha *World-Herald* labeled the proposed authority "a colossus which would be operated completely by the bureaucracy." The Miles City, Montana *Star* stated flatly that the bill had been written by the same "curly-headed Harvard boys" who ran the TVA. The Anaconda Copper Company's *Montana Standard* felt that the basin could be developed without "placing an irresponsible economic dictatorship" over the people.

From Helena, Murray's ally, Leif Erickson, wrote the senator that "the Company" had erected huge billboards extolling "from hell to breakfast" the virtues of private ownership of power.[10]

Countering such vocal opposition, Murray had some influential allies. Editorials in the Bismarck, North Dakota *Tribune*, the St. Louis *Star Times*, the Chicago *Sun*, the Philadelphia *Record*, and *The New Republic* all endorsed the senator's bill. In Montana the liberal journal *The People's Voice* kept up a steady campaign to win residents over to the valley authority. Early in 1945 Joseph Kinsey Howard, Montana's most reputable journalist, wrote a detailed article for *Harper's Magazine* lauding the MVA proposal.[11]

More organized assistance came from the National Farmers Union, led by its dynamic young president, James G. Patton. Over half the Farmers Union membership resided within the Missouri Basin, so naturally the organization took interest in any legislation affecting irrigation, flood control, and land use. By 1944 Benton J. Stong was serving as Patton's administrative assistant and editor of the NFU newspaper. As a journalist in Tennessee, Stong had been a leading spokesman for the TVA. As Patton's right-hand man he helped Murray draft the several MVA bills.

The Missouri Valley Authority became the hottest issue in the 1944 gubernatorial campaign in Montana. Leif Erickson, a young populist from the eastern part of the state, opposed one of Senator Burton K. Wheeler's Republican friends, Sam Ford. Ford and Wheeler excorciated the MVA as communistic and a threat to state sovereignty. An avid proponent of the MVA, Erickson attempted to counter their charges. In several statewide broadcasts Murray defended his authority scheme. He condemned the Montana Power Company for its "short-sighted policy" of opposing river valley development. Many interpreted Ford's decisive victory over Erickson as a critical setback for Murray's bill.[12]

Outside Montana the MVA did not do much better. Many congressmen felt that development of the basin could be handled just as efficiently by the pending Rivers and Harbors and Flood Control bills. Yet they realized that the Army Corps of Engineers and the Bureau of Reclamation must integrate their conflicting plans. In mid-October, responding to congressional pressure and the threat of a possible Missouri Valley Authority, two representatives from each agency met in Omaha to resolve their differences. This hasty conference produced the Pick-Sloan Plan, which retained nearly all of the Missouri basin projects contemplated in both the old Pick and Sloan schemes. The six-page document was more a peace treaty than a comprehensive development program. The Bureau of Reclamation received authority over all irrigation and reclamation, most of which was on the tributaries and upper valley; the Corps of Engineers was to control all of the main stem navigation projects. The new plan said nothing about how the water would be proportioned to meet conflicting needs. It called for the "fullest development" of the basin's hydro-power potential, but said nothing about how that power should be marketed.

Reactions of MVA proponents ranged from skepticism to hostility. Murray predicted that Pick-Sloan would not mark the end of fighting between the bureau and the corps. Patton labeled the agreement "a shameful loveless shotgun wedding" and concluded that the entire "scandalous performance should arouse the people of the valley . . . to the necessity of a new type of administration where people's needs are given at least minor consideration."[13]

When Congress reconvened after the 1944 elections, the battle lines formed. Murray announced that he would fight any legislation prejudicial to the MVA. John Overton, who had long represented the interests of navigationists in water matters, vowed to ram through the omnibus Flood Control bill complete with the Pick-Sloan Plan. The powerful Louisiana Democrat was determined to keep the Missouri Valley Authority bill bottled up in his Senate committee. During floor debate on the Flood Control bill, Murray engaged in heated exchanges with Overton and his ally, Missouri's Senator Bennett Clark. Overton curtly denied the Montanan's charge that backers of the flood control measure had entered into an agreement with the army engineers and the Bureau of Reclamation to block the MVA. Clark then rose and denounced the attempt by MVA supporters to tack their bill onto the flood control measure as an amendment. The Missouri senator accused Murray of closeting himself in his office with representatives of the CIO to draft legislation without the benefit of committee hearings. Murray firmly denied ever having offered a single bill sponsored by the CIO. His usually soft voice carrying to the galleries, the Montanan accused the Missouri senator of casting aspersions on his character.

Facing overwhelming opposition, Murray planned to withdraw his MVA amendment before it reached a vote. Then on November 28, the Senate received a letter from President Roosevelt recommending that the Pick-Sloan Plan be authorized only as the general engineering program "to be developed and administered by a Missouri Valley Authority." The president's message boosted the confidence of MVA supporters, and Murray renewed his attempt to push the bill through as an amendment.

Overton and his Louisiana colleague Allen Ellender then promised the Montanan that if he would withdraw his contemplated amendment, the Missouri Valley Authority would receive committee hearings "at an early date" in the next Congress. Murray expressed justified fear that if Pick-Sloan passed, Congress would feel no need to create a new agency to carry on unified development of the river. Alabama's Lister Hill and Elmer Thomas of Oklahoma assured Murray that such was not the case. Thus mollified, the senator agreed to forgo consideration of his amendment. Unknowingly Murray had sacrificed his only opportunity to bring the Missouri Valley Authority to a vote by the full Senate.[14]

On December 1 the Senate passed the massive Flood Control bill without a roll call. The president signed it three weeks later. He emphasized that he was approving the measure only "with the distinct understanding" that it would not jeopardize creation of a Missouri Valley Authority. The new law authorized development of the Missouri basin by the combined efforts of the Corps of Engineers and Bureau of Reclamation.

Shortly after Congress convened in 1945, Murray reintroduced his MVA bill. The new measure was virtually identical to the 1944 bill. Again the senator denounced the Pick-Sloan scheme as an "incompletely engineered compromise hastily agreed upon." Immediately after its introduction, Murray's bill received a deathblow. The Montana senator requested that the measure be referred to the Agriculture and Forestry Committee which earlier had considered the Tennessee Valley Authority legislation. Instead, Vice-President Truman let South Carolina senator Josiah Bailey persuade him to send the MVA bill to his Senate Commerce Committee. The conservative southerner was an avowed opponent of valley authorities.

While campaigning for the vice-presidency, Harry Truman had endorsed all of the Roosevelt domestic program including the MVA. So his action on the Murray bill came as a shock. Yet ever since his days as a local official in Kansas City, Truman had been a close ally of the Army Corps of Engineers. To those who criticized his handling of Murray's bill, the vice-president simply replied, "I'm here to send bills introduced in the Senate to the committees where they belong." In responding to one constituent, Truman did not veil his hostility toward the MVA. "The Missouri River cannot be handled in the same manner as the Tennessee, or the Columbia, or the Colorado," he wrote. "It is not a project to be worked out by demagogues or dreamers."[15]

Murray privately admitted that as long as his bill remained in Bailey's committee it would "be licked to a frazzle." The senator decided to attempt a resolution discharging the Commerce Committee from considering the MVA measure. When he presented his resolution, Bailey countered with a motion to allow three separate committees sixty days each to consider the Missouri Valley Authority bill. Murray consented to Bailey's compromise offer since it would at least prevent the powerful southerner from freezing the bill in his Commerce Committee.

Bailey's committee still received the first shot at the MVA measure. John Overton chaired the subcommittee hearings. A longtime crony of Huey Long, the Louisiana senator had recently become president of the Mississippi Valley Association, an organization formed with the declared purpose of blocking the creation of river valley authorities.

James E. Murray (left) with Franklin D. Roosevelt, 1942. Courtesy K. Ross Toole Archives, Mansfield Library, University of Montana.

Throughout the hearings, Overton allowed opponents every opportunity to label the measure totalitarian and fascist. The adverse report from the Commerce Committee surprised no one. The committee recommended that all provisions affecting navigation and flood control be stricken from the Murray bill in order to preserve the jurisdiction of the Army Corps of Engineers over these areas.[16]

The crippled Murray bill then went to the Senate Irrigation and Reclamation Committee chaired by none other than John Overton. Overton again presided over subcommittee hearings on the measure. He appointed MVA opponents to the other subcommittee positions. In arguing again for his bill, Murray cited a recent Gallup Poll showing that three-fourths of the respondents favored creation of a Missouri Valley Authority. During the two weeks of hearings, the Montanan received support from various local farmers unions, Mayor of Minneapolis Hubert H. Humphrey, and Joseph Kinsey Howard. Murray's aide Dewey Anderson lined up many of the friendly witnesses and briefed them prior to testifying. Leading the opposition were politicians from several basin states including South Dakota Congressman Francis Case, Congressman William Lemke of North Dakota, Colorado's Governor John Vivian and Governor Sam Ford of Montana. Ford reiterated the views of other hostile witnesses in declaring, "The enactment of S.555 would create a super-government placing in the hands of three men power to dictate and control the social and economic life of the Missouri River Basin. It would be a long step toward state socialism." Again, the adverse committee report came as a foregone conclusion. Senator Overton completed the emasculation of the Murray bill which he had begun in the Commerce Committee. His last report recommended that the jurisdiction of the Bureau of Reclamation over irrigation be maintained.

Stunned by the Overton committee's total condemnation of his bill, Murray objected that the report should not be filed until the minority could submit its views. The Montanan decried the "atmosphere of hostility" which had prevailed throughout the hearings. The Louisiana senator overruled Murray's protests. The MVA bill then went to the Agriculture and Forestry Committee. By then, Murray recognized that the heavy opposition his bill had aroused during the two Overton subcommittee hearings had virtually destroyed its chances of passage in the Seventy-ninth Congress. The senator persuaded members of the Agriculture Committee to postpone the hearings indefinitely.[17]

As the Murray bill stumbled through the Senate committees, President Truman did little to bolster its chances. Shortly after the new president took office, Murray wrote him a long letter which outlined the provisions of Senate Bill 555 and asked for a public letter of endorsement. Truman refused, but he did include an appeal for valley authorities in both the Missouri and Columbia basins as part of a message to Congress in September. Later, speaking before the National Reclamation Association in Denver, the president again shied away from endorsing the MVA. In January he informed a press conference that he would do everything he could to gain approval of the MVA in 1946. Then three months later he told a similar gathering that the diverse nature of the Missouri River placed it "in a different class from the Tennessee or Columbia River."[18]

While the president vacillated over the MVA, powerful foes were of one voice in condemning the proposal. Foremost among these were the private utilities. The price of electricity to Missouri Basin residents was two to three times the amount paid by dwellers of the Tennessee Valley. Power companies in the region saw no reason to change that situation. The threat posed by the MVA led 167 private utilities from throughout the nation to band together to form the National Association of Electric Companies. The power companies launched an expensive nationwide advertising campaign.

A variety of special interest groups supported the power companies. Upper basin cattlemen and farm bureau officials feared MVA dams would ruin valuable rangeland. Railroads felt that development of river transportation might hurt their business. State and local officials saw the valley authority concept as an infringement of state rights. The Missouri Basin States Committee, formed in 1942 by the governors of the region, played a prominent role in pushing the Pick-Sloan Plan. D. J. Guy of the United States Chamber of Commerce reflected the fear of many when he warned that the Missouri Valley Authority would have the power "to do everything but coin money, wage war, and amend the Constitution." A coalition of local reclamation and land and water development associations formed yet another powerful lobby fighting the MVA. Throughout 1945 the so-called water lobby organized letter writing campaigns and issued anti-MVA pamphlets with such catchy titles as "Totalitarianism on the March" and "Bureaucracy Rides the Rivers."[19]

To counteract these alliances, Murray relied on the assistance of several organizations. Patton's National Farmers Union and the St. Louis *Post-Dispatch* each maintained a steady drumbeat to popularize the MVA idea. Various state labor groups endorsed the Murray bill. Morris L. Cooke helped organize the Friends of the Missouri Valley to mobilize public opinion behind the MVA. In July 1945 valley authority proponents from every Missouri basin state except Wyoming met in Omaha and formed the Regional Committee for the MVA. The group elected unsuccessful Montana gubernatorial candidate Leif Erickson as its president and launched a petition campaign to get congressional approval of Murray's measure.

Murray naturally spoke as frequently as possible in support of his bill. In June 1946 the Montanan introduced a Senate resolution demanding a full investigation of the "strongly financed and unscrupulous lobby maintained by the private power interests of the country." The resolution went to the Military Affairs Committee where it was promptly pigeonholed.

Murray did not fare well in Montana politics either. The 1945 Montana state legislature, at Governor Sam Ford's bidding, passed a resolution condemning the MVA. R. C. Bricker, a former manager of real estate interests for the Montana Power Company, had introduced the resolution. In June the voters of Montana's eastern congressional district chose a congressman to replace Democrat James O'Connor who had died suddenly. The Missouri Valley Authority became a central issue. Republican candidate Wesley D'Ewart ran on a platform advocating the Pick-Sloan Plan. Murray rushed back to his home state to defend his project and to endorse Democratic candidate Leo Graybill. Heavy rains on election day led to a light voter turnout and helped D'Ewart emerge as eastern Montana's first Republican congressman since 1932.

Things did not improve for Murray and his valley authority in the 1946 general election. In the June senatorial primary MVA spokesman Leif Erickson edged out Burton K. Wheeler in one of the most stunning upsets in Montana political history. But, in November Erickson fell victim to the nationwide Republican trend and lost to Zales Ecton. Montana's first popularly elected Republican senator, Ecton served six uneventful years as an unabashed spokesman for the private utility industry.[20]

Despite the disastrous results of the 1946 elections, Murray was determined to reintroduce the MVA in the new Congress. The senator's aide, Dewey Anderson, spent months revising the 1944 bill hoping to satisfy some of its critics. The new measure established an advisory committee consisting of residents of the region and representatives of several federal agencies. The group would serve as a check on the three people of the MVA board of directors which critics had charged would have enjoyed dictatorial powers under the original bill. Over Murray's objections, his bill went to the Senate Public Works Committee chaired by West Virginia Republican Chapman Revercomb. In July Revercomb delivered a detailed indictment of the MVA proposal from the Senate floor. The West Virginian then shelved the Murray bill for the duration of the Eightieth Congress.[21]

Murray had no illusions about getting the Missouri Valley Authority measure through the Senate. "The job this year," he wrote a constituent, "is to continue the educational processes in the Missouri Valley area." Late in the spring of 1947, the Missouri River went on its annual rampage again causing millions of dollars in damage. The floods revived Murray's hopes that the Republican Congress might be goaded to take drastic action.

The Montanan introduced a resolution demanding the Senate investigate the floods and propose remedial action. Murray and Ben Stong met with Truman and urged him to push the valley authority program, but the president only promised to think it over. In a subsequent press conference, reporters pressed Truman on the Missouri Basin issue. "Murray was in here . . . just the other day," he told one questioner, "and I told him to push the [MVA] bill . . . I have always actively supported it." When the reporter replied that most of the Missouri Valley crowd did not feel that he was actively backing the MVA, Truman shot back, "I shall support the comprehensive flood control program. That is the emergency at the present time, not the Missouri Valley Authority." Truman's remarks prompted Murray to telephone the White House. He told presidential assistant John Steelman that he feared that the president's contemplated flood control program could jeopardize the MVA. Murray warned, "I wouldn't recommend them a God damned dollar now for flood control unless they come in on this bigger program."[22]

Despite Murray's admonition, Truman, in July, asked Congress for four billion dollars to continue the flood control program in the Missouri Basin. He threw in a general word of endorsement for valley authorities, but critics realized that the requested funds all would go toward further implementing the Pick-Sloan Plan. Supporters of the MVA felt betrayed. "It is obvious," wrote Murray's executive secretary William Coburn, "that although the President said he is in favor of an MVA, what he is most interested in is navigation and flood control." In *The Nation*, Ernest Kirschten reminded readers that Roosevelt had strongly endorsed the MVA, but his successor had given it "only lip service."[23]

Murray remained convinced that a groundswell of local support could win over both the president and Congress. To generate such pressure the senator and his congressional aides traveled to Montana at their own expense and conducted a series of informal hearings. Governor Ford and Congressman D'Ewart accused Murray of using the sessions as a vehicle to launch his reelection campaign. Nearly everyone attending the five hearings endorsed the Missouri Valley Authority.

While Murray was busy encouraging grass roots backing for the MVA, the Pick-Sloan Plan moved forward. In January, 1948, members of the Missouri Basin Inter-Agency Committee adopted a six-year program for water resources development. The plan sought to coordinate the activities of all government agencies working in the valley. The Army Corps of Engineers and the Bureau of Reclamation continued to let contracts for dam construction. Even the *New York Times*, which had endorsed the MVA, admitted that Pick-Sloan was "a bustling reality."[24]

Senator Murray remained unconvinced. In March he informed the Senate that "new and alarming evidence" indicated that upstream farmers would be deprived of irrigation water under the Pick-Sloan Plan. He introduced a resolution calling for immediate review and revision of all irrigation, navigation, and flood control programs planned or underway within the basin. Although his resolution went nowhere, the senator did manage to persuade Truman to declare all of eastern Montana a disaster area after the river went on its annual flooding spree.

The thwarting of the Missouri Valley Authority by the Eightieth Congress provided Murray with an issue during his 1948 reelection campaign. Speaking in Great Falls in October, the senator charged that Republicans in Congress had joined utility lobbyists "in a scheme to destroy the western program of reclamation, flood control and rural electrification." Following his decisive reelection, Murray told Joseph Kinsey Howard, "You can say this definitely. MVA is back on the map." Murray's bill received a further boost in Montana when John Bonner ousted Sam Ford from the governor's seat. Outside the state, fifteen new congressmen and at least two new senators won election after endorsing the MVA. Foremost among these was Minnesota's freshman senator Hubert H. Humphrey. In December, Murray confidently wrote Ben Stong: "We urge that you and the supporters of the

James E. Murray and Harry S. Truman examine Missouri River Basin, 1950. Courtesy K. Ross Toole Archives, Mansfield Library, University of Montana.

MVA throughout the Missouri Basin area prepare for a fight that will have only one outcome—the passage of the MVA this session."[25]

In January senators Murray, Humphrey, and Guy M. Gillette of Iowa visited Truman in hopes of gaining a firm endorsement. Murray assured the president that his new MVA bill would emphasize local control. He even proposed to change the word "authority" to "administration" because of the negative connotation attached to the former term. On March 2, Murray introduced the revised measure. It called for five men instead of three on the board of directors. The governor of each basin state would be placed on the MVA advisory committee. Of even greater significance, Murray's 1949 bill agreed to use existing agencies and programs in the basin. This was done largely to avoid disruption of the Pick-Sloan projects which by then were well underway. In his first formal Senate address, Hubert Humphrey endorsed Murray's bill as "a symbol of liberalism."

The new MVA measure went to the Senate Public Works Committee. Despite the newly elected Democratic majority, the committee still contained a majority hostile to valley authorities. Five of the eight Democrats on the body were from the South. The bill lay dormant, and by July cosponsor Guy Gillette admitted that there would not be "the slightest chance" for hearings during the 1949 session. "We had hoped that the November 2 mandate would be written into law," Murray lamented to a supporter. "We did not reckon with the reactionary coalition which has blocked not just an MVA, but nearly all truly liberal measures."

The conservative coalition aside, Harry S. Truman deserved much of the blame for the continued frustration among MVA's supporters. Weeks before introducing the legislation, Murray observed that the bill would not receive a favorable committee report "unless the President really gets behind the measure." In his annual state of the union message, Truman vaguely endorsed authority plans, but did not mention the Missouri Basin. Later, when asked at a press conference if his flood control report to Congress would contain an MVA recommendation, the president replied "no." After Truman had urged passage of a Columbia Valley Authority bill, a reporter asked if he planned to make a similar endorsement for the MVA. The president retorted, "Not at the present time." In January, 1950, he was asked whether he felt that Pick-Sloan eventually would envelop the MVA. He answered, "Yes, I am very sure it will."[26]

While friends of the MVA continued to hit roadblocks, opponents moved to kill the authority idea for good. In March, 1949, the Missouri Valley Development Association announced that it would work for legislation within each basin state to prohibit river authorities from developing natural resources. A year later the National Rivers and Harbors Congress passed a resolution condemning the concept of regional authorities. In a *New Republic* article, "The Rivers and Harbors Lobby," Ben Stong exposed the powerful alliances which he and Murray had been fighting. The article revealed the many close ties between the NRHC and contractors, power companies, big landowners, and the U. S. Army Corps of Engineers.

Early in 1949 the Rivers and Harbors Congress suffered a setback when the Commission on Organization of the Executive Branch of Government, chaired by former president Herbert Hoover, released its final report. The Hoover Commission called the compromise between the corps and bureau in the Missouri Basin a mere "division of projects" which could prove "more costly to the public than disagreement." "Successful regulation of the Missouri and its tributaries," the report concluded, "can only be managed on a basin-wide scale." Heartened by such powerful ammunition from an unexpected source, Murray had large sections of the report read into the *Congressional Record.* But the startling conclusions of the Hoover Commission persuaded neither Congress nor the president to scrap the five-year-old Pick-Sloan program.[27]

Undaunted, Murray saw the annual spring floods in 1951 as an "opportune" time to reintroduce his bill. Again it went to the hostile Public Works Committee, and Murray realized that it stood little chance. Truman's attitude continued to disappoint the Montana senator. Not only did the president ignore the wishes of liberals to create valley authorities, but with the outbreak of the war in Korea he came out against the start of any new large reclamation projects. In August 1951 Murray and four other western Democratic senators sent the president a strong warning. "Slashing of reclamation on whatever theory," they concluded, "spells political disaster in the West."

The death and destruction caused by the flooding Missouri River during the early 1950s was so serious that Truman realized, war or no war, something would have to be done. By the end of 1952, the Army Corps of Engineers and Bureau of Reclamation had spent more than a billion and a quarter dollars on huge dams, canals, and levees. Yet the cresting waters were higher than ever. After nearly eight years of effort, the agencies had brought only twelve thousand new acres of land under irrigation, even though Pick-Sloan had promised to irrigate five million acres. Irrigation advocates still feuded with downstream navigationists, and battles between public power and private power interests continued unabated.

In January 1952 Truman, by executive order, created a Missouri Basin Survey Commission. He directed the body to study the basin's land and water resources and to draft a plan for their coordinated development. Murray lauded Truman's decision. Several months earlier he had co-sponsored a Senate resolution calling for just such a commission. Truman appointed the Montana senator one of the new body's congressional members.[28]

In April the president gave valley authority advocates further hope that he might be changing his attitude. During the spring floods he invited Murray and pro-MVA senator Tom Hennings of Missouri to join him in an aerial inspection of the damage. But by then, Truman had already announced that he would not seek reelection. Republican presidential candidate Dwight Eisenhower was calling for a Missouri River flood control program that would give "as much authority as possible" to the individual states.

By the time the Missouri River Survey Commission released its report, Eisenhower was in the White House. After holding seventeen public hearings, the commission recommended a plan that would treat the entire basin as a single unit. The report fell far short of recommending a Missouri Valley Authority, however. Instead it called for the creation of a Missouri Basin Commission of five members to supervise the activities of existing federal agencies in the region, and give them "unified and coherent direction." Murray was disappointed that the Survey Commission had not endorsed the MVA, but he urged the establishment of the suggested five-member body as "a long step forward toward a unified plan and administration." Eisenhower neither endorsed nor condemned the report's proposals. During each Congress of the Republican administration, Tom Hennings introduced bills embodying most of the Survey Commission's recommendations. Each time they went to the Senate Public Works Committee where they died.

James E. Murray remained in the Senate until the end of 1960. During his final six years in office he chaired the powerful Senate Interior Committee. Yet, faced with a hostile president, the Montanan did not bother to reintroduce his Missouri Valley Authority Bill during the Eisenhower years. Instead, he consoled himself with the limited gains that had been made while congressional conservatives were forestalling the total victory, for which he had so diligently labored. "If we step back and take a historical view," he rationalized in 1954, "it is clearly evident. . .how we have all come to look upon these problems —flood control, irrigation, domestic water supply, electrical production, economic stimulation, and a dozen other problems—as common problems in regional development programs." While the MVA had forced a "shotgun wedding" of feuding parties in the Missouri Valley, he added, in other basins the government agencies had entered "wedded bliss" more or less voluntarily.[29]

NOTES

1. Thomas H. Langevin, "The Missouri Basin: A Study in Multiple-Purpose Water Development" (Ph.D. dissertation, University of Nebraska, 1951), pp. i, ii; Marian E. Ridgeway, *The Missouri Basin's Pick-Sloan Plan: A Case Study in*

Congressional Determination (Urbana: University of Illinois Press, 1955), pp. 3–4; Edward J. Skillin Jr., "Missouri Valley Authority: America's Greatest Single Peace Project," *The Commonweal*, 24 Aug. 1945, p. 446; Joseph Kinsey Howard, "Golden River," *Harper's Magazine*, May 1945, pp. 511–513.

2. For further information on Murray's early career see Anna Roth, Ed., *Current Biography, 1945* (New York: H. W. Wilson Co., 1945), p. 414; Forrest Davis, "Millionaire Moses," *Saturday Evening Post*, 8 Dec. 1945, p. 10; Donald E. Spritzer, "New Dealer From Montana: The Senate Career of James E. Murray" (Ph.D. dissertation, University of Montana, 1980).

3. "United for Victory," Murray Campaign Pamphlet, 1942; Small Business Committee press release, 6 July 1944; James E. Murray, Senatorial Papers, University of Montana Library Archives, Missoula, Montana, hereinafter cited as Murray MSS; Ridgeway, p. 73.

4. Elmo Richardson, *Dams, Parks, and Politics: Resource Development and Preservation in the Truman-Eisenhower Era* (Lexington: The University Press of Kentucky, 1963), p. 9; Langevin, p. 42.

5. Rufus Terral, *The Missouri Valley: Land of Drouth, Flood, and Promise* (New Haven: Yale University Press, 1947), pp. 188–203; Kyle Howard, pp. 513–15.

6. Murray to W. F. Flinn, Miles City, 14 Feb. 1944, Murray press release 16 Feb. 1944, Murray MSS; "One River—One Problem," St. Louis *Post-Dispatch*, 15 May 1944, clipping in Murray MSS.

7. Murray to John D. Pope, 24 Feb. 1936, Murray to David E. Lilienthal, Knoxville, Tennessee, 7 June 1944 and 15 Aug. 1944, Murray MSS; U. S. Congress, Senate, 78th Cong., 2d sess., S.2089, 18 Aug. 1944.

8. U. S. Congress, Senate, 78th Cong., 2d sess., 18 Aug. 1944, *Congressional Record* 90:7082–88, hereinafter cited *CR*.

9. 78th Cong., 2d sess., House Doc. No. 680, Message from the President of the United States, 21 Sept. 1944; Charles A. Murray interview with the author, Portland, Oregon, 19 May 1978, transcript in University of Montana Library Archives, Missoula, Montana.

10. Leif Erickson to Murray, 14 Jan. 1945, Murray MSS; *Miles City Star*, 3 Sept. 1944, Omaha *World-Herald*, 14 Oct. 1944, clippings in Murray MSS.

11. Bismarck *Tribune*, 12 Sept. 1944; St. Louis *Star-Times*, 25 Oct. 1944; Chicago *Sun*, 7 Nov. 1944; *Philadelphia Record*, 23 Sept. 1944, clippings in Murray MSS; *The People's Voice* (Helena) files passim; Howard, p. 517; "For a Missouri Valley Authority," *The New Republic*, 4 Sept. 1944, pp. 266–68.

12. James E. Murray radio addresses, Butte, 30 Oct. 1944, 6 Nov. 1944, Great Falls, 4 Nov. 1944, Murray MSS; B. K. Wheeler to William Honey (undated), Burton K. Wheeler Papers, 1910–1971, Montana Historical Society, Helena, Montana; Michael P. Malone and Richard Roeder, *Montana: A History of Two Centuries* (Seattle: University of Washington Press, 1976), p. 239; Ridgeway, pp. 241, 278; James G. Patton, taped answers to questions sent by the author, 10

April 1978, transcript in University of Montana Library Archives, Missoula, Montana.

13. U. S. Congress, Senate, 78th Cong., 2d sess., Senate Doc. No. 247, *Missouri River Basin: Report of a Committee of Two Representatives Each from the Corps of Engineers, U. S. Army and Bureau of Reclamation, Supplemental to Sen. Doc. No. 191 and House Doc. No. 475, 78th Cong.*, 21 Nov. 1944; *New York Times*, 9 Nov. 1944, p. 31; National Farmers Union press release, undated, 1944, National Farmers Union Papers, University of Colorado Western History Library, Boulder, Colorado.

14. 78th Cong., 2d sess., 28 Nov. 1944, 30 Nov. 1944, *CR* 90:8374-79, 8616-26; Allen Drury, *A Senate Journal, 1943–45* (New York: DaCapo Press, 1972), pp. 298–301.

15. U. S. Congress, 78th Cong., 2d sess., Pub. Law No. 534, *Statutes at Large*, 58:887-907; U. S. Congress, Senate, 79th Cong., 1st sess., S.555, 15 Feb. 1945, 79th Cong., 1st sess., 15 Feb. 1945, *CR* 91:1121-26; Harry S. Truman to E. L. Clary, Cleveland, 30 Mar. 1945, Harry S. Truman, Vice-Presidential and Senatorial Papers, Harry S. Truman Library, Independence, Missouri; *New York Times*, 13 Oct. 1944, p. 15, 2 Dec. 1944, p. 14, 16 Feb. 1945, p. 16.

16. U. S. Congress, Senate, Subcommittee of the Committee on Commerce, *Hearings...on S.555, To Establish a Missouri Valley Authority*, 79th Cong., 1st sess., 16–27 Apr. 1945; 79th Cong., 1st sess., Senate Report No. 246, *Report on S.555 from the Committee on Commerce*, 7 May 1945; Murray to Judge Homer T. Bone, San Francisco, 23 Feb. 1945, Murray MSS; Ernest Kirschten, "From TVA to MVA," *The Christian Century*, 30 May 1945, p. 649.

17. U. S. Congress, Senate, Subcommittee of the Committee on Irrigation and Reclamation, *Hearings...on S.555, To Establish a Missouri Valley Authority*, 79th Cong., 1st sess., 18–28 Sept. 1945, pp. 1–44, 622–30; U. S. Congress, Senate, 79th Cong., 1st sess., Sen. Report No. 639, *Missouri Valley Authority Act Adverse Report, Committee on Irrigation and Reclamation*, 18 Oct. 1945; 79th Cong., 1st sess., 18 Oct. 1945, *CR* 91:9760; Langevin, p. 91; Ridgeway, p. 256.

18. Murray to Truman, 24 Apr. 1945, Presidential Secy. Matthew J. Connelly to Murray, 2 May 1945, Harry S. Truman Presidential Papers, Harry S. Truman Library, Independence, Missouri; Truman News Conferences, 19 Jan. 1945, 18 Apr. 1946, Harry S. Truman, *Public Papers*, 1946 volume, pp. 34, 210; *New York Times*, 27 Nov. 1945, p. 27.

19. Ernest Kirschten, "MVA: Stalled but not Stopped," *The Nation*, 17 Aug. 1946, pp. 183–84; Omaha *World-Herald*, 7 Apr. 1945, p. 1; *Washington Daily News*, 17 July 1945, p. 19; Langevin, pp. 98–109; Ridgeway, pp. 12–13, 173, 264–68; Terral, pp. 179–81, 218–19.

20. 79th Cong., 2d sess., 18 June 1946, *CR* 92:7046-51, Index, p. 593; Omaha *World-Herald*, 7 July 1945, p. 1, 8 July 1945, p. 1; Leif Erickson, interview with the author, Swan Lake, Montana, 26 Aug. 1976, transcript in University of

Montana Library Archives, Missoula, Montana; *The Great Falls Tribune*, 24 May 1945, p. 9, 1 June 1945, p. 2, 6 June 1945, p. 1; Message of Gov. Sam C. Ford to Twenty-ninth Legislative Assembly of the State of Montana, 1945, text in Murray MSS; Ridgeway, pp. 180–81, 272–77.

21. Dewey Anderson to Claude B. Ricketts, St. Louis, 24 Sept. 1946, to George Sehlmeyer, Sacramento, 28 Aug. 1946, Murray MSS; U. S. Congress, Senate, 80th Cong., 1st sess., S.1156, 24 Apr. 1947; 80th Cong., 1st sess., 23 Apr., 26 July 1947, *CR* 93:3854,10354.

22. Transcript of telephone conversation between James E. Murray and John R. Steelman, 12 July 1947, Murray MSS; Drew Pearson, "The Washington Merry-Go-Round," *Washington Post*, 7 July 1947; Truman News Conference, 10 July 1947, *Truman Public Papers*, 1947 volume, p. 330; Murray to Phillip Murray, Washington, D. C., 19 Apr. 1947, Murray MSS; Benton Stong interview with Dale Johnson, Washington, D. C., 15 Feb. 1978, transcript in University of Montana Library Archives, Missoula, Montana.

23. William H. Coburn to Richard Shipman, Helena, 11 Aug. 1947, Murray MSS; Ernest Kirschten, "Hell, High Water, and the MVA," *The Nation*, 9 Aug. 1947, pp. 139–40.

24. Murray to Benton J. Stong, Denver, 8 Sept. 1947, Murray MSS; *The People's Voice* (Helena), 3 Oct. 1947, p. 1; *Lewistown Democrat News*, 30 Sept. 1947; *Miles City Daily Star*, 4 Oct. 1947; *The Dillon Daily Tribune*, 27 Sept. 1947; *The Glasgow Courier*, 2 Oct. 1947, clippings in Murray MSS; *New York Times*, 17 Oct. 1947, p. 29; 22 Jan. 1948, p. 9; 23 Jan. 1948, p. 45; Langevin, pp. 92–93.

25. Telegram Murray to Truman, 22 June 1948; Address, James E. Murray, Great Falls, Mt., 4 Oct. 1948; Murray to Benton Stong, 14 Dec. 1948; "MVA Wins in the Missouri Valley," undated memo, Murray MSS; U. S. Congress, Senate, 80th Cong., 2d sess., S.J.R.197, 16 Mar. 1948; Joseph Kinsey Howard, "Make Way for MVA," *The Progressive*, Jan. 1949, pp. 4–8.

26. U. S. Congress, Senate, 81st Cong., 1st sess., S.1160, 2 Mar. 1949; 81st Cong., 1st sess., 2 Mar. 1949, *CR* 95:1705-25; *New York Times*, 6 Jan. 1949, p. 4, 15 Jan. 1949, p. 2, 9 July 1949, p. 15; Truman press conferences, 8 Jan. 1949, 14 Apr. 1949, 5 Jan. 1950, Truman, *Public Papers*, 1949, 1950, 1951 volumes; Murray to Jerome G. Locke, Helena, 7 Feb. 1949, 2 May 1949, Murray MSS.

27. Benton J. Stong, "The Rivers and Harbors Lobby," *The New Republic*, 10 Oct. 1949, pp. 13–15; Edward S. Skillin, "Missouri Valley Task Force," *The Commonweal*, 20 May 1949, pp. 145–46; 81st Cong., 1st sess., 30 Mar. 1949, *CR* 95:2403; Ridgeway, p. 293.

28. "Memorandum for the President by Western Democratic Senators," 29 Aug. 1951, Murray press release, 4 Jan. 1952, Murray MSS; Statement of President Truman announcing creation of Missouri Basin Survey Commission, 3 Jan. 1952, Truman Presidential Papers; 82nd Cong., 1st sess., S.1883, 23 July 1951; S.J.R.93, 20 Aug. 1952; U. S. Cong., Senate, 82nd Cong., 1st sess., 23 July 1951,

CR 97:8654-59; Jean Begeman, "Misery on the Missouri," *The New Republic*, 28 Apr. 1952, pp. 13–14.

29. Murray to Truman, 21 Apr. 1952, Truman Presidential Papers; Missouri Basin Survey Commission, "Missouri; Land and Water," 20 Feb. 1953, text in Murray MSS; Murray press release, 20 Feb. 1953, Murray MSS; 83rd Cong., 2d sess., 17 July 1954, *CR* 100:10774; *New York Times*, 8 May 1952, p. 25, 8 Feb. 1957, p. 16.

9 /
THE COPPER PEN
Butte in Fiction

RICHARD B. ROEDER

The appellation "Richest Hill on Earth" usually describes Butte's wealth in copper, silver, and other precious metals. But Butte's treasure was not limited to the products of the earth. Just as ores yielded mineral riches, so the city's literary output surpasses that of any other area of the state. Richard Roeder, professor of History at Montana State University, examines Butte as a source of fictional writings. Roeder analyzes nineteen separate Butte novels written between 1902 and 1980. Not surprisingly, the quantity of published works corresponds roughly to the size and vitality of the community itself. While Butte flourished during the early twentieth century, novels appeared with some frequency. As mining declined, so did the output of Butte-inspired fiction.

Historical events in Butte's past inspire many of the stories and characters in Butte novels. The War of the Copper Kings, miners, gamblers, and prostitutes, diverse ethnic groups—all appear with varying literary clarity and historical accuracy. Roeder argues that this vibrant inspiration produced, at best, only mediocre literary works—"Butte has not been the source of a great American book." But many of the novels have factual and social validity. None deal with the profound impact of the metal mining industry on the lives of Butte's people, but through these pages are scattered real glimpses of Butte's working-class men and women. If there is a lasting contribution to these volumes, it is the slice of life they permit us to sample.

No other city or part of Montana can compare with Butte as a source of inspiration for those who would try their hand at fiction. As the extent of its ores attracted seekers of wealth, so the richness of its varied culture has tempted individuals to use it. Observers of life in Butte were attracted by its vibrancy and yet worried by its sin. Great Falls writer Joseph Kinsey Howard revealed this basic ambivalence. Howard referred to the city as the "Black heart of Montana." Yet his fondness for it is revealed by the fact that some of his best writings were about Butte.[1] Between 1902 and 1980 numerous writers, native and non-native, have sought to mine Butte's color as a setting for their stories. The result has been a considerable body of imaginative writing, very uneven in artistic merit and importance, but in aggregate revealing of Butte's past.[2]

Butte received its introduction to the world of writing with the greatest literary sensation in its history. In 1902 Mary MacLane, an 1899 graduate of Butte Public High School, rocked the nation and her fellow Montanans with the publication of *The Story of Mary MacLane*.[3] The book appears to be a journal of her mental life between January 13 and April 11, 1901. The nineteen-year-old Mary MacLane proclaimed that she was unhappy and that she would do anything to find happiness in this world. She announced that we could not find real happiness by following conventional norms. Never would she sew or mend clothes. Nor would she accept the institution of marriage. She observed that not two in a hundred Butte marriages produced any happiness. She also rejected the idea that conformity with community norms was real virtue. To her this was nothing more than the cowardice of people willing to accept the power of public opinion, for which she did not give a damn.

MacLane also eschewed traditional religious beliefs. She declared that Christianity was "full of hatred." She admitted that the life of Christ as depicted in scripture was beautiful, "but it is a lie." At the same time she frankly accepted the pleasures of sensual gratification; she delighted in her young body, which she tried to enhance by padding her breastline and accentuating her hips. She also revelled in oral gratifications by dwelling on the satisfactions of eating, whether a single green olive or full meals of porterhouse steak and young green onions.

Even more shocking was her frank expression of sexual urges. Some of this was in the form of her love for high school English teacher, Fanny Corbin, whom she called her "anemone lady." But she also longed for heterosexual love. She looked for a man to come and lead her "to what would be technically termed my ruin." In the absence of a flesh and blood lover, Mary MacLane had to be content with frequent fantasies of encounters with the Devil, whom she called upon to ravish her and to marry her.

But her yearnings went unfulfilled. Life was empty. Here Butte itself is significant as an ambiguous symbol of her failure to find happiness. In her frequent wanderings about the city she commented upon Butte's "sand and barrenness," a phrase that runs through the book. She felt terribly alone because there was no one in the city able to understand her. But her feelings about her hometown were not completely negative. Even Butte's ugliness had its positive side. Since the city was the "perfection of ugliness," it was "not to be despised." Moreover, MacLane was fascinated by Butte's diversity of neighborhoods and peoples. Like herself, many of these people rejected bourgeois ways. She liked what she called Butte's "Bohemianism."

Mary MacLane's book was an immediate national sensation. Some responses were positive. Writer Hamlin Garland, for example, thought Mary was "entering upon a startling career."[4] A few reviewers were able to see the significance of Mary's striving for self-expression and her refusal to accept marriage and motherhood. But the overwhelming response was shock. The reactions of the reviewer for the *New York Times* reflected the feelings of many and revealed as well an assumption of eastern cultural hegemony. Although MacLane was too old to be spanked, he thought her fellow Montanans ought to devise some condign punishment. After giving vent to his horrors at MacLane's iconoclasms, he declared that to be "a good wife and mother is not to fail in life." He could find no better reason why the book should have been written than "a maidenly desire for notoriety." He concluded that it was appropriate that such literary trash should be composed in Butte, Montana, and published in Chicago.[5]

The book also inspired a number of parodies. One such, *The Story of Willie Complain*, appeared in Butte, the product of Robert J. Shores, a local writer of verse.[6] Shores assumed that MacLane had no sufficient reason for her unhappiness. Consequently, he regarded her as insincere and the book as at best an expression of "ridiculous egotism" and at worst a pose and a sham.

That most of Mary MacLane's readers were shocked is now readily understandable. Writing might be an appropriate outlet for women, but only if they pursued their craft within the limits imposed by what most people still thought of as the canons of true womanhood. The woman writer must subscribe to piety, purity, submissiveness, and domesticity. These were precisely the virtues MacLane would not accept. As Barbara Welter has written, "If anyone, male or female, dared to tamper with the complex of virtues which made up True Womanhood, he was damned immediately as an enemy of God, of civilization and of the Republic."[7]

Mary MacLane wrote two more books. In 1902 she came out with *My Friend Annabel Lee,* a record of conversations she had with a porcelain statue of a Japanese woman whom she called Annabel Lee.[8] Butte enters the book very little, although she insists that as a place it is still her first love. The financial success of her first book enabled MacLane to leave Butte, but in December 1909 she returned. That she was not finding the happiness she sought is evident in her last book, *I, Mary MacLane.*[9] MacLane said that now (1917) she knew true loneliness and despair, and she felt that her life had become immoral because of its total futility. The "sand and barrenness" of Butte figures in the book as it did in *The Story.* But in her last work she places more emphasis on the beauty of the hills and mountains surrounding Butte. MacLane was fascinated by the moods of the city at different hours and seasons, and by the play of the sunlight and especially the lights at night. The emphasis on Butte in her last book reveals that her return home was an attempt to give some orientation to her life, but she failed in that attempt.

The next author to use Butte as a setting was also a woman and one of six people Mary MacLane said she most admired. MacLane had called the people of Butte the "Devil's playthings." California novelist Gertrude Atherton titled her Butte novel *The Perch of the Devil.*[10] Atherton's was the first of a series of Butte novels that celebrated mining as a way for the self-made man to acquire wealth. She also introduced a theme used by several subsequent authors. Mining, although risky to the individual in both a physical and financial sense, tended to create a stimulating community by attracting a population that was energetic and willing to take a long shot.

The hero of *Perch of the Devil* is Gregory Compton, product of a ranch background. Compton had his education at the School of Mines interrupted by the death of his father and the necessity of taking charge of the ranch. He takes with him a new wife, Ida Hook, daughter of a miner and a dressmaker for Butte's fashionable West Side women. Ida is a beauty whom Compton married in a sudden infatuation. Ora Stratton, whose father had been a mining company lawyer, grew up in Butte's high society, and with her mother (of southern background) makes the grand tour of Europe. However, Ora is left virtually penniless by the death of her father, who had mismanaged family finances. Ora marries Mark Blake, whose mother used to work for Ora's mother as a seamstress. Mark is now a rapidly rising lawyer and Compton's best friend.

Gregory discovers rich mineral deposits on his ranch which he later develops into a prosperous mine in the face of opposition from the Company. In anticipation of rising status, Gregory hires a tutor to transform Ida into a lady. The process of transformation is completed when Ora—"the European aristocratic type of woman"—takes Ida—"the evolving middle class woman of the 'West' "—on a tour of Europe. Ora and Gregory are secretly in love. Ora divorces her husband, and her freedom is complete when an old mining claim of her father's (conveniently located next to Gregory's ranch) pans out, thereby making her rich. Ora's and Gregory's love for each other cannot work out, however, because Ida will not accept a divorce. So Ora returns to Europe and a backup marriage, while Ida and Gregory, realizing there are few, if any, ideal marriages, carve out a mutually acceptable and lasting relationship.

The above plot outline fails to convey the fact that this is a remarkable book which in some ways is akin to Mary MacLane's writings. Atherton uses her story as a vehicle for social commentary. In the first place, she points out regional and national cultural differences. The East (and Europe) is contrasted with the West to the favor of the latter. In the West one's ancestors count for nothing. Eastern snobberies and social rigidities disappear in the democratic atmosphere of the West, where it is not who one is but what one can do that counts. William Cullen Whalen, the New England-born Butte high school English teacher whom Gregory hires for Ida's tutor, is one of the symbols of the East. Whalen is affected, ineffectual, and effete. Ida, who spiritually and even physically pushes him around, is the natural western woman who is natively bright and perspicacious in her judgments about individuals and institutions. Before she is culturally transformed by Ora and the European tour, her slangy manner of speech is a delight. But even after her reformation, she does not lose her natural shrewdness. Ora, by contrast, is too Europeanized and loses out in her fight to steal the husband of her friend.

In Atherton's novel there are exceptions to democracy even in the West. The broad acceptance of people of different backgrounds did not stretch to include recent immigrants from southeastern Europe, whom Butte residents called collectively "Bohunks" and regarded as inferior miners. When Gregory opens his mine, he proudly employs only the

Butte, Montana—The Richest Hill on Earth and a source of literature as well as copper. N. A. Forsyth photograph. Courtesy Montana Historical Society.

highest type of men while his corporate competitor employs eastern Europeans and loses the battle.

The democratic ethos of the West also did not fully include women. Like the writings of Mary MacLane, Atherton's novel reflects the discontents of some women. Conversations between Ora and Ida frequently reflect dissatisfaction with the very limited socially condoned outlets for their energy and their displeasure with the less than rewarding relationships between men and women at this stage in society's development. Ora especially craves adventure and wishes she were a man so she could prospect for new ore bodies. Her living at her mine site, while partly a ploy to stalk Gregory, is also a reflection of her desire to run the mine herself. In fact, it is limited economic opportunity and necessitous circumstances that push both Ida and Ora into hasty and inappropriate marriages. Their unsatisfactory marriages lead Ora and Ida into some very unflattering remarks about American men and what stupid mates they make. Ida remarks that a woman immediately acquires a child at the marriage altar. Gregory and Mark pursue wealth (success) with such single-mindedness that they make totally insensitive and inadequate husbands, and neither woman can find fulfillment in merely being kept as a well-off wife.

While the first to use Butte in their writings were women literary figures, the next several books were the work of newspaper men who, like Atherton, where fascinated by mining. Amidst great labor strife in Butte, Charles C. Cohan, an Anaconda newspaper man, wrote *Born of the Crucible*.[11] This is the story of Dan Bradshaw, a self-made mining man whose success was inspired by a woman. Bradshaw is a good example of the western man, democratic yet inherently a gentleman, with a drive for success tempered by inflexible principles of rectitude. In both body and soul, writes Cohan, Bradshaw is a "velvet covered rock." But when Bradshaw first comes to Butte, he is corrupted by his association with un-American radicals of foreign and low-class background. Dan flees Butte and undergoes moral and physical rehabilitation by working on a farm. While doing so he finds and later develops a mining claim located in a beautiful mountain setting. Under the influence of the arcadian circumstances of the farm and the picturesque setting of the mine, Dan's natural qualities of a gentleman emerge. He creates an idyllic company town in which management policies based on benevolent paternalism toward workers achieve industrial peace and harmony and prosperity for all.

Sulfur Fumes by essayist George Wesley Davis is probably the worst of a group of books about Butte appearing after World War I.[12] Anthony Dunlap, nephew of a mining magnate, inherits his uncle's fortune. Within the corrupt atmosphere of Butte—which Davis calls the "Garden of Hell" because of the sulfur fumes and the moral rot of gambling, prostitution, and hard drugs—Dunlap has been corrupted by two villains, one simply an uncouth man, the other a Jewish pawnbroker. Under this influence Dunlap cheats his cousin Howard, an illegitimate son of the dead mining magnate, of his just share of his father's estate. With the aid of an avuncular private detective and a benevolent district judge, Howard avoids Dunlap's evil friends and the corruption of Butte by fleeing to the Sunshine Ranch. Here the prudent and studious Howard prospers and becomes a successful rancher in his own right. Having proved himself a self-made man, Howard secures his rightful fortune by marrying his beautiful second cousin, Anthony Dunlap's daughter. After the marriage, the young couple, now rich and happy, flee the Garden of Hell for Howard's ranch.

Berton Braley, a journalist in Butte before World War I and a writer of light verse for popular middle-class periodicals, wrote two novels with Butte as the setting—*The Sheriff of Silver Bow* and *Shoestring*.[13] In writing the former Braley says he followed a schedule of producing a chapter a day and completing the book in six weeks. He later said that he was able to do this by "using the dime novel technique of putting my hero into successive messes and then dragging him out again."[14] The present-day reader has no trouble accepting Braley's recollection. The story begins with a train robbery of the "Great West Limited" at Homestake on the continental divide above Butte. The incident introduces the main characters, William Broderick, the incorruptible sheriff, and Mike Parks, a recent University of Wisconsin graduate who is seeking employment and adventure. While posing as a newspaperman, Parks works as an undercover agent for the sheriff. This enables him to explore Butte, including the city's underworld. Except for users of hard drugs, Parks finds redeeming features in the city's vice because it "came not from weariness and over-sophistication, but from the super-abundant energy of a town that worked and roistered at top speed. It wasn't pretty, it was evil, but the evil was Rabelaisian and rampant, not subdued and cloying." Parks quickly gains leads on the crooks responsible for the train robbery and other crimes. But before they can be brought to justice, the reader has to follow the hero through chases, gun battles, and rescues in Butte's underground labyrinth as Parks, the sheriff, and his beautiful daughter Celia break up the ring of crooks. Justice is done and Parks marries Celia.

In the *Shoestring* the protagonist is Steve Randall, a twenty-five-year-old mining engineer whom the author has obviously drawn from the career of mining magnate F. Augustus Heinze. Randall pursues wealth in the city of Maverick, a he-man town were bars do not have keys because they never close but a town where decent women can walk the street, day or night, without fear of being accosted. Through his prowess as a gambler Randall wins the Sally Dobbs, a no-account mine which Randall, through know-how and pluck and luck, turns into a producer. But he then has to fight the Consolidated Mining Corporation. The incidents of the battle, under and above ground, are familiar to readers who know their Butte lore. The legal and physical battles are interlaced with a love plot between Steve and Nancy Van Zile, a New Yorker who has family connections with Consolidated. With Nancy as intermediary, Steve negotiates a sale of the Sally Dobbs to Consolidated. Against the advice of his friends, Steve uses the proceeds to set himself up on Wall Street. Here some of the same people he had defeated in Maverick fleece him. Steve asks Nancy to marry him and the story ends where it began with Steve sitting down to a poker game to win himself a new stake.

Although the four books by Cohan, Davis, and Braley have no lasting literary merit, they do reveal widely held values, prejudices, and myths. The female characters are cardboard in their unreality. But they accurately reflect the nineteenth century cult of true womanhood. They are virtuous and genteel, with only an occasional touch of daring. For the most part, they are just things for the hero to possess in the end. The heroes are he-men who in their democratic values are juxtaposed with snobbish, class-conscious easterners. The heroes are also embodiments of the myth of the self-made man who overcomes obstacles and evils on the road to economic success. In doing so they sometimes find it necessary to flee the corruption of the city for redemption by a return to rural life. The evils of Butte are not inherent but are the result of corrupt men. Sometimes this corruption is the product of an excessive passion for wealth, but it also comes from characters of recent eastern European origin, characters who are portrayed as dark, swarthy types. These same types are also the source of unwanted and unnecessary political, social, and economic radicalism. The troublemakers are drawn in stark contrast with the good Anglo-Saxon miners who work hard and loyally for the hero employers. Finally, the incidents of these novels reflect a basic nineteenth-century optimism and innocence which continued to dominate the thinking of many people during the Progressive period of our history. All four books convey the message that we live in a secure world where the universe is essentially benevolent, things do get better, and romantic love is real.[15]

The next book to use Butte for its setting conveys a fundamentally different point of view. More than any other writer Dashiell Hammett changed the detective story and helped create the formula of the hard-boiled detective.[16] For a time Hammett worked in the Butte area as a Pinkerton operative, and his experiences there may have played a part in molding the views he reflects in his novels, including his first, *Red*

Harvest.[17] The book is generally regarded as set in Butte. Actually, Hammett's descriptions suggest Anaconda, but the place could just as well be any number of medium-sized western industrial cities. The city is a gray and ugly place dirtied up by mining and smelting. Equally important, it is the personal town of mining baron Elihu Willsson, hence the city's name "Personville." An unnamed private detective agency operative tells the first person story in the lingo of the prohibition era underworld. At a point in time before the story begins, old man Willsson had imported thugs to break the power of organized labor, including the Industrial Workers of the World. He then lost control of his town to his mercenaries and had to hire the detective to extricate him from the clutches of the mobsters.

The unlikely hero is forty years old, five feet six or seven, and one hundred and ninety pounds—"a fat, middle-aged, hard-boiled, pig-headed guy" as he is described by his call girl friend and informant. The tough hero smokes heavily, drinks excessively, and at one point even uses laudanum to take himself out of things. The local police are unkempt, dumb, untrustworthy, and led by dishonest and brutal officers. Similarly, the courts cannot be used since they too are controlled by Willsson's former hirelings. Consequently, there is no law but what one makes for oneself. The operative proceeds to use the methods of Italian city-state politics. He fans intermob rivalries and gets them to rub each other out. But he is unable to control the fury of violence, and a chain reaction of killings litters the landscape with bodies of murder victims. It ends in one grand finale of mutual St. Valentine's Day-type massacre. The unexplained loose ends are picked up in the last page or so, and calm is restored by a national guard-imposed martial law.

Hammett uses the city as a causative element. The city's name is appropriately mispronounced "Poisonville." It corrupts the hero and makes him willing to accept a "blood simple" solution to the problem of law and order. While this aspect of the book is not convincing, the book's message is clear. The city has no rules. Therefore, because we live in an unprincipled universe, the operative has to ignore his agency's rules and to sidestep the scrutiny of his agency boss. As John G. Cawelti has put it, Hammett's work reflects a "vision of a godless naturalistic cosmos ruled by chance, violence, and death...."[18]

In 1935 R. Francis James brought out *High, Low and Wide Open*.[19] Who James was is not clear at this point. The *Book Review Digest* says the name on the title page is a pseudonym for James Francis Rabbitt.[20]

In any case the author appears to have been familiar with earlier Butte books because he borrowed words (Butte is "Perch"), phrases, and plot elements. If the dust jacket can be believed, this was James's first writing for publication. It also describes him much as James portrays his hero in the novel, as a well-traveled character who has held down an amazing variety of jobs.

In its melodramatic plot *High, Low and Wide Open* is reminiscent of the books by Cohan, Davis, and Braley. It begins with the murder of Mark Broderick, assistant foreman of the Big Sweat Mine, one of the properties of the Golconda Copper Mining Company. The hero, Ray McFarlane, is a drifter who is a former Northwestern University student, boxer, soldier, and private detective. He came to the city of Perch to hire on as a mine guard, but had to settle for a job as station tender underground. Broderick's father, head of the largest bank in town, puts up a $10,000 reward for capture of the murderer. While the police try to frame the wrong man, McFarlane pursues the murderer because he needs the money to return to Northwestern.

By wining, dining, and loving the police stenographer, McFarlane secures information on the widow, Therese DuBois Broderick. He then pursues Therese, to whom he is immediately attracted sexually. During a wild night at her apartment he learns that she hates Perch because it is ugly and gossipy and that she plans to leave it for Hollywood just as soon as she gets her insurance money. McFarlane learns that Morgan Evans, his shift boss in the mine, and the libidinous Therese had had an affair. Evans was also a former assistant foreman who was demoted to shift boss to make room for Broderick. McFarlane tricks Evans into revealing his having committed the murder by letting him hear McFarlane's explicit description of his lovemaking with Therese. Evans takes the bait. McFarlane takes the reward, and Therese's implication in the murder is left uncertain by a hung jury.

Obviously, James's book marks some departures from the journalistic novels of several years before. The story is told more effectively with a writing style that employs short, direct sentences and convincing descriptions. He has also cast aside the simple moralism of the earlier stories. He discusses gambling and prostitution, but matter-of-factly. His frankness about sex is a throwback to Mary MacLane. He is also sympathetic to the wage earners. He says he has never met a miner who really liked being one. The reader sees something of the men at work in the mine and hears some of the cadence of the miner's language. Finally, not all characters with non-Anglo-Saxon names are bad guys.

James's writing bears some resemblances to Hammett's *Red Harvest*. The hero is full of self-assurance and is too worldly to be taken in by the wiles of the likes of Therese. He is a tough guy, an ex-operative who drinks and parties constantly while not actually in the mine. He bears little resemblance to the prudent, bourgeois heroes of earlier stories. While Perch is not the totally lawless city of Poisonville—it is less violent and even the gambling is run on the up and up—it is a very insecure place for the hero, who has no choice but to stand up for himself.

Before James brought out his novel, Montana's most prolific novelist, Myron Brinig, had already published several novels set in Butte; over a period of more than twenty years he employed Butte as the main setting in five of his books. Myron Brinig was born in Minneapolis but grew up in Butte.[21] His father, a Romanian Jewish immigrant, ran a clothing store on East Park Street. The youngest of seven children, Myron left Butte after high school for college on the East Coast. Army service in World War I interrupted his education. After the war he returned to the East and attended several Ivy League schools but did not complete his degree. He began writing while a college student. After selling stories to popular middle-class magazines and literary journals, he followed the trend of young writers of the twenties and went to Europe. There he wrote his first novel, *Singermann*, which appeared in 1929, the first novel published by the firm of Farrar and Rinehart.[22] Brinig wrote for the movie industry, and after returning from Europe he lived for a time in Hollywood. He moved about a great deal. In the early thirties he lived in Taos, New Mexico, as part of the artist circle of Mable Dodge Luhan. Later he made New York City his home. But from time to time he returned, figuratively, to Butte for the setting of his stories.

Singermann is heavily autobiographical. It is the story of Moses Singermann who leads his family from Romania to Minneapolis, where Moses meets with modest success as a huckster. At age forty-five he uproots his family to pursue real wealth in the West of the late nineteenth century. Brinig tells how Moses, his illiterate wife Rebecca, their daughter and six sons fare in the Butte environment. Moses wins the greater wealth he sought, but at a cost. What warmth and happiness there had been in the family back in his huckster days are sacrificed to an all-consuming concern for his dry goods store. Moreover, he painfully watches the Americanization of his children—even of himself. Moses becomes confused and sometimes angry in the face of changes.

The stress further sours his relationship with Rebecca. In describing these changes, Brinig shows their impact on the lives of each of the seven children, each life being an interesting story of widely divergent personalities.

Brinig's second Butte novel, *Wide Open Town*, is mostly about Butte's Irish world.[23] The main characters—Roddy Cornett the spieler (town crier) of magnificent voice, his nephew John Donnelly, an Irish immigrant turned miner, and Zola Peterson, a girl of the line with whom John is helplessly in love—are memorable. There are numerous minor characters who are also well drawn, such as Christian Weber, the elderly bibulous musician whose genius, like the artistic genius of thousands like him, goes unrecognized and undeveloped in smalltown America. Of the lesser characters perhaps the best is Angelina, Roddy's daughter who "lived in a small world whose extent was the length of her nose, and she judged all men by her own small standards." The antiseptic Angelina in her prim religiosity tries to insulate herself from the riffraff of her father's world of Butte streets, theaters, and saloons.

Brinig provides descriptions of the physical beauty surrounding Butte. But the city's atmosphere is mostly oppressive. To seek renewal both John and Roddy have to flee to the countryside below and above the city. Furthermore, the characters lead lives that are blighted by misfortune and fate. No one has a future any more than do Christian Weber, who remembers musical days in Europe, or Sammy Pickens, who likes to recall his early-day exploits as a baseball pitcher. There are also class, ethnic, and religious hatreds. Exploitation of the workers by what John calls the "suckin' rich" leads to a strike and a lynching of an IWW organizer. Brinig's handling of his characters as they pursue their fates is reminiscent of Thomas Hardy.

In Brinig's subsequent Butte novels the city becomes less vivid. In *This Man Is My Brother*, a sequel to *Singermann*, Michael Singermann, who is now a New York novelist, returns to Butte twenty years after his father's death to gather material for a new novel.[24] The story is one of decline, of the disappearance of traditions and the loss of Jewish culture just as Moses had foreseen in *Singermann*. Joseph, the oldest son, after an unsuccessful attempt to return to his religion, finds solace in endless hours of working at the family store, as does his ex-prize-fighter brother Sol. Harry, the business brains of the family, openly accepts the fact that technology has carried man further and further from the earth in which tradition grew. Harry willingly accepts this fact with a good riddance to tradition. With Moses' grandchildren the loss of Jewishness is more or less complete. Son David's adopted son is a Christian and one of the few healthy members of the family. Sylvia marries a Christian, and cousin Nina is seduced by one. Ralph, who among the grandchildren is the most tradition oriented, ends up in a mental sanitarium, a symbol of the decline of Moses Singermann's sturdiness.

The Sun Sets in the West is Butte during Hoover's presidency and the Great Depression.[25] Like the economy, Butte is in a state of decline. This novel has little of the lusty and hearty characters of Brinig's earlier books. It is, in fact, a gloomy book. Nothing works out well for most of the characters. Their fates are determined by compulsions and circumstances they cannot control. Of the older generation only Adam Mendelssohn, the junk dealer and still very much a Jew, is a sympathetic character. The people who control affairs in Butte are depicted as stupid, narrow-minded people whose false values and prejudices gum up the lives of the few admirable people. Such is the case with Gertrude Field, forty-year-old spinster who works at the public library where seventeen-year-old David Sandor spends much of his time. They develop a tender and warm relationship which is ended when people in the community demand that Miss Field be dismissed from her job for corrupting David.

As Brinig lived in other worlds far removed from the one of his youth, he used Butte less and less for his settings. In *The Sisters*, a story of the fortunes of three Elliott sisters who grew up in Butte, the setting is shared with San Francisco, New York, and other places.[26] While Butte's openness and lack of social barriers is contrasted with other cities, especially New York, it is not a personal or real force in the story as it was in his earliest Butte books. *With Footsteps on the Stair* Brinig used Butte for the last time as the main setting.[27] The story begins in 1908 and carries forward over several decades. It is a tale of the melding of the heavily male world of the Jewish family of Moses and Nettie Benjamin with the female-dominated Irish family of John and Mary Joyce through the marriage of son Joseph Benjamin and daughter Anna Joyce. Some of the characters and incidents are reminiscent of earlier books, but there are some wonderfully new characters such as the witty and sarcastic John, the father of the Joyce family, and his obese and brilliant son, lawyer Charles. Butte is less vivid and without much character compared to earlier books. Brinig seems to have given in to nostalgia, to one more fond return to his home town. In the process, the decadence of *The Sun Sets in the West* gives way to a delightful eccentricity in most of the characters. Except for young Stephen Benjamin, who permanently leaves Butte to become a writer, other characters who leave Butte return to it as a place of repose.

Brinig's novels are without doubt the best that have been inspired by Butte. But they are not great novels. It disturbed Brinig that reviewers, while saying that he showed talent ("promise" in his earliest books), never bestowed unqualified praise on his books. There is no question that he had an eye and ear. His books are full of human drama, and some of his characters are powerful and memorable. He wrote about women sympathetically and with uncommon sensitivity. He was also among the first writers in the country to deal openly with male homosexuality. And some of his descriptions are beautiful. On the other hand, he had a tendency to overwrite to the point of prolixity. But that does not explain the fact that reviewers hesitated to endorse his work wholeheartedly. After all, not all great novelists were flawless writers. Brinig's Butte novels are anchored in historical fact, and mostly they ring with authenticity. What Brinig lacked was a world view with which to give the incidents of his stories real meaning. Neither historian nor novelist can let the facts speak for themselves.[28] Brinig is too detached, too aloof. He is, perhaps, like Harry in *The Man is My Brother*, for whom tradition was out of place in the modern world and had been replaced by the machine. However, with the loss of tradition Brinig appears to have been left with an enervating moral neutrality.

Between Brinig's *The Sisters* and *Footsteps on the Stair*, Clyde F. Murphy produced *The Glittering Hill*, one of the most successful of all Butte novels.[29] The book was widely reviewed, and within a few months of its release it was in its third printing. It won the first Lewis and Clark Northwest Contest prize awarded by E.P. Dutton and Company, the book's publisher. A Hollywood group headed by Sam Jaffe bought the movie rights, and rumors circulated that Humphrey Bogart would play the lead role. Murphy was born in Great Falls and raised in Anaconda. A graduate of the University of Montana Law School, Murphy in 1939 closed down a successful Los Angeles law practice of seventeen years to take up writing.[30] Murphy's title reflects a theme that runs through much of the writing about Butte: during the day it was unquestionably ugly, but Butte lights at night gave it a real charm.

The story involves several groups of characters who are brought together on the same train into Butte. There is the overly ambitious Nick Stryker who uses a family inheritance to stake himself for a gamble on a really big fortune in the mining business. Stryker is smitten by Evelyn Shannon of Chicago, fresh and virginal from a Catholic midwest girl's school, whose Uncle Pat is a good friend of Magnus Dunn (Marcus Daly), the hero of Butte's Irish. There are also Denny O'Shea and Tom Gary, young Irishmen from the Midwest who are seeking better-paying jobs than they could get at home. O'Shea is a happy-go-lucky hellion whose shenanigans endear him to irresponsible Irish saloon buddies. Tom is quiet, strong, stern, and determined to get ahead in this world as he flees a narrow and superstitious Irish background. O'Shea's wild escapades get him into serious scrapes from which the stoical Tom, loyal in his friendship, must extricate him—usually at cost to himself.

Murphy uses some historical devices which will appear familiar to those who know their Butte lore. Dunn is contrasted, needlessly so far as the story is concerned, with Walter M. Cole (William A. Clark). In Heinze fashion, Stryker uses Populism (which Murphy portrays as a mere laughable political phenomenon) to his own end of electing Judge Porky Sullivan, uses his control of the Carmelita mine to cut into the Python's ore, and introduces the eight-hour day to erode Dunn's popularity.

In a convincing way Murphy probes the world of Butte's Irish culture. He portrays the snobbery of the "Lace-Curtain Irish" toward their low-class compatriots while revealing that the rich have their problems, like what to do with their women who are oppressed by leisure. Within the wage earning class itself we see an intense pecking order. At all levels of the Irish community the author shows the problem of too much whiskey. Members of the working-class Irish are always clouting each other. Murphy's descriptions of violence are very graphic. In fact, this is one of the book's most salient features. The violence, debauchery, and general earthiness of the book produced rumors that it would be banned in Boston.[31] One reviewer cautioned readers to remember that Murphy was depicting the "lowest type of immigrant 'shanty' Irish."[32]

Murphy's writing shows a real feel for some aspects of everyday life in Butte in the 1890s. The reader is exposed to the workings of such important institutions as the boarding house, saloon, and wake. The story reveals how institutions, habits, and the rhythms of life give cohesion to the community. But Murphy also shows how the city was beset with serious social tensions. The barely submerged hostility of the Irish toward other national groups is especially evident. Corporate conflicts also divide the community, as Stryker and the Python Company use undercover agents to spy on friends as well as foes. Tensions mount when Stryker is able, momentarily, to weaken allegiance to Dunn, formerly the heroic symbol of the city's unity.

While some aspects of *The Glittering Hill* are convincing, the book is seriously flawed. The love story is ridiculous, and the women are characterless and unreal. More seriously, the story involves an improbable sequence of events and a reversion to the old plot formulas of the novels from earlier in the century. Stryker's uncontrolled ambition to succeed forces him to use pirated ore. His questionable ethics result in the death of Denny O'Shea and also mean that he cannot have the hand of the totally virtuous pasteboard heroine, Evelyn. He must be satisfied instead with marrying Ruby, the good whore. Tom, whose abstemiousness, discipline, and quiet loyalty to the Python Company make him suspect among the roistering Irish, jumps with one leap from mucker to mine manager and wins the heroine's hand. The wedding of Tom and Evelyn is a great rite of democracy which brings together, at least temporarily, all classes of the Irish into the union of a nuptial celebration.

Almost twenty years elapsed between Brinig's *Footsteps on the Stair* and the appearance of the penultimate Butte novel. Richard K. O'Malley's *Mile High Mile Deep* is an account of Butte during the Prohibition era.[33] The book has a heavy autobiographical flavor. The first half, titled "Summer," is a picaresque boy's tale as Dick, the narrator of the story, and his sidekick Frank roam the environs of Butte. In the process they undergo a series of adventures while the reader learns many details about life in Butte. This is a multilingual world in which English is the language of the school and polite society but for many families is not the language of the home. It is a world of gambling dens, whorehouses, saloons, and outside toilets. The city is peopled with characters dubbed with nicknames such as Dynamite the Dog, policeman Puddinhead VanPelt, swineherd Filthy McNabb, and some familiar to those who have been exposed to Butte lore such as Shoestring Annie, Nickle Annie, and police chief Jerry the Wise. We see the men dress up in freshly washed bib overalls, white shirts, and blue serge jackets for festive occasions such as Miners' Field Day at Columbia Gardens, Fourth of July Miners' Picnic at Nine Mile, or the Croation pre-Lenten Mesopust. But life is also punctuated by episodes of violence—suicide, fights, and accidents.

The second part of the book, "Winter," is suddenly a man's world as Dick and Frank take what they assume will be temporary jobs in the mines. The story contains a great deal about life below the surface, and the greenhorn reader learns about mining and the miner's jargon. Dick responds to this world by becoming lost in an abandoned mine, an episode O'Malley describes in good, scary writing. Dick also learns that this man's world is beset with problems for which there seem to be no easy solutions. The miners' union lacks solidarity and real vitality but nevertheless calls a strike, which begins as something of a holiday. But as it drags on this atmosphere dissipates and the situation becomes very ugly when management imports strikebreakers and gunmen. Meanwhile, Butte's union men try to coerce local scabs into staying away from work by breaking up their home furniture. This part of the book culminates in the death of Frank and others in a cage accident. It ends with Dick vowing that the mines, which by now have consumed several generations of men, will never get him.

O'Malley's book has authenticity. The pictures of Butte life in the twilight of the underground mining days are compelling. The reader gets the impression that the writing is based on firsthand experience. This can hardly be said of the most recent Butte book. *The Butte Polka* is among the least successful of Butte novels.[34] In some respects it is a reversion to the journalistic novels of the World War I period. Like some of those stories, the book deals with radicalism. The setting is 1946 and twenty-four-year-old Jimmy Mulholland is thrust into trying to solve the disappearance of his friend and brother-in-law Joel Kangas, a former Wobblie and long-standing anti-company radical. In his quest Jimmy is assisted by newspaper reporter Gail Stinson, with whom Jimmy, predictably, has an affair. The two find the remains in a steamboiler furnace. While there is a prime suspect, the perpetrators of the foul deed are not clearly established and brought to justice.

While earlier works of a similar sort deal with the strokes of luck and genius by which a hero becomes a self-made mining magnate, Butte-born author Donald McCaig tries to center his story on the lives of working people. Miners have been on the job about six months without a contract. There are repeated ominous rumors of an impending strike. The company tries to manipulate the situation by using toadies, informers, spies, and thugs. The reader is also exposed to the split between younger and more radical men and older union men, such as Jimmy's father, who have middle-class aspirations. Jimmy, who is supposed to be a night student at the School of Mines, hates work in the mines; but in the end he refuses to leave Butte and, like his father who is wracked by miner's consumption and dies in a mine disaster, will be trapped in an economic system that has little good to offer.

There are a few positive sides to the book. The one convincing episode is the love scene with Gail. For anyone who has read Murphy and O'Malley the wake scene will be familiar. But the author's description of the "keeners" at Joel's wake is good. There are also a few examples of Butte lingo which sound real: Joel's partner was "as quiet as a Protestant at a wake" and "The only thing dumber than a dumb miner is a smart cowboy." The latter was so good it had to be repeated.

But for the most part the book fails to convey any convincing sense of the lives of Butte wage earners. The book is hodgepodge of now well-worn Butte lore: barkeeps and madams, boozing and whoring, job insecurity, and a corporate power that deals heavy-handedly and stupidly with its opposition. All of this is thrown together without regard to historical sequence into an unconvincing plot. There are pointless digressions and occasional time sequences that become a disorganized mess. Much of the time the dialogue is senseless. Consequently, the characters are flat. There is not a memorable one in the book. Some of these failings might be overlooked were it not for the fact that the book is just plain dull.

If McCaig's book is the best that Butte can now inspire, it must stand as a symbol of Butte's decline. With the passing of the first phase of the metals industry, a major chapter in the state's history has drawn to a close. The variegated population and the boisterous way of life the industry once supported has faded. At its height Butte called forth a diverse collection of imaginative writings. The very number of books is impressive evidence of the fascination its once teeming life held for those who experienced it.

Except for Mary MacLane, who wrote about the city only as it related to her own egotism, those who wrote about Butte looked at different parts of the social structure. Up to Brinig's *Wide Open Town* writers focused on the romance of mining as a means by which the ambitious could achieve financial success. These first books reflect the fascination of earlier generations with the extraordinary historical figure—the Marcus Daly, William A. Clark, or even F. Augustus Heinze. By contrast, most of Brinig's Butte novels recreate the lives of people tied to a mercantile world in the late nineteenth century and the early decades of the twentieth century. In them we see the day-to-day world of shopkeepers and their families. *Wide Open Town* and the books by others since focus on the lives of wage earners. Except for O'Malley's *Mile*

High Mile Deep the more recent books describe mostly the lives of unmarried people rather than families.

Butte has not been the source of a great American book. In no one volume do the elements of literary greatness come together. However, some of the books are of lasting significance as historical documents of their times and others as reflections of historical fact. The writings of Mary MacLane, who is now being rediscovered, deserve recognition in the history of feminism.[35] Atherton's *Perch of the Devil* reflects some of the same themes and remains one of the Butte novels that should continue to attract readers. Similarly, Hammett's *Red Harvest* marks a recognizable turning point in the evolution of the genre of the detective story.

Because of their factual accuracy, the writings of Brinig, Murphy, and O'Malley are still worth reading. Above all, Brinig's books, especially the first two, come closest to being works of lasting literary merit. None of these authors deals profoundly with how the mining-metals economy shaped the lives of the working class—their hopes, fears, frustrations, victories, and defeats. But collectively, Brinig, Murphy, and O'Malley capture slices of the lives of men and women of the working class over several decades. From them contemporary readers can derive some notion of what life must have been like and share the experiences of earlier times.

NOTES

1. Joseph Kinsey Howard, *Montana High, Wide, and Handsome* (New Haven: Yale University Press, 1943); "Butte, City with a 'Kick' In It," in *Our Fair City*, ed. Robert S. Allen (New York: Vanguard Press, Inc., 1947); "What Happened in Butte," *Harper's Magazine*, 194 (August 1948), pp. 89–96.

2. There is some question about what books should be included in a discussion of Butte in fiction. The closest thing to an authoritative list appears in Mary Murphy and Bill Walker, *Butte, Montana: A Select Bibliography* (Butte: n.p., 1980), p. 47. This list misses a few novels. It also includes Dan Cushman, *The Old Copper Collar* (New York: Ballantine, 1957) which the following discussion does not. While Cushman's story is part of Butte lore in that it is based on the Clark-Daly feud, Butte does not really figure in the story, since the events transpire in Helena. The following discussion does include some references to the works of Mary MacLane which Murphy and Walker list under "Biography." MacLane's writings, while deeply self-centered, are not historical in the sense of being an attempt at conveying a factually true account of either Mary's own life

or events in the life of the city. Therefore, her works are included as "imaginative" writings. Butte lore is codified (and embellished) in *Copper Camp: Stories of the World's Greatest Mining Town Butte, Montana* (New York: Hastings House, 1943), one of the books produced by the Work Projects Administration's Montana Writers Project. A good sample of the pictoral record can be found in Don James, *Butte's Memory Book* (Caldwell, Idaho: Caxton Printers, Ltd., 1975). The best description of Butte in its heydey is chapter 4, "Boom Town," in Michael P. Malone, *The Battle for Butte: Mining and Politics on the Northern Frontier, 1864–1906* (Seattle and London: University of Washington Press, 1981), pp. 57–79.

3. Mary MacLane, *The Story of Mary MacLane* (Chicago: Herbert S. Stone and Company, 1902). The following discussion draws upon two complementary articles: Leslie A. Wheeler, "Mary MacLane: Montana's Shocking 'Litr'y Lady'," *Montana: The Magazine of Western History*, 27 (July 1977), pp. 20–33 ably discusses MacLane's life and works; Carolyn J. Mattern, "Mary MacLane: A Feminist Opinion," *Ibid.*, 27 (October 1977), pp. 54–63 places MacLane's writings in the context of the history of feminism.

4. Hamlin Garland, *Companions on the Trail: A Literary Chronicle* (New York: The Macmillan Company, 1931), p. 147.

5. *New York Times Saturday Review of Books and Art*, May 10, 1902, p. 314.

6. Robert J. Shores, *The Story of Willie Complain, by Himself* (Butte: Inter-Mountain Publishing Company, 1902), pp. 30, 31, 49.

7. Barbara Welter, "The Cult of True Womanhood: 1820–1860," *American Quarterly*, 18 (Summer 1966), p. 151.

8. Mary MacLane, *My Friend Annabel Lee* (Chicago: Herbert S. Stone and Company, 1903).

9. Mary MacLane, *I, Mary MacLane: A Diary of Human Days* (New York: Frederick A. Stokes Company, 1917).

10. Gertrude Atherton, *Perch of the Devil* (New York: Frederick A. Stokes Company, 1914). Discussions of Atherton can be found in: "Atherton, Gertrude Franklin (Horn), October 30, 1857–June 14, 1948," John A. Garraty and Edward T. James, eds., *Dictionary of American Biography Supplement Four 1941–1950* (New York: Charles Scribner's Sons, 1974), pp. 30–31; Elinor Richey, "The Flappers Were Her Daughters: The Liberated, Literary World of Gertrude Atherton," *American West*, 11 (July 1974), pp. 4–10, 60–63; Elinor Richey, *Eminent Women of the West* (Berkeley: Howell-North Books, 1975), pp. 97–123; Charlotte S. McClure, *Gertrude Atherton* (Boise, Idaho: Boise State University, 1976); and Leslie A. Wheeler, "Gertrude Atherton: Montana and the Lady Novelist," *Montana: The Magazine of Western History*, 27 (Winter 1977), pp. 40–51.

11. Charles Cleveland Cohan, *Born of the Crucible* (Boston: The Cornhill Company, 1919). Cohan was also author of the lyrics to "Montana", the state song. Cohan vertical file, Montana Historical Society.

12. George Wesley Davis, *Sulphur Fumes or In the Garden of Hell* (Los Angeles: the Times Mirror Press, 1923). The problem of inheritance in the novel appears to be based on an incident in Davis's life. Davis also wrote *Sketches of Butte* (Boston: The Cornhill Company, 1921).

13. Berton Braley, *The Sheriff of Silver Bow* (Indianapolis: The Bobbs-Merrill Company Publishers, 1921); *Shoestring* (New York: Sears Publishing Company, 1931).

14. Berton Braley, *Pegasus Pulls a Hack: Memoirs of a Modern Minstrel* (New York: Minton, Balch and Company, 1934), p. 264.

15. The journalistic novels reflect what Henry F. May called "The Nineteenth Century Intact." Henry F. May, *The End of American Innocence* (New York: Alfred A. Knopf, 1959), pp. 3–117.

16. John G. Cawelti, *Adventure, Mystery, and Romance: Formula Stories as Art and Popular Culture* (Chicago and London: The University of Chicago Press, 1976), p. 139. For a discussion of how this new formula with its twentieth-century urban western setting parallels the nineteenth-century rural cowboy and Indian formula see Joseph C. Porter, "The End of the Trail: The American West of Dashiell Hammett and Raymond Chandler," *The Western Historical Quarterly*, 6 (October 1975), pp. 411–424.

17. Dashiell Hammett, *Red Harvest* (New York: Alfred A. Knopf, Inc., 1929). Lillian Hellman, *Scoundrel Time* (Boston: Little, Brown, 1976), pp. 47–48.

18. Cawelti, *Adventure, Mystery, and Romance*, p. 173.

19. R. Francis James, *High, Low and Wide Open* (New York: The Macaulay Company, 1935).

20. Mertice M. James and Dorothy Brown, eds., *The Book Review Digest Thirty-Second Annual Cumulation March 1936 to February 1937 Inclusive* (New York: The H.W. Wilson Company, 1937), p. 793.

21. Brinig vertical files, Special Collections, Montana State University and Montana Historical Society.

22. Myron Brinig, *Singermann* (New York: Farrar and Rinehart, 1929).

23. Myron Brinig, *Wide Open Town* (New York: Farrar and Rinehart, 1931).

24. Myron Brinig, *This Man is My Brother* (New York: Farrar and Rinehart, 1932).

25. Myron Brinig, *The Sun Sets in the West* (New York: Farrar and Rinehart, 1935).

26. Myron Brinig, *The Sisters* (New York: Farrar and Rinehart, 1937). There are also incidental Butte scenes in two other Brinig books: *The Gambler Takes a Wife* (New York: Farrar and Rinehart, 1943) and *You and I* (New York and Toronto: Farrar and Rinehart, 1945).

27. Myron Brinig, *Footsteps on the Stair* (New York and Toronto: Rinehart and Company, Inc., 1950).

28. Jackson K. Putnam, "Historical Fact and Literary Truth: The Problem of

Authenticity in Western American Literature," *Western American Literature*, 15 (Spring 1980), pp. 17–23. Surprisingly, Brinig's novels, at least those set in Butte, have not attracted commentary. The one exception is Harry H. Jones, "The Mining Theme in Western Fiction," *University of Wyoming Publications*, 20 (July 1956), pp. 101–129.

29. Clyde F. Murphy, *The Glittering Hill* (New York: E.P. Dutton and Co., Inc., 1944).

30. Box 1 of the Clyde F. Murphy papers, University of Montana Archives and Special Collections, contains a voluminous scrapbook of reviews and news items.

31. *Saturday Review of Literature*, November 18, 1944, p. 18. *Saturday Review of Literature*, June 9, 1945, p. 23 has a cartoon showing *Glittering Hill* as one of four books for sale just beyond the Boston city limits.

32. *Saturday Review of Literature*, November 4, 1944, p. 23.

33. Richard K. O'Malley, *Mile High Mile Deep* (Missoula, Montana: Mountain Press Publishing Company, 1971).

34. Donald McCaig, *The Butte Polka* (New York: Rawson, Wade Publishers, Inc. 1980).

35. Patricia Meyer Spacks, *The Female Imagination* (New York: Alfred A. Knopf, 1975), pp. 171–181.

10 /

A MURMURING OF VOICES
Historic Preservation and the Search for Montana's Past

GEORGE M. LUBICK

Written histories and public monuments are traditional ways for nations and states to preserve the past. They constitute *ex post facto* documentation of events and personalities deemed important. Actual physical evidence of day-to-day life, however, has largely disappeared in America—lost to "progress" or decay. Surviving relics of the colonial or early national eras are exceptions, the products of chance, not purposeful preservation. Only in recent years have Americans come to appreciate the need to preserve buildings and artifacts characteristic of early social activities.

George Lubick, associate professor of History at Northern Arizona University, traces the preservation process in Montana since its origins in the 1940s. Begun by private parties interested in old Virginia City, the idea of preservation took hold in the 1950s and 1960s, when federal stimulation and state response produced the State Historic Preservation Office, now located at the Montana Historical Society and staffed by full-time professionals. The results—in properties preserved and sites documented—have been impressive. Future success depends heavily on federal funding rather than state commitment.

"We have our monuments, Williamsburgs, vast museums, historic houses, even our tombs, to remind us of our heritage," K. Ross Toole mused in the last pages of *The Rape of the Great Plains*. But such institutions, he continued, seemed "in some root kind of way, sterile," and attempts to "recreate" or commemorate our national heritage remained "somehow synthetic."[1] Montana's heritage, he suggested, could be better appreciated by avoiding "monuments," however grand and pains-takingly constructed, in favor of a visit to the barely visible, rutted re-mains of the Whoopup Trail, or to Elkhorn, a ghost town overlooking the Boulder Valley from its location high atop a nearby mountain. Few visitors to that deserted mining camp would notice more than rusted pieces of mining equipment, sagging buildings, and long-abandoned houses. "But listen carefully," Toole instructed his readers, "and you will hear with your inner ear, the sound of boots on the boardwalks, the sound of a piano, and everywhere the murmuring of voices."[2]

Ghost towns like Elkhorn eventually vanished; some were restored and carefully preserved, attracting tourists equipped with cameras and clad in tennis shoes, pink shorts, and golf hats. Toole wondered whether throngs of such visitors could gain much appreciation of Montana's unique heritage by wandering through restored mansions, ghost towns, or military forts. "Their noise destroys the capacity really to hear," he lamented, "and they cannot see for the seeing of their own day and their own kind."[3] His misgivings about carefully preserved sites, whether restoration projects or national parks, reflected the criticisms of others, from John Muir to Edward Abbey. In *Desert Solitaire*, for example, Ab-bey bemoans the "industrial tourism" exhibited by so many national park visitors, who refuse to leave their air-conditioned automobiles to experience the natural beauty of Arches National Park or any other scenic area. But such tourists, regardless of their attire and devotion to material culture, have largely determined the success of historic preser-vation over the last several decades. Without them, America would have little need for Colonial Williamsburg, Albuquerque's "Old Town," Montana's own Virginia City, or any of dozens of restored sites designated as "old" or "historic."

While such restored and frequently commercialized sites remain to some extent monuments or museums, they also function as windows in-to the past—perhaps the only means by which America's urban, highly mobile, and increasingly nonreading society can come in contact with its heritage. It is one thing to read history, John De Hass observes in *If These Walls Could Talk*, "but quite another to experience it walking the same streets and looking into the same rooms where it was made." And despite his aversion to monuments, Toole supported such projects as "worthwhile and educational."[4]

The need to provide Montana with just such an experience—to pre-serve some tangible evidence of the state's history—provided the impe-tus for Charles A. Bovey's reconstruction of Virginia City. Years before

Fairweather Inn, Virginia City, 1972. Courtesy K. Ross Toole Archives, Mansfield Library, University of Montana.

there was a National Trust for Historic Preservation or a National Register of Historic Places, Bovey began his efforts to restore Montana's territorial capital and the hub of placer mining and vigilante activity in Alder Gulch in the mid-1860s.

When restoration began in the late 1930s, Virginia City's buildings were only about eighty years old, and many of them dated back to the early days in Alder Gulch. The old part of town had never been devastated by fire, and its structures remained well preserved in Montana's semiarid climate. The area's bitter winters may have been a burden for the Gulch's residents, but the cold temperatures eliminated an infestation by termites and the threat they posed to wooden buildings. Snowfall, fortunately, had never caved in roofs.[5]

Bovey's decision to preserve the historic town was fortuitous. Virginia City could not have withstood the effects of weather indefinitely, nor could its historic buildings have counted on continued immunity from the forces of modern highway builders and developers. Highly sensitive to the heritage of the past and motivated by a sense of responsibility to preserve the details of mining camp life, Bovey had no intentions of purchasing buildings only to lock them up—a practice common to many privately restored sites. Instead, he and his wife foraged through dry goods and hardware stores, finding in obsolete inventories the authentic merchandise to furnish the restored commercial establishments of Virginia City.[6] As a result, Virginia City provides Americans with a tangible model of life during one of the most exciting and ephemeral periods in the history of the American West. The town's boom period from 1863 to 1865, the aspect of its life preserved by Bovey's restoration, accounts for only a small fraction of its 120-year history. But fully one-third of Virginia City's history has been shaped by restoration and preservation.[7]

Historic preservation was at best a vague concept in the late 1930s—not only in Montana but throughout the country. Scattered groups in the South and New England had achieved some notable successes. The Mount Vernon Ladies Association purchased George Washington's home in 1856, relying on funds solicited through a carefully organized campaign. This early project set a precedent for later generations of preservationists, who have focused on buildings associated with important figures and events. And the purpose of contemporary historic preservation also reflects the idealism of the Mount Vernon project—the hope to educate, motivate, and inspire Americans who visit such landmarks.[8]

The tendency to establish historic places like Mount Vernon as museums continued into the early twentieth century, when William Sumner Appleton established the Society to Preserve New England Antiquities. Concerned that so many of New England's eighteenth century buildings had deteriorated sadly over the years, Appleton was determined to save and restore as many as possible. Some of the structures lacked historical significance, but the S.P.N.E.A. hoped to preserve them for their unique and beautiful architecture. Because of the large number of buildings involved, the traditional museum approach was abandoned in favor of purchasing, restoring, and then selling the structures for use as private residences. In this way New England preservationists introduced in a primitive fashion the "adaptive use" concept of historic preservation.[9]

Preservation of historic districts, rather than single buildings, began in the late 1920s with the restoration of Williamsburg, the cultural and political capital of colonial Virginia. Generous funding from John D. Rockefeller, Jr. sustained this ambitious restoration, organized as an open air museum for the benefit of all Americans. Lacking such funding, other preservationists developed alternative means both to finance and protect their historic districts. Charleston, South Carolina, in 1931 developed a revolving fund to purchase, restore, and sell significant properties, while relying on strict covenants and historic district zoning to prevent the incursion of incompatible buildings. Later in the decade, New Orleans successfully employed such measures to restore and protect the Vieux Carré district.[10] Virginia City, later designated the Virginia City Historic District, could draw on the accomplishments of its predecessors in the South and East, and it shares the open air museum concept characteristic of historic district preservation.

For much of the twentieth century, local preservationists could count on little aid from the federal government. Washington had preserved scenic wonders in various national parks since 1872, and the 1906 American Antiquities Act directed Congress to preserve objects of historic or cultural interest located on federal land. President Theodore Roosevelt earned the lasting respect of preservationists when he used the 1906 statute to establish national monuments at Devil's Tower, Wyoming; Petrified Forest and Montezuma Castle in Arizona, and El Morrow, New Mexico.[11] In 1916, the administration of national parks and some national monuments was consolidated in the new National Park Service, but until the 1930s the organization's preservation activities remained limited to administering a few prehistoric and historic sites in the West.[12]

Franklin Roosevelt transferred historic sites belonging to the federal government to the National Park Service in 1933, and two years later Congress passed the Historic Sites and Buildings Act. The definitive legislation before the 1960s, the act established the preservation of historic sites as national policy and directed the secretary of Interior to secure data, conduct surveys, acquire property, enter into contracts, restore buildings, erect markers, and develop programs relating to the preservation of historic sites.[13] Another Roosevelt program, the Historic American Building Survey, employed architects to record through photographs and measured drawings the country's historic structures. Initially proposed as a six-month project, by 1941 the survey had collected 23,756 sheets of measured drawings and over 25,000 photographic negatives of 6,389 buildings.[14]

World War II brought a general halt in preservation activities, but the movement resumed in the late 1940s with the National Council for Historic Sites and Buildings, the predecessor of the National Trust for Historic Preservation. Established in 1949, the National Trust sought to stimulate public participation in the preservation of historic sites, buildings, and objects of national significance. The organization was empowered to receive donations of sites, buildings, and objects and to administer them for public benefit.[15]

Establishment of the National Trust represented a landmark for historic preservation, but on the state level comparatively little had been accomplished. In Montana, responsibility for the conservation of scenic, archeological, scientific, and recreational resources rested with the State Parks Division of the Highway Department, which could acquire for the state any sites and objects which its officials felt should be improved or maintained as state monuments or historic sites. In addition to supervising Montana's state parks, the Highway Department had erected roadside markers along principal highways with highly readable texts by author Robert H. Fletcher.[16] Such historic place markers represented only a minor commitment to historic preservation, but they effectively informed both tourist and native Montanans of important sites throughout the state.

The Montana Historical Society was equally active in conserving the state's historical resources, primarily through collecting manuscripts, documents, and other materials pertinent to historical research. Beginning in the 1950s, the historical society, under the directorship of K. Ross Toole, also operated the newly constructed museum in Helena which housed the Charles M. Russell collection of bronzes and paintings. The society, however, was excluded from most activities concerning preservation of historic sites. The director of the historical society was not a member of the State Parks Division, and the trustees of the society lacked authority to acquire historical sites except through donations or gifts.[17]

A variety of local groups, primarily county historical societies and such organizations as the Daughters of the American Revolution, marked historic sites from time to time. In Fort Benton, local residents sought to preserve the remains of the original fort, and a similar group was actively marking Indian and U.S. troop positions on the Bear Paw Mountain Battlefield. The Beaverhead County Museum Association purchased the Bannack townsite and also established a small museum in Dillon. The Yellowstone County Historical Society and several other local associations also demonstrated an interest in preserving historic sites.[18] But their activities were exceptions to the general lack of historic preservation in the state. More often than not, important sites had been destroyed over the years. The old Paul McCormick home in Billings, an

1888 Victorian structure regarded as one of eastern Montana's outstanding residences, was leveled to make room for an office building. Farm buildings were constructed over the site of Fort Ellis near Bozeman, and old Fort Custer became part of a golf course. Fort Peck Reservoir inundated a number of locations associated with the Lewis and Clark Expedition and with early steamboating on the Missouri River, but officials failed to conduct a survey of such sites before beginning construction of the dam. Periodic floods on the Missouri had buried old forts from the fur trade era, and wind erosion badly damaged adobe structures at Fort Benton and Fort C. F. Smith.[19]

While state and local preservationists had accomplished comparatively little outside of Bovey's continuing work on Virginia City, the federal government had not neglected its role in historic preservation. The National Park Service administered two important sites at Custer Battlefield National Monument and Big Hole National Monument. In addition, the site of the 1877 Battle of the Bear Paw Mountains was owned by the federal government, while the Bureau of Indian Affairs operated the Museum of the Plains Indians at Browning.[20]

Before Montana could begin restoring or preserving its historic sites and buildings, it first had to find them. The stimulus for developing an inventory of state historic sites came from the National Park Service as part of a larger survey of the recreational resources in the Missouri River Basin in the mid-1950s. National Park Service Historian Ray H. Mattison supervised the survey of Montana's historic sites and relied upon K. Ross Toole and personnel at the state historical society for advice. The resulting list of places "Worthy of Preservation" included only twenty-eight historic sites which were placed in six broad categories. Pompey's Pillar, Fort McKenzie, and Fort Benton comprised the extent of Montana's role in exploration and the fur trade, while the missions of St. Paul, St. Xavier, and the Holy Family were evidence of its participation in the Indian frontier. Sites relating to the military frontier included the Custer, Big Hole, Bear Paw, and Rosebud Battlefields, along with Forts Shaw, Assinniboine, Keogh, and C. F. Smith. The I. G. Baker Store in Fort Benton, the Bedford Mill near Townsend, and the Grand Union Hotel in Fort Benton reflected the growth of commerce and industry in the state. Under the heading of "Cultural" were four Helena buildings—Ming's Opera House and the homes constructed by T. C. Power, Joseph K. Toole, and Samuel T. Hauser. Robbers' Roost near Laurin defied categorization and was simply listed as "miscellaneous." In addition to the twenty-eight places designated as worth preserving, Mattison's report listed fourteen sites for the placement of historic markers.[21]

Mattison's "preliminary inventory" was not an exhaustive survey of Montana's historic sites since it was limited to the Missouri River Basin. But the document indicated the state's neglect of its historic places and recommended a general expansion of preservation activities, not only by the state but also by local organizations most familiar with sites in their vicinity. In particular, Mattison recommended that the state take advantage of the growing tourist trade to increase visits to its historic sites. And towns like Helena and Fort Benton, he noted, needed surveys to determine which buildings merited preservation. Since many of these structures were built between 1880 and 1900, Mattison advised that some might qualify for the Historic American Building Survey.[22] Montana was one of several states not represented in the survey, and the inclusion of any of its historic buildings would clearly promote the cause of preservation. HABS distributed no funds, but it requested the plans of historic buildings for the Library of Congress and awarded owners a certificate citing their property's historic value.

While Mattison's report contained a useful, early inventory of sites, a number of other factors continued to hamper historic preservation in Montana. Public indifference remained an enduring problem, and the lack of funds invariably impeded progress on the few projects undertaken. Like most states, Montana had no central agency that was even aware of the diverse activities, much less capable of providing any direction. No group of professionals had been designated to review preservation plans to ensure that existing standards were met.[23]

The state's immense distances and the small size of its towns presented an additional difficulty. The widely dispersed communities usually lacked funds for restoration work, and distances hampered effective communication among preservation groups. "The number of people which can be gathered on any one occasion to give enthusiasm and encouragement is limited," a state official complained in 1970.[24]

With state offices providing relatively little encouragement or leadership, historic preservation in Montana relied extensively on the initiative of local organizations. Historical societies flourished in some counties, particularly in Yellowstone County, where Billings residents undertook development of a civic gallery. Restoration of Virginia City and nearby Nevada City continued under private direction, while Great Falls established its Russell Gallery. By the end of the 1960s,

Montana boasted forty community museums as well as a state organization, the Montana Association of Museums. The growth of the Montana Institute of the Arts and the Montana Archeological Society provided additional sources of expertise for preservation projects. Local residents also initiated the restoration of "old town" in Great Falls, while St. Mary's Church in Stevensville and St. Ignatius Church benefitted from local care and the support of state and regional Catholic organizations. The major preservation activity of state government focused on the development of Headwaters State Monument at the Three Forks of the Missouri.[25]

Historic preservation in Montana received its greatest impetus in 1966 with passage of the National Historic Preservation Act, one of four major pieces of preservation law passed by the Eighty-ninth Congress. The new law broadened the national preservation policy of the Department of Interior and provided important new tools for its implementation, among them an expanded National Register of districts, sites, buildings, structures, and objects significant in American history, architecture, archeology, and culture. The expanded Register provided Washington with a record of the national patrimony that merited preservation and also served as a guide to aid preservationists in determining which properties deserved restoration and protection.[26]

In addition to continuing existing programs, the law sought to identify signficant state and local properties. States were given the responsibility to conduct surveys, compile registers, and nominate properties to the secretary of Interior for inclusion in the National Register. Criteria for the latter were broadly framed to permit considerable latitude for professional evaluation, and state governments also were required to nominate evaluators and advisory boards. Another section of the law provided for an Advisory Council on Historic Preservation to inform the president about administrative and legislative matters to enhance preservation policy. The Advisory Council also retained the major responsibility for safeguarding National Register properties.[27]

Perhaps the most important aspect of the National Historic Preservation Act was the program of grants-in-aid to states to help finance surveys of historic sites, statewide preservation plans, and individual projects. Both public and private property qualified for grants so long as it was listed on the National Register, consistent with the state preservation plan, and approved by the secretary of Interior. At that time, fourteen historic sites in Montana were listed on the Register.[28]

Montana officials reacted quickly to the provisions of the Historic

Preservation Act. Late in 1966, Governor Tim Babcock designated the Fish and Game Commission as the state agency responsible for preparing surveys, receiving grants, and generally carrying out a state preservation plan. The chief of the commission's Recreation and Parks Division then contacted local historical societies and public service groups, requesting information about historically significant property in their localities. Because only a few dozen organizations replied, the state engaged Robert A. Murray as a historical consultant to prepare an inventory of historic sites that met the criteria for inclusion on the National Register.[29]

In preparing his inventory, Murray selected sites to reflect various phases in Montana's history, including the Indian frontier, the fur trade, the Lewis and Clark Expedition, missionary activity, mining, the military frontier, river transportation, and trails. In all, he proposed sixty-seven sites for Registered National Historic Landmark status, in addition to the Helena Historic District, the Pryor Mountains Historical and Archeological District, and several related sites at the mouth

Isdel Mercantile Building, Pony, MT, 1972. Courtesy K. Ross Toole Archives, Mansfield Library, University of Montana.

of the Judith River. Another sixty properties were judged as meeting the National Register criteria for either state or local significance.[30]

During the next two years, Montana established a Governor's Advisory Committee for the Preservation of Historic Sites and also submitted its official Historic Preservation Plan to the National Park Service, fulfilling two of the requirements of the National Historic Preservation Act. Developed by the Fish and Game Commission, the Governor's Advisory Committee, and Robert H. Fletcher, the *Montana Historic Preservation Plan* of 1970 was described as a "comprehensive survey of historic sites," and its authors intended that the document serve as a state guide for future preservation activities. The appointment of a preservation review committee soon followed, drawing its members from the ranks of professional historians, architects, and archeologists. Its major task concerned the review of restoration and preservation plans to ensure that such projects met state and federal guidelines.[31]

The prospect of receiving matching grants-in-aid from Washington provided much of the incentive for historic preservation in Montana. Upon acceptance of the Montana Historic Preservation Plan by the director of the National Park Service, Montana could then nominate properties to the National Register from its inventory of historic sites. Once listed in the Register, the sites then became eligible for the matching federal funds, and restoration and preservation work could begin in earnest. The federal assistance for historic preservation and the ensuing state planning came at a propitious time in Montana's history. Not yet a century old, much of its past was still within the memory of its older residents. The future promised accelerated change, making it important to begin an extensive preservation program "while the past still lingers within our grasp." While preservation of a historic site was not the sole means of understanding the past, the philosophy of preservation in Montana was based on the "inspirational experience" of a visit to a site of historical importance. Such a "glimpse of history" might inspire or sadden, one preservation official explained, but it invariably caused a person to pause and reflect on the present and the future.[32]

In developing guidelines for its preservation program, the advisory committee and its associates emphasized the need for proper research to guarantee the authenticity of any contemplated project. They defined "historically signficant" to mean an event "of such importance that it became a turning point in history or which had a major influence on subsequent events." In other fields—architecture, archeology, culture —preservation might include sites that were deemed "representative or typical of an era or a field of endeavor." Generally, the state sought to develop a balanced program with appropriate attention given to all elements of Montana's historic and cultural background. Actual preservation was to receive preference over reconstruction and restoration, and the protection of a historic site was interpreted to mean inclusion of the national landscape as well as buildings.[33]

Included in the preservation plan of 1970 was a historic sites inventory of 310 locations, many of them taken from Murray's earlier compilation. Southeastern, southwestern, and north-central Montana counted the largest number of sites, with the remainder scattered across the state map. Most of the state's historical buildings were located in the capital city of Helena.

Historic preservation was not the sole preserve of the Governor's Advisory Committee and the Fish and Game Commission. Eighteen additional federal and state agencies shared to some degree in the preservation of historic sites. In some instances, the operation of such agencies directly threatened historic sites; on other occasions they clearly complemented the program. The Soil Conservation Service, for example, occasionally began construction projects unaware of the existence of a historic site. To limit damage caused by such negligence, the agency began developing policies to identify historic sites and to consider the public interest in preservation. The Army Corps of Engineers, the target of criticism from environmentalists over the years, frequently found historic sites impeding its projects. Although the corps had overlooked environmental and historic issues in the past, by 1970 it emphasized that current policy considered "all aspects of historical, geological, archeological, paleontological, architectural, cultural, ecological, and other sites with regard to their preservation or development for human needs."[34]

Another agency often damned by environmental groups and preservationists, the Federal Highway Administration, acquired a distinct responsibility for historic preservation through the 1966 Department of Transportation Act and the Federal-Aid Highway Act, both passed by the "Preservation Congress." The laws declared that special efforts be made to preserve the natural beauty of the countryside, public parks, recreational lands, wildlife and waterfowl refuges, and historic sites. If federal transportation projects threatened such land, the secretary of transportation and the federal highway administrator were required to consider alternative plans to avoid or minimize damage.[35] The Department of Housing and Urban Development had similar responsibilities for historic preservation and also operated a number of programs important to protecting and maintaining historic sites. Included among HUD's administrative responsibilities were urban renewal projects with funds to acquire and restore historic and architecturally valuable buildings, urban renewal demonstration grants, and grants for historic preservation. The Demonstration Cities and Metropolitan Development Act of 1966 provided an additional asset to historic preservation in urban areas, since it relaxed restrictions on the use of urban renewal funds for historic preservation and authorized several new programs.[36]

Like HUD, the Army Corps of Engineers, and the Federal Highway Administration, other agencies acquired broad commitments to the preservation movement. In Montana, responsibility for historic preservation extended to the U.S. Forest Service, the Bureau of Sport Fisheries and Wildlife, the Bureau of Reclamation, and the Bureau of Land Management, among others; state offices with similar authority were the Montana Historical Society, the Office of State Forester, the Montana Highway Commission, the Montana Water Resources Board, the State Board of Lands and Development, the Bicentennial Commission, and the Montana Arts Council.[37]

Assured of federal funding by 1970, Montana embarked on a ten-year program of historic preservation, designed to be both comprehensive and balanced. Its long-range goals focused on the preservation of historic sites of the greatest importance to the state and nation, as well as architectural, archeological, and cultural property deemed significant. Specific projects considered for the 1970s were the marking of the Lewis and Clark Trail, preservation of several sites at the mouth of the Judith River, and similar work on the Big Horn Post and other sites at the mouth of the Big Horn River.[38]

State officials also announced a short-term plan to be undertaken within three years. The Bannack Historic District, Pictograph Cave, Chief Plenty Coups Memorial, Beaverhead Rock, the Chief Joseph Battleground of the Bear Paw Mountains, the Three Forks of the Missouri, and the Two Medicine Fight location were all scheduled for preservation work in fiscal years 1972 and 1973. Estimated costs for the acquisition, rehabilitation, restoration, and protection of the seven sites amounted to $160,000, with the largest sums going to Bannack ($50,000) and Pictograph Cave ($40,000).[39]

The combination of federal legislation and the enthusiasm generated by the 1970 Preservation Plan enhanced the cause of preservation in

Montana, and by 1975 the state could point to considerable success. Thirty-four Montana locations were added to the National Register in the four years following the Preservation Plan, and the National Park Service expanded its activities with the acquisition of the Grant-Kohrs Ranch for future development. Another federal agency, the Bureau of Land Management, undertook the preservation of the ghost town of Garnet.[40]

State government had been active as well, designating as state monuments the Bannack Historic District, Pictograph Cave, the Three Forks Site, Chief Joseph Battleground in the Bear Paws, Chief Plenty Coups Memorial, the Madison Buffalo Jump, the Ulm Pishkun, the Medicine Rocks site, Fort Owen, and the Makoshika archeological site at Glendive. Local governments had also taken the initiative in preserving historic sites in their localities. Fort Benton adopted a comprehensive preservation plan for the city and also acquired the Kluge House. The City of Wibaux drew up plans for preservation of the home of early Montana cattleman, Pierre Wibaux, while in Virginia City the preservation of Madison County Court House was financed by a historic sites grant-in-aid. The 1875 building represented a particularly important example of neoclassical New England architecture, and county officials had carefully preserved its facade.[41] Preservation of sites by private individuals was equally impressive. To such older sites as Pompey's Pillar and the missions at St. Mary's and St. Ignatius were added W. A. Clark's "Copper King" mansion, Camp Disappointment near Browning, the Fort Logan Blockhouse, and the site of the Battle of the Rosebud.[42]

The grants-in-aid programs for preservation of historic sites had been particularly helpful in Montana's preservation program. Although funding had been modest, it was sufficient to help acquire Beaverhead Rock, along with several properties at the Bannack and Fort Benton historical districts. A dozen historical buildings in Helena benefitted from such funding, and preservation officials in 1975 estimated that over $1,000,000 would be committed to exterior restoration in the state's capital city.[43]

Between 1970 and 1975, historic preservation in Montana had acquired a considerable public following. Newspaper accounts of the vandalism of ghost towns and desecrations of archeological sites were particularly effective in stimulating public concern. The 1973 legislature passed the Montana Antiquities Act, which established a state historic register and extended protection to registered properties and to all sites on state-controlled land. It also authorized agreements to protect sites on private land, if the owners desired it. In the years following the 1970 Historic Preservation Plan, Montana twice revised its inventory of historic sites. The 1975 survey expanded the earlier list of sites to embrace over 2,700 locations.[44]

While accomplishments in the early 1970s appeared substantial, Montana's preservation program, in reality, was limited. Staff shortages hampered efforts severely, and the limited funds restricted inventory work and reduced the state's ability to protect historic sites. Frequently, the latter task was added to the duties of state game wardens. The state had not yet developed a standardized system to determine the feasibility of preserving specific sites and resources. Consequently, field personnel and owners of historic properties lacked guidelines for use in preliminary evaluations of sites.[45]

Acts of vandalism became increasingly common, as "weekend doorknob hunters" and commercial pot hunters pilfered sites. On other occasions, preservationists witnessed the destruction of historic buildings to make room for modern structures, and archeologists found ancient pictographs covered with spray paint. While intensive enforcement of laws against vandalism suggested a short-term solution, such incidents indicated a continuing lack of public understanding and support for preservation. State officials hoped to remedy these problems through an educational program to explain the values of historic preservation and to stimulate additional participation.[46]

More serious than vandalism was the lack of coordination and communication—"the greatest incipient danger to Montana's historic preservation program," according to one source. State agencies had grown in size, and projects frequently produced far-reaching and unanticipated consequences. Compounding such problems was the large number of local, federal, and state agencies involved in preservation and their lack of knowledge about procedures. The problem was partially solved by the 1969 Environmental Protection Act which required federal officials to cooperate with state historic preservation officers. Distribution of the State Preservation plans to state and local agencies also increased awareness of the state's commitment to preservation and encouraged some coordination of efforts.[47]

As Montana preservationists initiated projects and expanded surveys in the 1970s, they encountered unanticipated difficulties. Even in Montana, with its small population spread across a wide expanse of territory, population pressure had a decided impact. New demands on state resources and the increased need for additional water storage facilities

Gillian Hall (left) and Fraternity Hall, Elkhorn, MT. Courtesy Don Miller, Western Montana Ghost Town Preservation Society. Courtesy K. Ross Toole Archives, Mansfield Library, University of Montana.

threatened historical resources. Owners of recreational vehicles damaged the terrain and vandalized archeological sites, while urban sprawl and urban renewal projects destroyed important historic sites.[48]

Strip mining of coal reserves in eastern Montana presented a major problem for preservationists in the 1970s. While energy companies quickly drew up plans for the extraction of Montana coal, neither the state nor private groups undertook a survey of the area's archeological sites. The acute conflict between resource use and historic preservation left no middle ground. "A site will be either destroyed or saved"; the 1975 Historic Preservation Plan noted, "a choice must be made."[49]

Owners of historic buildings and other properties also encountered impediments to their restoration work. The repairing of old buildings, many of them learned, was exceedingly expensive. State government could provide them with no financial aid because it was prohibited from granting money to private organizations or individuals. Consequently, even the owners of Pompey's Pillar and other National Historic

Landmark properties had to finance restoration and preservation expenses from their own resources. State officials hoped to remedy the problem by proposing a state-funded loan program to aid such private restorations.[50]

By the mid-1970s state officials had alleviated some of the most pressing problems. A professional historian had been hired on a temporary basis, and negotiations were underway to secure the services of an archeologist on an "on-call" basis. The Archeological Survey was designated for incorporation in the Preservation Office, and funding increases allowed the director of the Recreation and Parks Division to expand its preservation staff. To enhance cooperation among state agencies, officials planned to offer "historic preservation workshops" and scheduled the first session at the Fish and Game Department. With the hiring of additional personnel, the state anticipated adding 300–500 properties, most of them archeological sites, to the state inventory. The Governor's Advisory Council approved the nominations of thirty sites to the State Register and thirty-five to the National Register in the 1975–1976 fiscal year.[51]

Congress provided additional financial aid for preservation with the Tax Reform Act of 1976 and the Revenue Act of 1978 which granted tax advantages to owners of commercial and income-producing historic properties who undertook the rehabilitation of such structures. Two years later President Jimmy Carter signed the National Historic Preservation Act Amendments, thereby authorizing the historic preservation program through 1987. The new legislation represented the first significant modifications in the state-federal historic preservation program since 1966. Owners of private sites or buildings listed in the National Register were now given an opportunity either to object to, or concur in, the inclusion of their property. The Amendments also authorized distribution of grants from the Historic Preservation Fund on the basis of programs rather than specific projects, and for survey and planning activities a seventy percent federal/thirty percent state matching grant was available. The new legislation also reflected an important change of attitude toward historic preservation; federal agencies henceforth were required to view preservation as an "active" rather than reactive part of their responsibilities.[52]

Major changes had occurred in Montana in the meantime. Administration of historic preservation was transferred from the Fish and Game Department to the Montana State Historic Preservation Office in the Historical Society. The governor designated the director of the Historical Society as the State Preservation Officer, while actual operation of the office was managed by his deputy who also functioned as the staff historian. The 1979 Montana Antiquities Act assigned to the new office the tasks of securing federal money for preservation, conducting a continuous survey of historic resources, and maintaining an inventory of heritage properties and paleontological remains. The State Historic Preservation Office also nominated Register properties, annually reviewed the state preservation plan, disseminated information, and assisted state agencies and individuals in preservation activities.[53]

While the new office could rely on the groundwork laid by its predecessor, it was, in fact, a new office and did not immediately acquire a full complement of professionals. Local preservationists around the state were slow to recognize that the state's preservation activities were housed in a new agency and that some procedures had changed. The transition caused some frustration, leading one state official to explain: "We are still fighting for contacts, wide name recognition, and chances to assure people that changes we propose are rational and will be seen in the context of previous official decisions."[54]

A related problem concerned the lack of university personnel, architects, planners, and engineers who understood that historic preservation involved planning to cover a wide range of sites. Too frequently such people and local historical associations thought of preservation as "embalming." Consequently, many ardent proponents never really understood the issues involved in complying with state and federal standards. For many Montanans, the tasks associated with nominating sites for the National Register seemed to be a "difficult, Federally complicated, relatively unrewarding process." When Washington declared a moratorium on nominations to the National Register of privately owned property, preservation efforts in Montana sustained a serious blow. When combined with uncertainty about federal grants in the early 1980s, the moratorium meant that "Registration, as a tool in the preservation process, has virtually disappeared."[55]

While such restrictions undoubtedly frustrated personnel at the Historic Preservation Office, the new organization could point to substantial achievements. An inventory of historic bridges provided a record of more than 400 structures, 80 of which were identified as eligible for the National Register. In 1979, Livingston initiated a historic resources survey, the first of its kind in the state, and by the fall of 1981 twenty community historical and architectural surveys were in progress around the state.[56]

Perhaps the major achievement was the heightened visibility of the Historic Preservation Office. Through publication of a preservation supplement to *The Montana Post*, the newsletter of the historical society, information about historical preservation was widely disseminated. Beginning in August 1980, *Preservation* reached the 9,000 members of the Montana Historical Society, and additional copies were sent to architects, planners, and local officials. The Preservation Office also increased its educational and technical assistance efforts, hoping that generating enthusiasm for historic preservation might stimulate additional public support. In 1981, state preservationists presented twenty programs on the purposes of historic preservation, the activities of the Historic Preservation Office, historic architecture, and related topics.[57]

Although preservation officials in Helena worried about the public's perception of historic preservation and complained about the shortage of professional personnel, the real threat to Montana's preservation program came from America's newly elected, financially conservative president, Ronald Reagan. His proposed budget for fiscal year 1982 eliminated funding for State Historic Preservation Offices and for "re-grant" restoration projects and surveys. Funding was not simply trimmed; one preservationist moaned, "It has been eliminated." Reagan's retrenchment did not eliminate earlier regulations, but his proposed budget threatened to halt over forty years of successful work in Montana. In the spring of 1981, state officials were left wondering whether Montana would assume direct control of its historic resources, forfeit them to the Interior Department, or leave their existence to chance.[58]

For more than four decades, historic preservation in Montana had grown slowly and haltingly. Most restoration and preservation projects began through the initiative of local organizations and individuals, and the state did not even possess a rudimentary list of its historic resources until Mattison's 1955 inventory. Not until the federal government entered the preservation field in 1966 did Montana develop an extensive program to identify, inventory, restore, and preserve its heritage properties. The National Register listed only fourteen Montana sites in 1966, but the number of Montana properties grew each year. By 1971 the total had doubled, and in the Bicentennial year seventy-two state sites were included. The decade of the seventies closed with 111 National Register properties located in Montana, and the state's continuing survey included hundreds of other historically important locations.[59]

Such numbers suggest that the state's preservation program has been a major success, particularly considering that most of its preservation activity occurred in the sixteen years following the National Historic Preservation Act. Equally important, the accelerated pace of preservation after 1966 emphasizes the continuing need for federal financial assistance. The future of Montana's preservation program naturally requires state support and participation by local groups. But federal grants initially stimulated the movement, and they will largely determine its future successes—or failure.

NOTES

1. K. Ross Toole, *The Rape of the Great Plains: Northwest America, Cattle and Coal* (Boston: Little, Brown and Co., 1976), p. 240.

2. *Ibid.*, p. 241–42.

3. *Ibid.*, p. 242.

4. John N. DeHass, Jr., ed., *If These Walls Could Talk: The History of the Buildings of Virginia City* (n.p.: Montana Ghost Town Preservation Society, 1977), p. 2; Toole, *Rape of the Great Plains*, p. 241.

5. DeHass, *If These Walls Could Talk*, p. 3.

6. *Ibid.*, p. 2; *Ghost Towns of the West*, text and photographs by William Carter (Menlo Park, California: Lane Magazine and Book Co., 1971), p. 7.

7. DeHass, *If These Walls Could Talk*, p. 3

8. *With Heritage So Rich: A Report of a Special Committee on Historic Preservation under the Auspices of the United States Conference of Mayors* (New York: Random House, 1966), pp. 37–38.

9. *With Heritage So Rich*, p. 41.

10. *Ibid.*, pp. 46, 59–60.

11. Alfred Runte, *National Parks: The American Experience* (Lincoln, Nebraska: University of Nebraska Press, 1979), pp. 71–72.

12. Horace M. Albright, *Origins of National Park Service Administration of Historic Sites* (Philadelphia: Eastern National Park & Monument Association, 1971), p. 1; Runte, *National Parks*, pp. 103–105.

13. S.K. Stevens et al., "The Federal Responsibility in Historic Preservation," *Historic Preservation* 20 (1968): 9; Charles E. Peterson, "Historic Preservation: Some Significant Dates," *Antiques* 89 (February 1966): 232.

14. Charles E. Peterson, "Thirty Years of HABS," *AIA Journal* (Nov. 1963): 83–84.

15. *With Heritage So Rich*, p. 49; for a detailed account of the history of the National Trust, see David E. Finley, *History of the National Trust for Historic Preservation* (Washington, D.C.: National Trust for Historic Preservation, 1965).

16. U.S., Department of Interior, National Park Service, "Preliminary Report on Historic Sites of Montana in the Missouri River Basin," by Ray H. Mattison. (Washington, D.C., 1955), pp. 37–38, 44.

17. Mattison, "Preliminary Report," p. 37; Montana Department of Fish and Game, Recreation and Parks Division, *Montana Historic Preservation Plan* 2nd ed., vol. I (Helena, Montana, 1975), p. 70.

18. Mattison, "Preliminary Report," pp. 38, 45.

19. *Ibid.*, pp. 41–42, 45.

20. *Ibid.*, p. 43.

21. *Ibid.*, pp. 22–27.

22. *Ibid.*, pp. 46–48.

23. Montana Department of Fish and Game, *The Montana Historic Preservation Plan* (Helena, Montana, 1970), p. 8.

24. *Montana Historic Preservation Plan*, 1970, p. 9.

25. *Ibid.*, pp. 8–9.

26. Robert M. Utley, "Federal Historic Preservation Programs," *History News* 22 (1967): 214–215.

27. *Ibid.*, p. 215.

28. *Ibid.*, pp. 215–216; Montana, State Historic Preservation Office, "Preservation Funding Request" (Helena, Montana, 1981), p. 6. The sites listed on the National Register in 1966 included: Bannack Historic District, Big Hole National Battlefield, Butte Historic District, Camp Disappointment, Charles M. Russell House and Studio, Custer Battlefield National Monument, Fort Benton, Great Falls Portage, Hagen Site, Pictograph Cave, Pompey's Pillar, Three Forks of the Missouri, Traveler's Rest, and Virginia City Historic District.

29. *Montana Historic Preservation Plan*, 1970, pp. 17–19; Robert A. Murray, "A Montana Historic Sites Inventory" (n.p., September 1968), p. 1.

30. Robert A. Murray, "A Summary Listing of National Register Proposals for the State of Montana, As a Component of the Montana Historic Sites Inventory" (n.p., September 1968), pp. 1–8.

31. *Montana Historic Preservation Plan*, 1970, pp. i–ii, 10.

32. *Ibid.*, pp. 10–12.

33. *Ibid.*, pp. 15–16.

34. *Ibid.*, pp. 87–88, 90–91.

35. *Ibid.*, pp. 91–93; Utley, "Federal Historic Preservation Programs," p. 214.

36. *Montana Historic Preservation Plan*, 1970, pp. 93–97; Utley, "Federal Historic Preservation Programs," p. 214.

37. *Montana Historic Preservation Plan*, 1970, pp. 88–89, 97–107.

38. *Montana Historic Preservation Plan*, 1970, pp. 110–111.

39. Montana Fish and Game Department, "The Montana Historic Preservation Plan: Short-Term Program" (Helena, 1970), pp. 1–2.

40. *Montana Historic Preservation Plan*, 1975, I, p. 47; MSHPO, "Preservation Funding Request," pp. 6–7.

41. *Montana Historic Preservation Plan*, 1975, I, pp. 47–49.

42. *Ibid.*, pp. 49–50.

43. *Ibid.*, p. 51.

44. *Ibid.*, 61, 71–72, vol. III, pp. 25–26.

45. *Ibid.*, I, p. 62.

46. *Ibid.*, p. 62.

47. *Ibid.*, p. 62.

48. *Ibid.*, p. 62.

49. *Ibid.*, p. 62.

50. *Ibid.*, pp. 62–63.

51. *Ibid.*, III, pp. 30–33; Montana, Historic Sites and Antiquities Advisory Council, Meeting Summaries, 1967–1976, pp. 11–14.

52. *Montana Post Preservation*, November-December 1980, p. 4; February-March 1981, p. 4.

53. *Ibid.*, August-September 1980, p. 4; MSHPO, "Preservation Funding Request," pp. 2–3.

54. Montana, State Historic Preservation Office, Survey and Planning; "Applications, Approvals, Information, FY 82, Part III: Program Overview," p. 3.

55. *Ibid.*, pp. 2, 5.

56. MSHPO, FY 82, "Program Overview," p. 1; *Montana Post Preservation*, August-September 1981, p. 1.

57. MSHPO, FY 82, "Program Overview," p. 1.

58. MSHPO, "Preservation Funding Request," pp. 1–2.

59. *Ibid.*, pp. 6–8.

11 /

AN UNCOMMON HAND
The Writings of K. Ross Toole

No one will ever compile an exhaustive list of the writings of K. Ross Toole. Not even Toole himself could remember all the items he had written. He kept few copies of his personal letters; he wrote unsigned columns and fillers for historical magazines and museum journals; he even reviewed books pseudonymously. Sometimes he sent magazine copy off without saving carbons, and no record appears in his personal effects. He wrote letters to newspaper editors, innumerable speeches which were never published, and countless lectures, addresses, introductions, and book prefaces. No effort has been made here to track down these ephemeral pieces.

We present instead a list of the publications Toole wanted to be remembered for. These are the books, articles, and essays for which he sought or consented to publication, which his constituents read, and upon which his reputation as historian and polemicist rests. They range from his earliest, scholarly investigations, through promotional literature designed to advance the public's appreciation of history, to more politically and environmentally oriented work in the 1970s and 1980s. The bibliography is eloquent testimony to Ross Toole's thirty-one year effort to inform the present via the past—to explicate Montana and the West.

BOOKS

A History of Montana. With Merrill G. Burlingame. 3 vols.
  New York: Lewis Historical Publishing, 1957.
Historical Essays on Montana and the Northwest. With J. W. Smurr.
  Helena, MT: Western Publishing, 1957.

Montana: An Uncommon Land. Norman, OK: University of Oklahoma, 1959. American Association for State and Local History, National Award for Excellence, 1959.

Probing the American West. Santa Fe, NM: Museum of New Mexico, 1962.

An Angry Man Talks Up to Youth. New York: Award Books, 1970.

The Time Has Come. New York: William Morrow, 1971. Book-of-the-Month Club Alternate, 1971. Also: Arabic translation by Dar Nahdet Misr, under sponsorship of the U.S. Information Agency, 1977.

Twentieth-Century Montana: A State of Extremes. Norman, OK: University of Oklahoma, 1972.

The Rape of the Great Plains: Northwest America, Cattle and Coal. Boston: Little, Brown, 1976. Book-of-the-Month Club Alternate, 1976.

Montana: Images of the Past. With William E. Farr. Boulder, CO: Pruett Publishing, 1978.

ARTICLES AND ESSAYS

"The Anaconda Copper Mining Company: A Price War and a Copper Corner," *Pacific Northwest Quarterly,* vol. XLI, no. 4 (October 1950), 312–29.

"The Genesis of the Clark-Daly Feud," *The Montana Magazine of History,* vol. I, no. 1 (April 1951), 21–34. Reprinted in Michael P. Malone and Richard B. Roeder, eds., *The Montana Past: An Anthology* (Missoula, MT: University of Montana, 1969). Also reprinted in Michael P. Malone and Richard B. Roeder, eds., *Montana's Past: Selected Essays* (Missoula, MT: University of Montana Publications in History, 1973).

"Fort Benton: Hub of the Empire," *Out West Magazine,* vol. 2, no. 11 (December 1952), 12–13.

"When Copper Was King," *Out West Magazine,* vol. 2, no. 10 (November 1952), 26.

"Anne McDonnell: A Tribute," *The Montana Magazine of History,* vol. III, no. 4 (Fall 1953), 63.

"Early Montana Banking," *Out West Magazine,* vol. 3, no. 1 (February 1953), 26.

"Montana," *Daughters of the American Revolution Magazine,* vol. 87, no. 3 (March 1953), 440, 460.

"Montana's Potential," *Out West Magazine*, vol. 2, no. 12
(January 1953), 26.

"When Big Money Came to Butte: The Migration of Eastern Capital
to Montana," *Pacific Northwest Quarterly*, vol. 44, no. 1
(January 1953), 23–29. Reprinted in Michael P. Malone and
Richard B. Roeder, eds., *The Montana Past: An Anthology*
(Missoula, MT: University of Montana, 1969). Also reprinted in
Michael P. Malone and Richard B. Roeder, eds., *Montana's Past:
Selected Essays* (Missoula, MT: University of Montana
Publications in History, 1973).

"E. S. Paxson: Neglected Artist of the West," *The Montana
Magazine of History*, vol. IV, no. 2 (Spring 1954), 26–29.
Reprinted in *A Portfolio of the Art of E. S. Paxson, Montana
Heritage Series, No. 4* (Helena, MT: Montana Historical Society,
1954), 2–5.

"A Tribute to Dr. Paul C. Phillips," *The Montana Magazine of
History*, vol. V, no. 1 (Winter 1955), 68.

"The Impact of the Museum in the Hinterlands," *Clearing House
for Western Museums*, Newsletter 201 (November 1956), 991–96.
Reprinted in *Curator*, vol. I, no. 3 (Summer 1958), 36–42.

"The Other Side of the Montana Face," *Montana Opinion*, vol. I,
no. 1 (June 1956), 25–27.

"The Historical Society and Its Function Today," *Nebraska History*,
vol. 38, no. 3 (September 1957), 221–27. Reprinted in: *Bulletin of
the Detroit Historical Society*, December 1957.

"The Role of the Museum in the Great Plains," in Paul G. Ruggiers,
ed., *Cultural Leadership in the Great Plains: A Report of the
Great Plains Conference on Higher Education* (Norman, OK:
University of Oklahoma, 1957).

"Art in the Intermountain West," *The Lotus Leaf*, March, 1958, 3–5.

"Beloved Westerner: Charles M. Russell," *Montana: The Magazine
of Western History*, vol. VIII, no. 4 (Fall 1958), 3–5.

"Is Local History Really Important?," American Association of
State and Local History, *Ideas in Conflict* (Madison, WI:
AASLH, 1958).

"Address: Eulogy to Charles M. Russell," *Congressional Record*,
vol. 105, March 23, 1959, A-2575.

"Education and History," *Museum News*, vol. 37, no. 1 (March
1959), 12–13.

"Some Thoughts on the Great Plains," in University of North

Dakota, *Seventy-Fifth Anniversary and Faculty Convocation* (Grand Forks, ND: University, 1959).

"Surprizes for the Museum-going Vacationist," *New York Times,* May 24, 1959.

"The Tourist and the Museum," *New York Times,* May 14, 1959.

"The War of the Copper Kings," in *The Westerners: New York Posse Brand Book,* vol. 6, no. 1 (1959), 1, 3, 10, 12.

"Urban and Non-urban Museums: A Subjective Comparison," *Curator,* vol. III, no. 1 (Winter 1960), 20–25.

"Where Are the Ranch Records?," *Montana Stockgrower,* vol. 38, no. 10 (October 1966), 32–33.

"The Opening Door," *University of Montana, President's Newsletter,* Fall 1968. Reprinted in *Montana Business Quarterly,* vol. 6, no. 4 (Fall 1968), 9–12.

"A Microfilm Project in the Hinterlands," *American Philosophical Society Yearbook* (Philadelphia, PA: American Philosophical Society, 1968).

"Timber Depredations on the Montana Public Domain, 1885–1918," with Edward Butcher, *Journal of the West,* vol. VII, no. 3 (July 1968), 351–62.

"The Changing Winds of Montana," *Montana Business Quarterly,* vol. 7, nos. 1/2 (Winter/Spring 1969), 7–10. Reprinted in Patricia P. Douglas and Rauf A. Khan, eds., *Computers in State Governments* (Missoula, MT: Bureau of Business and Economic Research, 1969).

"Environmental Degradation in Montana," *Montana Business Quarterly,* vol. 8, no. 1 (Winter 1970), 5–9.

"Let's Put More Gap in the Generation Gap," *U.S. News and World Report,* April 1970. Reprinted in: *Editor and Publisher,* May 9, 1970; *Reader's Digest,* June 1970; Madeline H. Engel, *Inequality in America: A Sociological Perspective* (New York: Thomas Y. Crowell, 1971); Lloyd A. Flanigan and Slyvia A. Holladay, *Developing Style: An Extension of Personality* (Boston: Holbrook, 1972); Jean D. Grambs et al., *Education in the World Today* (New York: Addison-Wesley Publishing, 1972); Louis C. Reichman and Barry Wishart, *American Politics and its Interpreters* (Dubuque, IA: William C. Brown, 1971); and A. Scharback and R. H. Singleton, comps., *The Lively Rhetoric,* 2nd ed. (New York: Holt, Rinehart and Winston, 1972).

"Montana," in Joseph L. Morse, ed., *The New Funk and Wagnalls Encyclopedia* (New York: Funk and Wagnalls, 1970).

"To the Waiting Student," *New York Times*, September 24, 1970.

"Old Man Thomas and the Stuff of History," *Montana Historian*, vol. 3, no. 2 (Winter 1973), 21.

"The Yonlanders," *New York Times*, June 25, 1973.

"The Sandwich Man: A Hard Role," *Museum News*, vol. 52, no. 9 (June 1974), 41–42.

"How Montanans View America: Independent Cusses vs. Glittery Suits," *Montana Business Quarterly*, vol. 13, no. 2 (Spring 1975), 33–38.

"Is Local History Passe?," *Montana Historian*, vol. 6, no. 2 (June 1976), 54.

"Things Will Never Be the Same," *University Outreach*, vol. 1, no. 2 (1976), 1–2.

"Amateurs Can Abet Academic Historians," *Pacific Northwesterner: Spokane Corral of the Westerners*, vol. 22, no. 3 (Summer 1978), 46–48.

"The Future of the Northern Rockies," *Rocky Mountain Magazine* (November 1979).

"The Harney Scandal," *Montana Lawyer*, vol. 5, no. 3 (November 1979), 4, 14–15.

"The Honyockers," U.S., Small Business Administration, *SBA Directory*, 1979 (Washington, D.C.: SBA, 1979).

"Montana: The Peculiar Exclave," U.S., Small Business Administration, *SBA Directory*, 1979 (Washington, D.C.: SBA, 1979).

"The Montana Patterns," *Champion Magazine* (December 1979).

"The Northern Great Plains," in Brian W. Blouet and Frederick C. Luebke, eds. *The Great Plains: Environment and Culture* (Lincoln, NE: University of Nebraska, 1979).

"Notes: Why I Live Here," *Northwest America*, vol. I, no. 1 (May 1979), 22.

"The Future of Higher Education in Montana," *Rocky Mountain Magazine* (February 1980).

"Montana: The New Place and the Old," *Champion Magazine*, no. 6 (1980), 3–10.

"The Forty-Seventh Legislature in Review," *Montana Magazine*, vol. 11, no. 6 (July/August 1981), 10–16.

MISCELLANEOUS

Montana: The Magazine of Western History. Editor (1951–1957);
  contributor of a one-page feature entitled "Director's Roundup"
  (1953–1958); originator of several book reviews and "Letters to
  the Editor," published under various pseudonyms (1951–1958).
Our Town [New York]. Founder (1959), supervising editor
  (1959–1960), and contributor (1959–1960) for this quarterly
  juvenile magazine published by the Museum of New York City.
"Montana History." Ten-week newspaper series, under a grant from
  the U.S. Department of Health, Education, and Welfare, Fund for
  the Improvement of Post-Secondary Education. Appeared in: the
  Great Falls Tribune, the (Glendive) *Ranger-Review,* the *Livingston
  Enterprise,* the *Anaconda Leader,* the (Libby) *Western News,* and
  other Montana newspapers, 1975–1976. Reprinted, with some
  revisions, as a course manual: University of Montana, Office of
  Post-Secondary Education, *Montana History* (Missoula, MT:
  University, 1976).
"Montana As Science Sees It," script for film, under a grant from
  the Montana Committee for the Humanities, 1977.
"The Economics and the Myth: A History of the Western Cattle
  Industry," script and narration for one-hour television
  documentary, under a grant from the National Endowment for
  the Humanities, 1978.
"The Blue Sky Blues," script for film, under a grant from the
  National Endowment for the Humanities, 1979.

Contributors

HARRY W. FRITZ has taught early American history at the University of Montana since 1967. After Ross Toole's death, he took over "Montana and the West," and is now pursuing a variety of Montana topics. He earned an M.A. at Montana and a Ph.D. at Washington University in St. Louis.

DELORES J. MORROW received her B.A. and M.A. from the University of Montana. K. Ross Toole served as her advisor for both degrees. In addition to studying Helena's Jewish community, she has completed a history of Montana's lumber industry and is now photo curator at the Montana Historical Society.

W. THOMAS WHITE is curator of the James J. Hill Papers in St. Paul, Minnesota. He enrolled in "Montana and the West" as an undergraduate, took his B.A. and M.A. from the University of Montana, and his Ph.D. from the University of Washington. His work focuses on railroad labor history in Montana and the West.

DANIEL FROST GALLACHER received his M.A. in History under Ross Toole in 1980. He has museum experience at the Montana Historical Society and the Fort Missoula Historical Museum and currently works for Historical Research Associates in Missoula, a private consulting firm.

REX C. MYERS is associate professor of History at Western Montana College. A product of Ross Toole's "Montana and the West" in 1967, he went on to receive his M.A. and Ph.D. from the

University of Montana. With William Lang he authored *Montana: Our Land and People.*

A native of Ronan, Montana, FRANK R. GRANT is past Director of the Fort Missoula Historical Museum. His articles have appeared in *The Historian* and *Montana: The Magazine of Western History.* He is completing a biography of Robert Sutherlin, a topic first suggested by Ross Toole.

Born in Kremlin, Montana, ROBERT G. ATHEARN wrote his first book on Thomas Francis Meagher. Ross Toole praised him for never forgetting "that writing was invented to be read." He retired in 1982 after thirty-five years at the University of Colorado, and died in 1983.

Raised in Gunnison, Colorado, DONALD E. SPRITZER now heads the reference department of the Missoula City-County Library. He earned his Ph.D. from Montana in 1980, with a dissertation on the career of James E. Murray. He is also the author of *Waters of Wealth: The Story of the Kootenai River and Libby Dam.*

RICHARD B. ROEDER has been a History professor at Montana State University since 1962. He received his Ph.D. from the University of Pennsylvania, has written numerous articles on Montana history, and with Michael Malone is the author of *Montana: A History of Two Centuries.*

GEORGE M. LUBICK is an associate professor of History at Northern Arizona University. He received his B.A. and M.A. degrees in history from the University of Montana and his Ph.D. from the University of Toledo. His work has focused on American thought and culture.

Index